Also by David Sehat

The Myth of American Religious Freedom

THE JEFFERSON RULE

How the Founding Fathers Became
Infallible and Our Politics Inflexible

DAVID SEHAT

Simon & Schuster
New York   London   Toronto   Sydney   New Delhi

Simon & Schuster
1230 Avenue of the Americas
New York, NY 10020

First Simon & Schuster hardcover edition May 2015

SIMON & SCHUSTER and colophon are registered trademarks
of Simon & Schuster, Inc.

For information about special discounts for bulk purchases,
please contact Simon & Schuster Special Sales at 1-866-506-1949
or business@simonandschuster.com.

The Simon & Schuster Speakers Bureau can bring authors to your
live event. For more information or to book an event contact the
Simon & Schuster Speakers Bureau at 1-866-248-3049 or visit
our website at www.simonspeakers.com.

Interior design by Lewelin Polanco

Manufactured in the United States of America

10 9 8 7 6 5 4 3 2 1

Library of Congress Cataloging-in-Publication Data

Sehat, David.
  The Jefferson rule : how the founding fathers became infallible and our
politics inflexible / David Sehat. — First Simon & Schuster hardcover edition.
     pages cm
  Includes bibliographical references and index.
   ISBN 978-1-4767-7977-5 (hardcover : alk. paper) — ISBN 978-1-4767-
7978-2 (trade paper : alk. paper) — ISBN 978-1-4767-7979-9 (ebook)
1. Political culture—United States. 2. Founding Fathers of the United
States. 3. Collective memory—Political aspects—United States.
4. Persuasion (Rhetoric) I. Title.
  JK1726.S44 2015
  306.20973—dc23
                              2014034708

ISBN 978-1-4767-7977-5
ISBN 978-1-4767-7979-9 (ebook)

For Connie

CONTENTS

Contents

THE
JEFFERSON
RULE

PREFACE

American politics has its share of odd symbols, practices, and orthodoxies, but surely the most peculiar is the constant reference to the nation's Founders in contemporary debate. Everyone cites the Founders. Constitutional originalists consult the Founders' papers to decide original meaning. Proponents of a living and evolving Constitution turn to the Founders as the font of ideas that have grown over time. Conservatives view the Founders as architects of a free enterprise system that built American greatness. The more liberal-leaning, following their sixties parents, claim the Founders as egalitarians, suspicious of concentrations of wealth. Independents look to the Founders to break the logjam of partisan brinksmanship. Across the political spectrum, Americans ground their views in a supposed set of ideas that emerged in the eighteenth century.

But, in fact, the Founders disagreed with each other. They agreed to separate from Great Britain, and they agreed after much compromise, at least some of them, on the text of the Constitution. But beyond that, they had vast and profound differences.

1

They argued over federal intervention in the economy and about foreign policy. They fought bitterly over how much authority rested with the executive branch, about the relationship and prerogatives of federal and state government. The Constitution provided a nearly limitless theater of argument. The founding era was, in reality, one of the most partisan periods of American history.

How is it, then, in contemporary debate that conservatives, liberals, and libertarians cite these argumentative Founders as though they would all naturally support policies in the present? How did a bitterly divided generation become a cohesive group of visionaries?

It has been a pattern of long standing. From the early disputes about the role of the federal government in nation building, to the conflict over slavery and the Civil War, the debates over the New Deal during the Great Depression, the civil rights movement of the 1950s and 1960s, and the Reagan Revolution of the 1980s, everyone has called on the Founding Fathers. Today's Tea Party continues a habit common from the beginning of American political debate.

What is the result?

Founders talk degrades debate. It encourages intellectual dishonesty. It is both easy and destructive. The Founders' words and thoughts become weapons. Discussion of policy becomes ideological combat. If you disagree, you betray principle. Ultimately, citations from the Founders become partisan propaganda. In *1984*, George Orwell wrote: "Who controls the past controls the future; who controls the present controls the past." So it has been for much of American history, as successive generations of politicians impose their own meaning on the Founders.

Let's take up that history beginning with the Founders themselves, when Thomas Jefferson won the first round of debate and set the pattern for all succeeding ones.

CHAPTER ONE

The Quest for Unanimity

George Washington probably should have known better. In 1789, just after taking office, he faced a choice that would turn out to shape his two terms as president. The Constitution had been drafted nearly a year and a half earlier. After a bruising battle over its ratification, in which many people objected to what they saw as the Constitution's centralization of authority, Washington had been unanimously elected as the nation's first president. The moment was delicate. Everyone trusted in Washington as a leader, but not everyone trusted one another. And not everyone trusted in the government created by the Constitution.[1]

As Washington assumed the seat that many thought had been made for him, he needed to reassure concerned citizens that all was well. So he used his first inaugural to smooth over anxiety about the new government. It would be a force for national prosperity and national good, he promised. He would not allow the government to become despotic or to aid one section of the country over another. "No local prejudices or attachments, no separate views nor party animosities, will misdirect the comprehensive and equal eye which ought to watch over this great assemblage of communities and interests," he pledged to the nation's citizenry.[2]

But he also needed to use the new national powers of the government to confront the various and multiple problems that the nation faced. And he needed to appoint people to his cabinet who would use these new powers in a vigorous but politically circumspect manner. They would have to wield the new executive authority provided to the government without antagonizing those who had objected to the Constitution.

In that quest he did not hesitate, at least initially, to think big. His first appointment was Alexander Hamilton, for Treasury. The United States faced a number of economic problems that had been around since the end of the Revolutionary War. Under the Articles of Confederation—the wartime government that the Constitution replaced—the United States had been unable to coordinate the economic activity of the states. The nation, as a result, had no coherent program of economic development. And it struggled under debt from fighting the Revolution. If the United States was going to be successful as a nation, it would need to address its large debt, establish its credit in the eyes of other nations, and raise the capital to engage in still necessary national improvements.

Hamilton was perfect for that task. He was one of the most brilliant minds of the new nation, and he had a clear conception of the economic problems. But he also had a particularly clear vision of national power that was bound to antagonize those who feared a strong central government. More than anyone else among the founding generation, Hamilton believed that the new constitution provided, in his words, "streams of national power" that needed to be channeled to specific ends. Power was, for Hamilton, a good thing. Those who worried about strong governmental power, according to Hamilton, missed the more dangerous problems that arose out of a lack of governmental power. As he explained in the *Federalist Papers,* a series of newspaper articles written with James Madison and John Jay to support constitutional ratification, under a weak government "we are apt to rest satisfied that all is safe because nothing improper will be likely *to be done.*" But this view was, he believed, shortsighted. "We forget how much good may be prevented," he pointed out, "and how much ill may be produced, by the power of hindering the doing what may be necessary, and of keeping affairs in the same unfavorable posture in which they may happen to stand at particular periods."[3]

Such a view was at total odds with Washington's choice for secretary of state, Thomas Jefferson. It was here that Washington made his first mistake. State was also a vital cabinet position. Following the Revolution, several aspects of foreign relations needed attention. And because many future treaties would deal with commercial relations, some overlap in Hamilton's and Jefferson's respective portfolios was inevitable. The overlap would not have been a problem had they been in general philosophical agreement. But because Jefferson and Hamilton could not disagree more vehemently on any number of issues, conflict was also inevitable.

Jefferson had, in fact, long been uncomfortable with the Constitution. Though he did not have a hand in drafting it—he was away in Paris during the entire debate—when he first heard the plan he complained to his friend James Madison, "Primâ facie I do not like it. It fails in an essential character, that the hole and the patch should be commensurate. But this proposes to mend a small hole by covering the whole garment." Jefferson would have preferred to live under the Articles with perhaps a few amendments. "I own I am not a friend to a very energetic government," he acknowledged. And though he eventually made peace with the

Constitution, he did not abandon his belief that energetic government was always a threat to liberty.[4]

Jefferson's commitment to liberty, as he understood it, was bound to cause problems when he was paired with Alexander Hamilton, a man also not shy about his opinions. But Washington did not see the potential for conflict. In spite of the raucous debates that the nation had endured during the ratification process, Washington assumed—like many in his time—that any fair-minded gentleman politician would arrive at basically the same place as any other fair-minded gentleman politician, so long as they were both republican in outlook. He did not believe that two republican gentlemen could disagree on principle without one of them suffering from a fatal flaw in character. He thought that if he chose what he called "first characters"—those who made up the natural aristocracy of the United States and could be trusted to lead the nation—he would not need to scrutinize their views too closely.[5]

So he filled out his cabinet without regard to political inclination or orientation, and laid the seeds for bitter conflict in the future. Hamilton, a partisan of power, went to Treasury. Jefferson, a partisan of liberty, went to State. Edmund Randolph—one of three people who had stayed through the entire Constitutional Convention and then declined to sign the document—became attorney general, the chief law enforcement officer of the new government. And Henry Knox, Washington's successor as commander of the army after the Revolution and a secretary of war under the Articles of Confederation, stayed on as the secretary of war under the new government. Given the quality of the people he selected, and ignoring their obvious political differences, Washington looked forward to the future. His administration, he predicted, would shine in "the tranquil deliberations and voluntary consent" characteristic of a republican form of government.[6]

But in this, Washington would be sadly disappointed. And it is out of that conflict that we find the origins of our contemporary debate.

INTERNAL FRACTURE

The problems began almost immediately. Hamilton led the way. In keeping with his views of power, he entered office determined to aggressively use his command of the Treasury to set the nation on what he considered a proper economic path. His goal was the creation of a new American political economy. Faced with the threat of insolvency and neocolonial dependency after the Revolutionary War, Hamilton thought the national government should foster markets, prompt investment and entrepreneurship, and create a coherent national financial policy that protected public credit.

To that end, he put forward a series of economic reports in which he recommended an expansion of government that would occur in three steps. First, he proposed, the federal government should assume the debts of the states to create a large and consolidated national debt. Then it should repay those debts at face value, rather than downgrading the debt and hurting the nation's credit rating. Once those first two commitments were in place, he proposed that the government create a national bank that could collect new national taxes and use the subsequent capital flows to offer loans to the private sector in order to develop the economy. The net effect would be a powerful and centralized institutional control over American economic life.[7]

But Hamilton's proposals were controversial. His promotion of a national bank, in particular, made it clear that he wanted to use the government to favor the merchants of the North, who could aid in the economic development of the nation while simultaneously enriching themselves. To agriculturalists, particularly in the South, it seemed as though Hamilton was using his office to pick winners and losers in the new economy. Or, to put it another way, he was using the power of the government to endanger the agriculturalists' liberty.[8]

Jefferson and Madison, who both came from the agricultural state of Virginia, were upset. In the process of debate both emerged as Hamilton's opponents. Madison in particular used his immense prestige as the architect of the Constitution to call into question the constitutionality both of the bank and of Hamilton's entire economic system. He did so by arguing that the Constitution granted only limited powers to the Congress in section 8 of Article I. Because chartering a bank was not among those powers, Congress could not do it. This position became known as strict constructionism.[9]

As the split became clear, Washington grew disturbed. This was the first visible crack in the façade of agreement that existed in his administration. He had relied on both Madison and Hamilton in the initial part of his government, so a split between the two suggested a growing ideological divide that he did not understand and could not readily explain. But he grew even more disturbed after Madison directly appealed to him to veto the bank bill, once it had passed over Madison's objection in Congress. Uncertain of what to do, Washington solicited three opinions on the constitutionality of a national bank: one from his attorney general, Edmund Randolph; one from Jefferson; and, after he had consulted the other two, one from Hamilton. Everyone brought considerable legal powers to the task. The resulting opinions confirmed for Washington that a constitutional and political gulf was opening beneath him.

Jefferson and Randolph followed Madison in his strict constructionist argument, with Jefferson using his full rhetorical arsenal to defend what he had earlier called "the holy cause of free-dom." By rooting his opinion in the Tenth Amendment—which reserved all powers not delegated to the national government for the states and the people—Jefferson argued with Madison that the Constitution was like the Magna Carta, primarily a restraint on power that served as a charter of liberty. "To take a single step beyond the boundaries thus specially drawn around the powers of Congress," Jefferson complained, "is to take possession of a boundless feild [*sic*] of power, no longer susceptible of any defi-nition."[10]

But when Hamilton read the opposing opinions, he could barely contain his contempt. Jefferson was not even at the Consti-tutional Convention, and Randolph, who had been there, refused to sign it at the convention's end. And they were lecturing him on the Constitution's meaning! "Principles of construction like those espoused by the Secretary of State and the Attorney Gen-eral," Hamilton coolly responded in his own opinion, "would be fatal to the just & indispensable authority of the United States."[11]

Their disagreement was really about the nature and purpose of governmental power. For Jefferson, power always had a ten-dency toward malevolence that needed to be contained, but for Hamilton, power was the ability to do things that contributed to the public good. Precisely because the Constitution was de-signed to invigorate national government after the weakness of the Articles, Hamilton suggested that it was a charter of power, not merely liberty. It gave some powers to Congress by explicit statement and gave other powers to Congress by implication.

In essence, Hamilton argued that if Congress had the ex-press power to do one thing, such as collect taxes, it had the im-plied power to do other things, such as chartering a bank, that were a means of exercising that express power. To support his claim, Hamilton pointed to the so-called "necessary and proper" clause of Article I, section 8: "Congress shall have power . . . to make all Laws which shall be necessary and proper for carrying into Execution the foregoing powers." "The whole turn of the clause . . . indicates, that it was the intent of the convention, by that clause[,] to give a liberal latitude to the exercise of the specified powers," Hamilton wrote. This position became known as broad constructionism.[12]

Washington tarried for two days, uncertain what to do. Then he signed the bill. It appeared to be a clear victory for Hamilton. But, to Hamilton's consternation, the debate was just beginning.

FANATICAL PARTISANSHIP

Hamilton had pinpointed the exact questions of their debate, which would only grow more bitter in the future. Did the Constitution invigorate national government or constrain it? Did the framers trust or distrust power? And how exactly did they imagine that liberty would be maintained in this new federal system?

Those questions would soon grow more urgent, but in the meantime the debate itself was disturbing to many in Washington's administration. They expected consensus in politics. The Founders saw politics in terms of the deferential and rank-ordered society that they sat atop. Politics was supposed to be an expression of the enlightened governance expected by society's natural rulers. As Thomas Jefferson said in 1776, the goal of any political system is "to get the wisest men chosen [in government], and to make them perfectly independent when chosen." The voting masses would elect their betters, who could then, in tranquil deliberation, decide matters of public policy. And the Constitution had continued this idea. As Madison explained in *Federalist* No. 10, the Constitution used the principle of representation "to refine and enlarge the public views, by passing them through the medium of a chosen body of citizens." The best in society could then oversee "the permanent and aggregate interests of the [national] community."[13]

But it was not working. After the success of Hamilton's legislative program, Jefferson and Madison became convinced that the system had been overtaken by proto-despots. Hamilton had used his powers to aid not the permanent and aggregate interests of the national community, but the narrow interests of merchant capitalists. And he had done so with the overwhelming support of Congress. To resist what looked to them like the beginning of national degeneracy, Jefferson and Madison began canvassing New England and New York to seek support from regions other than Virginia. Their opponents claimed with some justification that they were trying to form a political party, but Jefferson and Madison admitted only that they were looking for other like-minded people to resist Hamilton's dangerous tendencies.[14]

The divide grew worse when Jefferson and Madison returned from their trip. The problem was not just their political organizing but also a gaffe Jefferson had made prior to leaving. As an ardent Francophile, he had long been excited by the French Revolution, which had been under way for three years. But he had been unable to read the best defense of the revolution, Thomas Paine's *The Rights of Man,* published originally in Great Britain. Just before the trip, after a Philadelphia publisher had decided to bring out an American edition, one of Jefferson's friends managed to get hold of the printer's copy. He gave it to Jefferson to look over with the simple request that Jefferson forward it to the publisher when he was finished. But rather than just sending the book along, Jefferson added a note—"to take off a little of the dryness," he later explained—that the publisher reprinted without permission at the front of the book. "I am extremely pleased to find . . . that something is at length to be publicly said against the political heresies which have sprung up among us," the note read. With Jefferson's name and comment at the front of the American edition, he appeared to be sponsoring the book's publication. And he seemed to be using *The Rights of Man* to air disagreements that he had with members of the Washington administration, especially Vice President John Adams, whose pamphlet criticizing the French Revolution, *Discourses on Davila*, had just been published.[15]

The response was fierce, as news of the fracture between the members of the administration leaked. Newspapers began alternately defending and attacking Jefferson, so much so that in early May he felt the need to justify himself to President Washington. He had, after all, betrayed proper decorum and the public commitment to consensual politics.

Jefferson wrote to Washington explaining his letter to the printer and assuring Washington that he did not consent to the publication of what was supposed to be a private comment. But he also admitted that he did in fact have John Adams in mind when he spoke of "political heresies." They had been friends of old, Jefferson said, and he expected that they still were. "Even since his apostasy to hereditary monarchy & nobility," Jefferson wrote of Adams, "tho' we differ, we differ as friends should do."[16]

Washington responded with an icy silence.

Jefferson's explanation was actually quite remarkable. He only offered regret that his pronouncement had been published, not for its sentiment that Adams had betrayed the republicanism of the American Revolution and had become a supporter of monarchy. Jefferson, it was now clear, had become obsessed with his opponents in government. He believed with a kind of fervent zeal that the true principles of government were fixed and known to all (though especially to him). In his own mind, he stood as a redoubt against dangerous error, a lonely crusader in a government that seemed, as he lamented in a letter around the same time, to "have apostatised from the true faith."[17]

With Jefferson's movement into partisanship, the Washington administration began to come apart. The final provocation came in December 1791, when Hamilton released his next major financial report, the Report on the Subject of Manufactures, which completed his vision for remaking the American economy. In his final proposal, Hamilton sought to use federal aid to promote manufacturing in the United States. He advocated, in particular, protective tariffs, that is, taxes on imported goods that would raise their cost in order to allow domestic industry to mature. Those taxes also would raise money that could be funneled through the national bank and then channeled into American industry. The result, he believed, would be the creation of a diversified, capitalist economy in which industry, commerce, and agriculture were mutually reinforcing in a feedback loop that would unlock the nation's tremendous resources and catapult it into international supremacy.[18]

But Jefferson again saw tyranny in Hamilton's plan. It would only further the government's favor for merchants while hurting the agriculturalists' liberty. Fortunately, he had already mobilized forces for his attack. During the summer of 1791, while he was dealing with the fallout from his heresy note—and while he remained a member of the administration—Jefferson had recruited the New York editor Philip Freneau to Philadelphia to start what would become an opposition newspaper against Washington's administration. The negative press coverage of his heresy note had convinced Jefferson that he needed a friendly organ that he could control.

Shortly after Hamilton's third report was made public, articles began appearing in Freneau's paper and elsewhere attacking Hamilton's policies. They asserted that his plan was aristocratic, because it sought to aid the mercantile class over others, and that it was a departure from republicanism. It was the beginning of a systematic newspaper campaign that began in earnest in mid-March and continued for eighteen weeks. Although Jefferson never wrote himself, he solicited contributions from Madison and supported the paper in numerous ways, including paying Freneau as a government translator for the Department of State.[19]

Jefferson's use of Freneau was a remarkable step in light of Jefferson's professed disdain for partisan politics. He was now managing the publicity arm of an opposition movement while he remained in the administration. And he sought to reach beyond his official portfolio of responsibility to interfere with a cabinet member who seemed to have the president's unquestioned support. The consensual norms of the period had begun to groan against the strain.

Finally, after maintaining several months of reticence, in August 1792 Hamilton pushed back and sought to expose Jefferson's partisan maneuvering. Writing under various pen names, he began a series of essays that ran until the end of the year. In one way or another, they all called into question Jefferson's private integrity and his public service. In the first, written as "An American," Hamilton complained, correctly, that Jefferson had brought Freneau to Philadelphia to serve as a mouthpiece for an opposition party led by Jefferson himself. Jefferson had also, Hamilton asserted, used public money to secure Freneau's services, thereby using his place within the administration to systematically and illegitimately obstruct its policies. "Is it possible," Hamilton wondered, "that Mr. Jefferson, the head of a principal department of the Government can be the Patron of a Paper, the evident object of which is to decry the Government and its measures?" "If he disproves of the Government itself and thinks it deserving of opposition," Hamilton continued, "could he reconcile to his own personal dignity and the principles of probity to hold an office

under it and employ the means of official influence in that opposition?" To make sense of the puzzle, Hamilton made a series
of damaging observations: that Jefferson had been something less
than a full supporter of the Constitution during ratification; that
he had systematically opposed nearly all the major initiatives of
the Washington administration even though they had been approved by large majorities in both houses of Congress and by
Washington himself; that Jefferson actually believed a national
government promoted "pernicious principles and dangerous
powers" that must be dismantled as much as possible to preserve
liberty; and that ultimately his long-standing opposition to the
Constitution made him wish that the government would fail.[20]

Although Jefferson was stung, as usual he did not need to lift a
pen in response. Madison, James Monroe, and other allies swung
into action, often at Jefferson's request. The resulting exchange
was a rare spectacle: two principal ministers of the Washington
administration unabashedly tearing each other apart in full view
of the public. It was an utter failure of consensual politics.

The Founders, it turned out, had deep and numerous disagreements in matters of policy, governance, and constitutional theory
and interpretation. Seemingly their strongest point of agreement
was that all parties and organized political conflict were evil. And
yet they were each outraged by the other and edging toward organized political opposition. That cognitive dissonance, in which
they found themselves doing something that they theoretically
deplored, produced more acrimony. Each believed the other side
responsible for the growing factionalism, which in turn fueled
more savage disagreement, and the process repeated itself with
great intensity.

Jefferson fumed in private even before Hamilton began his
public attack. He was particularly upset at Hamilton's "daring
to call the republican party *a faction*." His sense of self-righteous

grievance even led him to write to Washington, complaining of Hamilton and his policies. Jefferson cited, in a remarkably bold display of concealed partisanship, the newspaper coverage that he himself had procured as evidence of the public's concern over Hamilton's dangerous tendencies. He was still stewing a few months later, when he reiterated some of the charges in person to Washington. But when Washington signaled support for his Treasury secretary, Jefferson let the matter drop, at least to Washington's face.[21]

Things looked to be reaching an explosive climax. But, perhaps in recognition of the monster that they had unleashed, both sides drew back. Jefferson accompanied his complaint to Washington with a request. He wanted Washington to stand for reelection in the coming presidential contest. Washington received similar entreaties from Madison, Hamilton, and Edmund Randolph. Although Washington had endured the fracturing of his government and had watched in dismay as his first term ended in public acrimony and bitter partisanship, he remained the only figure not tainted by party who could be trusted by all sides. Urging him to remain in office was a way of holding back the party energies that Jefferson and Hamilton let loose and that threatened, they now feared, to run out of control.[22]

Though Washington eventually agreed to stand again for election, he wrote letters to Hamilton and Jefferson pleading for unity in the future. But he seemed unable to see just how vast the divide had become. Washington chastised Jefferson for seeking some "infalible [sic] criterion by which the truth of speculative opinions, before they have undergone the test of experience, are to be forejudged." To Hamilton, Washington urged a discussion of differences "without having the motives which led to them, improperly implicated." After all, he concluded, they all had "the same *general* objects in view."[23]

But, unfortunately for Washington, it was not at all obvious that they did have the same general objects in view, still less that they could agree on the means of attaining any particular object.

Hamilton responded that he wished only to support the government and indirectly confessed that he had entered into the public fray. He promised comity in the future, provided that Washington put forward a plan to unite the cabinet "upon some principle of steady cooperation." Two days later Hamilton was back in the *National Gazette* anonymously defending himself and obliquely reiterating his charges against Jefferson.[24]

Jefferson, too, professed a perfunctory regret at his role in the conflict before launching into yet another attack on Hamilton's policies and political philosophy. Implicitly rejecting Washington's advice, Jefferson complained that his disagreement with Hamilton was "not merely a speculative difference." Hamilton's plan "flowed from principles adverse to liberty, & was calculated to undermine and demolish the republic." Jefferson did promise that he had not been publishing (which was technically true, but a lie when his activities are taken in total view) and that he would remain out of the papers if he could. But he reserved the right at some point in the future to defend himself from "the slanders of a man whose history, from the moment at which history can stoop to notice him, is a tissue of machinations against the liberty of the country which has not only received and given him bread, but heaped it's [*sic*] honors on his head."[25]

Given such self-righteousness, peace would prove elusive, indeed.

REBELLION

The problem on both sides was not merely a difference in policy. Hamilton's and Jefferson's dislike for one another emerged out of a deep contradiction that they both suffered under. They had vast and seemingly unbridgeable differences in political philosophy and in their conceptions of government. But they shared a mutual commitment to consensual politics and a mutual antipathy to parties as a rejection of consensus. Their deep political conflict in the face of their expectations of political consensus gave a vicious cast to their disputes. Each side blamed the other for the breakdown. Each believed the other lacked legitimacy in their disagreement. And each regarded himself as the true standard-bearer of republicanism that was threatened by the opposite side.

Such animosity led to a curious phenomenon: the acceptance of party as a temporary measure to destroy the phenomenon of parties in general and to restore consensus back to American politics. Parties at this point existed more as informal groups of like-minded politicians. There was no party machinery, no political organizing, and nothing like campaigning that we would recognize today. The political system had been designed so that none of this was supposed to be necessary. But in the 1792 elections, large numbers of Federalist politicians—those who followed Hamilton and Washington—returned to office. Since Jefferson and Madison believed that theirs was the position favored by the electorate, the failure of their favored candidates suggested that Madison and Jefferson needed to take more proactive measures. They needed to mobilize the people into supporting their political positions through what we today would recognize as an organized political party.

In the spring and summer of 1793, they were aided in that goal by the sudden formation of what became known as Democratic-Republican societies. These were essentially political clubs or activist organizations that sought to mobilize public opinion against Hamilton's policies. Some societies were rooted in ethnic communities, some grew out of trade and workingmen's organizations, some were specific to cities such as Philadelphia, and some claimed to speak for an entire state. All claimed a common commitment to democratic-republican politics, and all asserted their prerogative to petition the government to uphold these principles.[26]

Since the Democratic-Republican societies combined support for limited national government with a suspicion of the Washington administration, it was natural that Jefferson and Madison watched their formation with excitement. But they had certain disagreements with the societies as well. After all, Jefferson had not entirely abandoned his earlier belief that the role of the citizen was primarily to vote—and then keep quiet. Now faced with a popular reaction against elected officials, Jefferson and Madison sought to harness this movement while maintaining their essentially elitist views.[27]

In April 1793, for example, just as the Democratic-Republican societies were forming, Madison wrote to Jefferson urging "an early & well digested effort for calling out the real sense of the people." If left to themselves, he warned, "there is room to apprehend they may in many places be misled." His letter betrayed an odd sense of the place of the people in this early turn to parties: the people needed to be simultaneously solicited and shaped.[28]

And even after a boisterous summer of Democratic-Republican society protest and a visit with James Monroe in Charlottesville, Virginia, where the two began making earnest plans for party organizing, Madison felt the same. "The Country is too much uninformed, and too inert to speak for itself," he wrote to Jefferson. Madison and Jefferson needed to mobilize the citizenry and then speak for them.[29]

Meanwhile, a crisis that had been forming for several years was about to come to a head. In 1791, after Congress passed a tax on spirits to fund Hamilton's program, large sections of Appalachia and especially several counties in western Pennsylvania had objected, complaining that the plan unfairly burdened them to the benefit of others. By the middle of the next year, four counties in western Pennsylvania had created an organization to obstruct collection of the tax. They hoped to eventually have the tax repealed.

President Washington was initially delicate in his response. In mid-September he issued a pronouncement. "Certain violent and unwarrantable proceedings" threatened the good order, he announced. They were "of a nature dangerous to the very being of a government" because everyone must abide by the rule of law for government to stand. Though he vaguely warned of coercive measures if they did not desist, he did not actually do much. He instead contented himself with a warning: "Now, therefore, I, George Washington, President of the United States, do by these presents most earnestly admonish and exhort all persons whom it may concern to refrain and desist from all unlawful combinations and proceedings."[30]

That hardly had the desired effect. The impasse had lasted through the formation of the Democratic-Republican societies in 1793 and into early spring 1794, as Jefferson and Madison began party organizing in earnest. Finally, in summer 1794, a federal marshal showed up with orders for tax-avoiding distillers to appear in federal court. In response, an armed mob burned an excise inspector's home, beat back federal troops, and began preparations to seize a federal garrison that could arm the region (they eventually abandoned this plan).[31]

The Whiskey Rebellion, as historians now call this uprising, further inflamed the growing partisan animosity. During the whole period, Washington still peppered his statements with admonitions toward "the careful cultivation of harmony" and "unprejudiced coolness" in government. He and his advisers distrusted the Democratic-Republican societies as expressions of factional politics bent on undermining consensual government. But the Whiskey Rebellion added to the administration's alarm by suggesting the revolutionary tendency of the Democratic-Republican movement. "I consider this insurrection as the first *formidable* fruit of the Democratic Societies," Washington wrote to an ally. He believed that factious men had created the societies "primarily to sow the seeds of jealousy and distrust among the people, of the government, by destroying all confidence in the Administration of it."[32]

So the first order of business was to crush the rebellion. In August he called up an army of thirteen thousand men from state militias and volunteers—a force roughly the size of the Continental Army during the American Revolution. Once it was assembled, he and Hamilton went with the army to western Pennsylvania, where the rebels simply melted away. In the end, the authorities rounded up a few ringleaders but the point was mostly symbolic, a weak end to what many feared could have become a powerful challenge to the federal government.[33]

But that did not mean that the Whiskey Rebellion was unimportant. The efflorescence of popular agitation actually brought the parties into clear relief. It showed that they disagreed about more than simply economic policy: they disagreed about the nature of governance and the prerogative of the people. Washington returned to the insurrection during his annual message to Congress in November when he explained what he saw as the larger issue. His objection was not to the mob in western Pennsylvania, he said, but to "certain self-created societies"—the Democratic-Republican societies—who had called themselves into existence in order to oppose a duly elected republican government. Washington believed that the societies violated "the true principles of republican government and liberty," which depended fundamentally on representation, not populist agitation. That was the design of the Constitution, and, he seemed to suggest, the Democratic-Republican societies were in constitutional violation.[34]

Madison was stunned at what seemed a clearly partisan

message from Washington, but he continued to see Washington as above parties and instead blamed Hamilton for the partisan rebuke. "The game was," Madison explained to James Monroe, "to connect the democratic Societies with the odium of insurrection—to connect the Republicans in Congs. with those Societies—to put the P[resident] ostensibly at the head of the other party, in opposition to both." He lamented what he saw as Washington's naïveté. By listening to Hamilton, Washington had committed "the greatest error of his political life."[35]

Others were less kind as the partisan dynamic solidified. "The denunciation of the democratic societies," Jefferson wrote to Madison, "is one of the extraordinary acts of boldness of which we have seen so many from the faction of Monocrats." The opposing side, which seemed to include Washington, had fallen from republican values and abandoned the true faith. Resistance was now the only option.[36]

For his part, Washington felt that he had been pushed into a critical position by the party activities of others, Jefferson especially. And given Jefferson's threat to a consensual political order, Washington did everything he could to sideline him. In March 1796, he decided to retire and informed his appointed successor, John Adams, of his plans. But he did not publicly announce his decision until September, which helped ensure Adams's election. Because Jefferson, who had resigned from the cabinet at the beginning of 1794, would wait for a signal from Washington before marshaling his own forces for the election, Washington's delay hampered the effectiveness of Jefferson's campaign.[37]

Washington also labored to set the terms of debate. During the summer of 1796, he began working with Hamilton, who had left the administration a year earlier, to draft Washington's announcement of retirement. The Farewell Address primarily urged the avoidance of two dangers: foreign entanglements and political parties. Again Washington reiterated a consensual notion of American government. "The unity of government," he suggested, is that "which constitutes you one people." Those who worked through a party were "destructive of this fundamental principle."[38]

But given the wider political context, the Farewell Address was actually a party act that denied its own partisanship by denying partisanship in general. Its clear message was that a vote for Jefferson was un-American and a denial of proper political principle. In the place of "consistent and wholesome plans, digested by common counsels and modified by mutual interests," Washington warned, party leaders sought "to organize a faction . . . to put in the place of the delegated will of the nation the will of a party." Such thinking would tear the nation apart. It risked pitting "the animosity of one part against another" and so tended toward the "riot and insurrection" that had, though he did not say so explicitly, been seen in the Whiskey Rebellion.[39]

With that parting shot, Washington stepped aside. The thin veneer of comity among the remaining Founders peeled painfully away. Jefferson's election team swung immediately into action but John Adams won the presidency. Jefferson had to settle for the vice presidency, which was awarded to the runner-up under the original constitutional rules. Now, in a system designed to suppress parties, the president and the vice president had diametrical political orientations. "The *Lion* & the *Lamb* are to lie down together," Hamilton mused to one of his allies. "Sceptics like me quietly look forward to the event," he continued, "willing to hope but not prepared to believe."[40]

TOWARD THE BRINK

Hamilton had reason to be concerned. The nation was about to enter one of its most dangerous periods. In the first eight years after the ratification of the Constitution, a familiar pattern had emerged. The beginning of the first party system featured a dominant party and the opposition. Each side saw the other as misguided. Each used means, both fair and foul, to advance their cause. Each party believed that they alone represented true republicanism and the other represented an aberration or a betrayal. Neither believed that their differences were merely a normal aspect of modern politics but something to be overcome through the utter destruction of the other side. Washington had stood as a figure of national unity within this conflict, even when he engaged in his own partisanship. But with his retirement to Virginia, the views that each side had of the other found no check. Both had to confront what they were willing to do if the other side won.

At least initially, everyone hoped to avoid faction in the coming change of office, even if they believed that the other would obstruct a functioning and nonpartisan government. Upon learning that he was to be vice president, Jefferson wrote a letter to Adams that offered both an overture and a warning. While in government Hamilton had made Adams and his friends "tools" for Hamilton's own purposes, Jefferson believed. He warned that Hamilton would likely continue his machinations even though he was not in office. Jefferson wished that he and Adams would work together for the good of the republic.[41]

He was at least mentally prepared to go even further. In a letter to Madison a couple weeks later, Jefferson considered an alliance with Adams against Hamilton. "If Mr. Adams can be induced to administer the government on it's [sic] true principles," Jefferson said, it might be better to unite behind him as "the only sure barrier against Hamilton's getting in." What he meant was that if they united with Adams, they might be able to keep Hamilton marginalized from the party machinery and unable to manipulate government.[42]

Adams responded by channeling Washington and seeking to rise above partisanship. "There is nothing which I dread so much as a division of the republic into two great parties," he had earlier said. In his inaugural address, Adams continued the theme. He worried about the place of parties in the late election and claimed that the rise of two parties might produce a government chosen by the party "for its own ends" rather than "the national good." The Constitution, he continued, sought to remove "the spirit of sophistry, the spirit of party, [and] the spirit of intrigue" from government. It was this constitution that Adams promised to up-hold.[43]

But, predictably, given his disdain of parties in a political world in which parties increasingly organized power, Adams was routed. In keeping with his nonpartisanship, he had decided to keep the cabinet that he had inherited from Washington, which was filled with people more loyal to Hamilton than to the president. And so, within the year, once Adams and Jefferson had sunk into a dysfunctional hostility, Hamilton was calling the shots.

The immediate context for the breakdown was a threat of war. Hostilities had begun to develop with the French as a result of the French Revolution. Jefferson continued his support for the French project, while Hamilton rejected it. Adams sought to maintain neutrality. But shortly into Adams's term, the United States descended into quasi-war with France—it was essentially a sporadic naval war. Many from Adams's party worried that France might land military forces in the United States. Prompted by Hamilton, they decided to raise an army of their own to repel the potential French invasion. To pay for it, Congress passed the first ever national tax on dwellings, land, and slaves—an expansion of federal authority that Hamilton championed and that Adams approved against his better judgment. But he still sought a way to marginalize Hamilton after the latter expressed interest in leading the army. Adams decided instead to ask Washington to be the commander, who agreed on one condition: Hamilton would have to be appointed second in command. That meant, given Washington's age, Hamilton would lead the army into any actual battle. Adams was thwarted again.[44]

With Adams frustrated at nearly every turn, Hamilton sought to use the war to destroy factions once and for all. He meant, in other words, to destroy Jefferson and his party. Hamilton had long seen Jefferson as dangerous, even as an anarchist, and he associated Jefferson with the Jacobins of the French Revolution. The quasi-war with France made Jefferson's proclivities more than just misguided, according to Hamilton. They tended toward treason.[45]

Now was the moment for Hamilton to press for victory. "You will have observed with pleasure a spirit of patriotism kindling every where," he wrote to a frequent correspondent, Rufus King. "The leaders of Faction," by which he meant Jefferson, would soon be destroyed. "And you will not be sorry to know . . . that there will shortly be *national unanimity*," he emphatically concluded.[46]

Such attitudes led almost directly to the Alien and Sedition Acts of June and July 1798. The former modified several citizenship laws and allowed the president to deport any alien who he believed presented a danger to the United States. The Sedition Act made it illegal to engage in organized resistance to federal law or to defame the president or Congress. The law was written so broadly that it suggested merely criticizing the president or Congress was a criminal act.[47]

In response, Jefferson and Madison began secretly drafting what would become the Virginia and Kentucky Resolutions, arguing that the Alien and Sedition Acts violated the Constitution when it was read in strict constructionist terms. It was clear, they suggested, that the Constitution was a compact among the states that gave limited powers to the federal government. The Alien and Sedition Acts had overstepped those limits, the resolutions complained, and as such they were unacceptable. Jefferson's Kentucky Resolutions even assumed that the states could somehow dissolve federal law—the exact mechanism for this was vague—and both the Virginia and Kentucky legislatures called upon other states to join in similar protests. Although none did, the resolutions suggested just how deep the divide had become. Partisans could not even agree on the nature of the union.[48]

That division nearly led to constitutional crisis. Even before the Alien and Sedition Acts had passed, Jefferson was actively calming his most die-hard partisans, who were entertaining the idea of secession. In June 1798, Jefferson wrote to John Taylor of Caroline County, a member of the Virginia legislature who had been pushing secession, to warn against such talk. "Our present situation is not a natural one," Jefferson assured him. Though the great body of the people was republican, a perfect storm had delivered the government over to Hamilton's party, the Federalists. "It was the irresistible influence & popularity of Genl. Washington played off by the cunning of Hamilton," he continued, "which turned the government over to antirepublican hands, or turned the republican members chosen by the people into antirepublicans." Secession was not the answer, Jefferson counseled, because the schism would not stop. The states that seceded would turn on one another, as Hamilton had long ago predicted, or fragment. "A little patience," he concluded, "and we shall see the reign of witches pass over, their spells dissolve, and the people[,] recovering their true sight, restore their government to it's [*sic*] true principles."[49]

But dire assessments of the situation continued in spite of Jefferson's assurances. After the Virginia and Kentucky Resolutions passed, Hamilton received a seemingly credible report that the legislature of Virginia had set aside money to purchase arms in order to resist the federal government. No such appropriation had been made, but it was widely believed by both parties at the time. Hamilton's correspondent explained the plan as follows: Stock up on arms. Find people "panting to become Martyrs in the *holy cause*." Let them violate the Alien and Sedition Acts in a way that would force prosecution. Resist with armed force after the federal government tried to enforce the acts. "And thus, the signal of Civil War will be given," he concluded.[50]

In the face of such reports, Hamilton thought about forcing a showdown with an army of his own. Writing to an ally in Congress, Theodore Sedgwick, Hamilton asked, "What, My Dear Sir, are you going to do with Virginia?" Hamilton, of course, had some ideas. He recommended that the matter be referred to a special legislative committee, a way of pretending action while actually doing nothing. "In the meantime," Hamilton continued, "the measures for raising the [national] Military force should proceed with activity. . . . When a clever force has been collected let them be drawn towards Virginia for which there is an obvious pretext—& then let measures be taken to act upon the laws & put Virginia to the Test of resistance."[51]

Things looked, again, to be approaching an explosive climax. But, in perhaps the signal achievement of the early national period, everyone took a big breath. Rather than following the French Revolution into violence, they redirected that potential for armed conflict into the political arena. Federalists became uncomfortable in the face of the upcoming presidential election, which Jeffersonians, now calling themselves Republicans, were quietly confident of winning. Adams disassociated completely from his own party by promoting peace with France. That undercut the major rationale for the army, the taxes, and the Alien and Sedition Acts.

Without the rationale of impending war, Federalists realized, they were vulnerable to the Republican charge that they were despots and betrayers of republican principles.

Hamilton was particularly uncertain how to respond. "The leading friends of the Government are in a sad Dilemma," he wrote to Rufus King. Adams had proven unstable, George Washington had recently died ("He was an Aegis very essential to me," Hamilton lamented at the time), and now an election loomed. Federalists in Congress became so concerned that they voted to demobilize the army by June 15, 1800, just before the election but too late to change anything. That left Hamilton complaining of Adams's "Perverseness and capriciousness."[52]

Once the election arrived, Federalist disarray combined with a popular backlash against taxes, a standing army, and the Alien and Sedition Acts to swing the election to the Republicans. They swept into a majority of both houses of Congress, with Jefferson squeaking into the presidency.

Hamilton's plan had failed miserably. Rather than achieving unanimity by destroying the opposing party, he had in fact badly divided the nation and destroyed his own party instead. The Federalists were soon to enter permanent decline, and Jefferson began to codify what he claimed were the true founding principles. The result would make it possible, in spite of all evidence to the contrary, to invoke the Founders as a unit defined by Republican consensus.

CONSOLIDATION AND ERASURE

Jefferson's election in 1800 marked the culmination of an interpretive stance toward the founding moment that has become so problematic today. His goal was the complete eradication of Federalism and the establishment of a new Republican political orthodoxy. But he submerged this goal under the guise of consensual respect that showed a lingering desire for unanimity. In his first inaugural, an address singularly pitched to ward off animosities and diffuse conflict, he called on everyone to "unite with one heart and one mind." Jefferson observed the "contest of opinion" that had happily been decided in his favor, but he abjured any celebration or sense of triumph. "Every difference of opinion is not a difference of principle," Jefferson proclaimed. "We have called by different names brethren of the same principle. We are all Republicans, we are all Federalists."[53]

It was possible to read Jefferson's statement as a gracious response in victory. By disclaiming partisan triumph, Jefferson could suggest that all true patriots of the founding generation were conjoined in their vision of the United States. To that end, Jefferson used his first inaugural to elaborate what he saw as "the creed of our political faith." It included a promise of equal rights to all individuals, support for state governments in their prerogatives, and vigorous promotion of a national government of limited authority. His statement of principles, though distinctly Republican, was not particularly narrow and might have suggested a more politically ecumenical attitude than Jefferson had earlier displayed.[54]

But his private sentiments of the time reveal a more merciless edge to his political faith. Immediately after his inaugural, Jefferson responded to many letters of congratulation from his political allies. He confirmed to them his belief that the Republican triumph had ended a giant con that the Federalists had been running. His fellow citizens had "been led hoodwinked from their principles." And in letter after letter he turned to Protestant religious imagery to suggest just how dangerous his opponents had been. "The leaders of the late faction" had formed into a "federal sect" that had, for a time, engaged in a reign "of bigotry."

"The barbarians really flattered themselves that they should even be able to bring back the times of Vandalism, when ignorance put everything into the hands of power & priestcraft," Jefferson marveled. His goal was "to obliterate" Federalism in order to attain "a perfect consolidation." "I shall . . . sink federalism into an abyss from which there shall be no resurrection," he explained to one correspondent. This "reformation," with Jefferson as its Martin Luther, would install a renewed political faith that would guarantee the nation in the future.[55]

Yet Jefferson, once in office, acted with pragmatism. He decided to leave in place the lower-level government officials that he inherited from previous administrations. By replacing only cabinet-level ministers, he hoped to peel off moderate Federalists who could then be absorbed by the Republicans. Federalist leaders, whom Jefferson considered reprobates, would then be left without followers. As he explained to James Monroe, "[The Federalists] are now aggregated with us, they look with a certain degree of affection & confidence to the administration, ready to become attached to it if it avoids, in the outset, acts which might revolt & throw them off."[56]

That did not mean that he intended to support Federalist policies in general. In his first message to Congress, he urged ending domestic federal taxes, shrinking expenditures, demobilizing the military, and paying off the federal debt. Contrary to the Federalist vision of a strong central government that fostered private economic enterprise, Jefferson initially urged a more laissez-faire approach. "Agriculture, manufactures, commerce, and navigation, the four pillars of our prosperity, are . . . most thriving when left most free to individual enterprise," Jefferson explained.[57]

But some were concerned that he did not go far enough. Although he laid out clear principles, he seemed too tentative in destroying his opponents. He even decided to leave Hamilton's bank, which dismayed some of his Republican supporters. To them Jefferson pleaded political realism. "When this government was first established," he responded to one critic, "it was possible to have set it going on true principles, but the contracted, English, half-lettered ideas of Hamilton destroyed that hope in the bud." Jefferson hoped "to introduce sound principles and make them habitual," but he warned, "what is practicable must often controul what is pure theory."[58]

That realism led to a surprising development. Rather than the small-state republicanism that he had advocated throughout the 1790s, Jefferson began to drift toward what could fairly be described as neo-Federalism. But he did so with his abhorrence of Federalists and his own sense of reformational mission fully intact.

He first compromised on his constitutional views. In 1803 Jefferson was presented with the opportunity to buy Louisiana from France, which would double the size of the United States and make way for territorial expansion in keeping with Jefferson's agrarian vision. Yet Jefferson saw no explicit grant of power in the Constitution for territorial expansion. According to his strict constructionist principles he should have declined the purchase. He instead resolved his dilemma by resorting to exactly the broad constructionist principles of Hamilton that he had earlier rejected: the president and the Senate had been given treaty power, he reasoned, and the purchase of land from France was, after all, a treaty.[59]

Jefferson's reelection in 1804 signaled the further collapse of the Federalists as a party, but it paradoxically confirmed his movement toward Hamiltonianism. At the beginning of his second term, Jefferson embraced government-sponsored economic development of the kind that he had earlier rejected. Unfortunately,

Hamilton had died in a duel with Jefferson's vice president in the summer before the election, so he was not around to comment on the obvious similarity between their two plans. The only difference was that Jefferson thought federal taxes ought to be divided among the states to support economic development and, now returning to his strict constructionist principles, that a constitutional amendment was needed to put the plan into effect. But the upshot of Jefferson's plan would inevitably involve the government in picking winners and losers in American economic life—the aspect of Hamilton's plan that he had earlier found so objectionable.[60]

By the end of his presidency, Jefferson even embraced a sweeping notion of national power that rivaled Hamilton's. It emerged out of his foreign policy. As the Napoleonic Wars engulfed Europe, Jefferson sought to keep the United States on the sidelines and out of harm's way. What that meant in practice was that Jefferson sought to continue commercial relations with all sides. The British objected to the neutral American position and used their superior navy to harass American ports, to interfere with trade, and to impress, or seize for mandatory naval service, people they considered British subjects but that the United States recognized as American citizens.

In July 1807, Jefferson issued a Proclamation of Neutrality in the Napoleonic Wars and included a decree: all British ships had to leave American harbors and could not return. He established, in effect, a reverse blockade. But rather than merely focusing on the British, Jefferson also requested that Congress pass a bill outlawing commerce with all foreign nations, which it promptly did. He then used various measures of compulsion against the many New England merchants who flouted the law, even mobilizing U.S. ships off the Atlantic coast to patrol for smugglers.

Critics claimed that the embargo was unconstitutional and even began to threaten secession. But Jefferson was untroubled by his position. Congress had the power to regulate commerce, Jefferson reasoned, and that power included the cessation of all commerce. A principle of such broad construction and the consequent use of national power would have made Hamilton proud—even though he would have deeply objected to Jefferson's actual policy on the grounds that it was self-destructive to inhibit commerce with the nation's dominant trading partner.[61]

In the end, Jefferson even embraced the system of domestic manufacturing that had grown up because of his policies. The embargo crisis made him see the problem of an agrarian republic, which left the nation dependent on foreign production. But the embargo also had the effect of diverting capital into domestic industry. "The extent of this conversion is daily increasing," Jefferson happily reported in his eighth annual message, "and little doubt remains that the establishments formed and forming will, under the auspices of cheaper material and subsistence, the freedom of labor from taxation with us, and of protecting duties and prohibitions, become permanent." Though it was not an organized program and certainly not Hamiltonian in scale, the growth of manufacturing was still the direct result of Jefferson's exercise of national power that he had earlier deplored.[62]

Jefferson had embraced or conceded many parts of Hamilton's economic system. He even lapsed into Hamiltonian constitutionalism when it suited him. Yet in 1807 he was still warning other Republicans of the dangers of falling into Federalist "heresy." The result was the progressive erasure of the Federalists from the realm of political legitimacy even as Jefferson appropriated their policies and principles.[63]

That trend continued when Madison was elected president in

1808. Jefferson left quite a few problems for Madison to clean up. The exigencies of governance had pushed him into adopting large portions of Hamilton's economic system without understanding or accepting that it could only work if relations with Great Britain remained positive. He had pushed the United States toward war with Great Britain and estranged New England with his embargo, neither of which worked with Jefferson's other policies. As a result, all of Madison's first term and most of his second were consumed with the increasing hostilities with Great Britain and the subsequent War of 1812.

The result was, yet again, a puzzle. The experience of war strengthened the emerging neo-Federalism in Republican ranks, though the Federalist Party itself utterly collapsed. Federalists remained in disrepute while their theories ascended. And in 1815, during his seventh annual message, Madison simply embraced Hamilton's economic system in its entirety. He urged a new national bank, tariffs to protect American manufacturing, and a system of national improvements undertaken by the federal government (not the states). Constitutionally speaking, there was little to nothing separating Madison's proposal from Hamilton's—except an interval of twenty-five years.[64]

By the time James Monroe came into office in 1817, the trend was complete. Federalism had triumphed in policy making while the Federalist Party had been utterly delegitimized and had long since faded from the national stage. Monroe continued to urge a Hamiltonian system of national economic development, which would "require the systematic and fostering care of the Government," even as he rejoiced that the political system had been at last restored to first principles. "The increased harmony of opinion" that now characterized the Union, according to Monroe, represented the security of Republican triumph and the restoration of the Founders' intentions.[65]

Jefferson himself could not have been more pleased. Monroe's election convinced him that the nation had finally arrived at "the complete suppression of party." The pretenders to American principle, who were "essentially bigoted in politics as well as religion," had been routed. Now Monroe's administration would "consecrate" republican principles so that they would be protected from change. At the end of the first party system and the beginning of a brief period of one-party rule, the new republican orthodoxy reigned supreme.[66]

But it was an orthodoxy filled with contradictions. Jefferson railed against Hamiltonianism in the 1790s, worked relentlessly to suppress Federalism from 1800 onward, and finally created a neo-Hamiltonian system through his successors.

In the end his orthodoxy consisted more of sloganeering and rhetorical posture than political platform. But that rhetorical posture turned out to be his most lasting contribution. In this nascent period of American politics, the Constitution was still indeterminate. The Founders had agreed on the wording but did not necessarily agree on what it meant or even its purpose. Hamilton had believed that it created an invigorated national government that enabled the promotion of a variety of public goods. Jefferson believed that it was a charter of liberty that sought to limit national power. Both had their followers. And both sides blamed the other for the breakdown in consensus.

If Hamilton had won, things would have turned out differently (though there would, no doubt, have been other problems). Given Hamilton's view that the Constitution was a grant of power to a strengthened national government, any disagreement over policy in a Hamilton administration would have remained simply a policy disagreement, not a larger disagreement over first principles. But Jefferson's victory redirected American politics into different channels by asserting a particular relationship to the Constitution and to the founding moment. His relentless search for political heresy and his promotion of his own political creed suggested that there was *a* meaning to the Constitution that all true Founders supported. The result of his constitutional stance turned differences over policy into life-and-death fights over first principles and made the early national period into one of the most partisan eras of American political history.

The Constitution had been saved, Jefferson proclaimed, by the destruction of the Federalists. His victory excommunicated all who disagreed with him and made possible the facile and somewhat perverse invocation of the Founders as a united authority who agreed on the Constitution. That triumph also obscured the deep disagreement that existed nearly from the moment that the Constitution was ratified and that continued to be present in the differences between Jefferson's initial principles and the ones he used in office.

Jefferson was actually a supreme political innovator. He was a central figure in the emergence of popular politics and political democracy. He rejected, at least partially, the condescending elitism of the founding era and the reflexive distrust of partisanship, political organization, and systematic opposition. But he promoted all of this innovation while claiming a mantle of restoration and dedication to the true principles of the past.

Many politicians have done this, but Jefferson set the pattern.

In the end, Jefferson's triumph consolidated the founding moment and handed to his successors an interpretive stance toward the founding era that would become the norm. He rhetorically turned the founding era into one of political purity that he himself had channeled. Henceforth, if Jefferson had his way, American politics would be fought by seeking a connection to Jefferson and, through him, to the Founders. Any innovation would, of necessity, require politicians to show that their policies were in line with the principles of the past. And it would go without saying that a departure from Jeffersonianism—now equated with the principles of the Founders—represented the beginning of national degeneracy.

CHAPTER TWO

Specters of Fracture

No one really expected controversy. In 1819, when Missouri Territory applied for statehood, the application should have been a matter of course, simply another state addition in a rapidly expanding nation. After all, the debates of the founding era had been settled. Political quietude prevailed. All had united behind Jefferson. Founding principles were restored. But when the debate on Missouri began, James Tallmadge of New York—a man not much remembered except for this one act—rose to offer two amendments to the bill permitting Missouri's statehood. Up until that point, the Congress had allowed southerners to bring their slaves to Missouri Territory. But Tallmadge proposed that before moving any further, Missouri should have to ban the future importation of slaves into the territory and that it should place its existing system of slavery on a path toward abolition.[1]

His proposal, delivered without preamble and without warning, was not just unexpected. It was unheard of. Congress had shied away from addressing the question of slavery in the vast reaches of Jefferson's Louisiana Purchase. In fact, the subject had never even come up.

But those who favored slavery's restriction had a simple, even elegant, argument to justify their departure from past practice. They pointed out that the Constitution required all states to have a republican form of government. That meant, at least minimally, that it had to be a government defined by equality. To prove their point, they called upon Jefferson's Declaration of Independence. "[The Declaration] defines the principle on which our National and State Constitutions are all professedly founded," Timothy Fuller of Massachusetts asserted. "All men are created equal," he read from the document, and "are endowed by their Creator with certain inalienable rights." Precisely because everyone had equal rights, slavery could not be allowed into the territories or any new states without violating this republican promise. As John W. Taylor of New York put it: "Are we willing to pronounce this declaration, for the support of which the Fathers of our Revolution pledged their lives and fortunes, a flagrant falsehood?"[2]

Unfortunately, the restrictionists' argument incensed their proslavery colleagues. In defining republicanism as inherently antislavery, restrictionists donned the mantle of the Founders while declaring that the existing slave states were an aberration from founding principle. They made invidious distinctions between states on the basis of slavery, even though slavery had been present at the founding. In response, slavery proponents sought to place the Declaration in historical context. When seen in that light, they argued, the Declaration did not support abstract individual rights but the inalienable rights of communities to self-governance.

"We agree with the Congress of 1776," Alexander Smyth of Virginia responded, "that men, on entering into society, cannot alienate their right to liberty and property, and that they cannot, by compact, bind their posterity." But slaves had never entered into society as such, Smyth claimed, so they could not be included in the Declaration nor could the Declaration be used to harass slave states. And, in a neat twist, Smyth drew on the Declaration to justify Missouri's right to slavery, which was a form of property rights that were, therefore, inalienable.[3]

An impasse loomed. Since the Declaration seemed to cut two ways and both sides could make plausible constitutional arguments, all sides returned repeatedly to Thomas Jefferson.

Restrictionists pointed out that Jefferson himself had acknowledged slavery as a moral barbarism. As Jefferson wrote in his 1785 work, *Notes on the State of Virginia,* "The whole commerce between master and slave is a perpetual exercise of the most unremitting despotism on the one part, and degrading submissions on the other." That sentiment had underwritten the Declaration, slavery opponents insisted, so keeping slaves from the territories was not really a political innovation. It was positively Jeffersonian. "I hold the good old Republican doctrines," William Darlington of Pennsylvania put it. Allowing slavery into the territories would be corrosive to those "first principles."[4]

But trying to use Jefferson to support antislavery was a little like deflecting a knife thrust by grabbing the blade. In the Senate, after several antislavery proponents had quoted Jefferson's antislavery statements, William Smith of South Carolina rose to object: "These observations . . . are the effusions of the speculative philosophy of his [Jefferson's] young and ardent mind. He wrote these Notes near forty years ago . . . and, during the whole time [since then], his principle [*sic*] fortune has been in slaves. . . . It is impossible, when his mind became enlarged by reflection and informed by observation, that he could entertain such sentiments, and hold slaves at the same time." That did not mean that Jefferson was a hypocrite, Smith was quick to say. Quite the contrary. Given Jefferson's place in "the promotion of civil liberty," his decision to hold slaves suggested to Smith that slavery was a positive good.[5]

As the debate dragged on, eventually stretching across several sessions and even a term change in Congress, acrimony increased and the stakes began to rise. In the final moments of the fifteenth Congress, they were still at it when William Cobb of Georgia rose. "Are the gentlemen aware of what they are about to do?" he asked. "Do they foresee no evil consequences likely to result?" At a minimum, he believed, the Tallmadge proposal strained the affection of the southern states for the Union. Looking into the future, though, it was clear that the entire debate lit "a fire which all the waters of the ocean could not extinguish." It would be put out "only in blood."[6]

Henry Clay of Kentucky, the Speaker of the House, watched the debate with a mounting sense of alarm. His job was to make sure that the legislative process was orderly and effective. In a Congress in which nearly everyone called themselves Jeffersonian, that should not have been too hard. But as the debate turned ugly, Clay realized that he had a problem. He finally spoke on February 6 for a full four hours. In broad strokes, Clay objected to the terms of debate. As a slave owner who was theoretically opposed to slavery, Clay renounced the ideological inflexibility that both sides displayed. And though he would occasionally refer to himself as a Jeffersonian, he leaned toward an instinctive pragmatism that emerged from his sense of historical change.

After all, as almost everyone recognized, over the course of the nineteen years since Jefferson's election the United States had been transformed. It had grown from a cluster of states on the Eastern Seaboard into a land empire that occupied half the continent. Rather than a rank-ordered society dominated by a landed gentry, it had become a bustling, commercialized, fluid, and even upwardly mobile society. In just a few more years the nation would be unrecognizable to its first political generation. Given this social, economic, and cultural transformation, Clay came to the conclusion that a forward-looking vision, rather than slavish devotion to the principles of Jefferson, would best serve the country as it addressed its many new problems.

So while trying to avoid the rancor and the ideology that pervaded the debate, Clay swung into action. First he identified the tricky nature of the problem, namely that one set of states was arguing what another potential state could and could not do. Then he identified the stumbling block for the South: that, as he told the Congress, "whilst our Federal Union is admirably fitted to accomplish all the national purposes for which it was intended, there are delicate subjects [that is, slavery], exclusively appertaining to the several States, which cannot be touched but by them."[7]

This last was essentially Jeffersonian, if Jefferson had an essence, in that Clay seemed to recognize the legitimacy of a states' rights argument. But, as he would later explain, Clay did not intend to suggest that there was "no remedy within the reach of the [national] Government" to address the newly emerging issues facing the United States. It was just a matter of figuring out where that remedy might lie.[8]

Like many in Jefferson's party, Clay moved toward a neo-Hamiltonian solution. On the slavery issue, he thought both sides should make some concessions. In particular, he proposed to allow slavery in the new state of Missouri so long as Maine, previously under control of Massachusetts, entered as a free state (to preserve the sectional balance) and so long as slavery was limited in the future to the southern portion of the United States. This Missouri Compromise staved off crisis. But Clay did not really believe that such a limited compromise was enough. The more he thought about the economic and political consequences of these sectional divisions, which were just then solidifying as a result of industrialization and the massive expansion of plantation slavery, the more he concluded that the only way to save the United States in the long term would be to bind the nation more tightly together.

To that end, in 1824 he proposed an economic development plan that was similar to Hamilton's original in many ways. It used tariffs to protect industry and relied on a national bank. But it combined the protection of northern industry with a desire to develop the West by building roads, canals, and other infrastructural improvement projects that would prompt more growth in an endless feedback loop. With the development of the North and West, Clay reasoned, the South would gain domestic customers for its cotton and its foodstuffs. Everyone would benefit in the end. So impartial was his proposal that he considered it "a genuine American system" that could boost the nation to hitherto unimagined levels of prosperity. It would also—and this is the key point—tighten the bonds of union by making all parts of the nation economically reliant on one another.[9]

In laying out his proposals, Clay referenced the Founders only in passing. "The principle of the system under consideration has the sanction of . . . our Franklin, Jefferson, Madison, [and] Hamilton," he assured the House. But this was hardly more than lip service that mushed all the Founders together and elided the obvious differences between and among them. For the most part Clay simply avoided the kind of Jeffersonian argument that had characterized earlier debates and that had become so problematic with the Missouri question. Those rigid concerns about political apostasy and those dangerous disputes over first principles could only have negative consequences given the new realities facing the nation.[10]

At least initially, others seemed to agree. In the 1824 election—the first to raise into the highest office someone not from the founding generation—nearly all of the presidential candidates supported the American System. There was little explicit discussion of the founding principles. John Quincy Adams, the son of John Adams, and a former Federalist who had come over to Jefferson's party when the Federalists collapsed; John C. Calhoun, a South Carolina planter who supported national development to increase domestic markets for southern agriculture; Andrew Jackson, a military hero from Tennessee who lacked a clear political platform; and Clay himself—all supported, or were presumed to support, national economic and infrastructural development.[11]

Only one candidate objected to national development on the basis of founding principles: William H. Crawford, a Georgia Republican of the states' rights school. His position reflected an emerging group of states' rights activists that rejected any attempt to strengthen the union, figuring these efforts would invariably be made at the expense of states' autonomy. But when Crawford suffered a debilitating stroke after announcing his candidacy, whatever momentum he could have generated came to an end.

To many a casual observer in 1824, then, the debates of the past generation appeared settled. With a shove from Clay, it seemed as if the nation was moving toward a kind of Republican Hamiltonianism that would make reference to the past disputes and founding principles no longer necessary. But this moment of political possibility was about to dim. Rather than heralding a new political sunrise, Clay's proposal set off a controversy that reinforced the Jeffersonian pattern of argument and marked the beginning of a series of crises that would trouble the nation for the next forty years. Those darkening clouds first began to gather through a problem of electoral math.

A NEW POLITICAL ORDER?

The 1824 election turned out to be messy. There were simply too many candidates for a majority in the Electoral College.

In accordance with the Constitution, the election went to the House of Representatives, which had to choose from among the top three vote getters. But the Constitution did not give clear guidance on how such questions were to be sorted out. Everyone began to jockey for advantage. Andrew Jackson believed he had a moral claim to the presidency, having won a plurality of both the popular vote and the Electoral College. John Quincy Adams, who came in second in both the popular vote and the Electoral College, was not willing to concede. Nor was William H. Crawford, who came in third, even in his stroke-debilitated state. John C. Calhoun remained aloof, having withdrawn from consideration in order to run for vice president. That left Henry Clay, who came in fourth in the Electoral College, as a king-maker.[12]

Clay lamented his options. "I consider whatever choice . . . [to] be only a choice of evils," he told an ally. Crawford he despised as a states' rights activist. Adams he disliked for personal reasons. Jackson represented to him a "Military Spirit," whose election would "wound" American political institutions. Ultimately, he decided to throw his support to Adams, believing him to be the least bad of the three candidates.[13]

The next day Clay called on Adams to discuss an alliance. As Adams later reported to his diary, "[Clay] wished me . . . to satisfy him with regard to some principles of great public importance, but without any personal considerations for himself." No doubt Clay wanted to be sure that Adams supported the American System. But it is hard to say because Adams provided no details and a studious vagueness hovers over the statement. Adams did, however, report the upshot of Clay's visit with a sense of triumph. "In the question to come before the House between General Jackson, Mr. Crawford, and myself," Adams wrote, "he [Clay] had no hesitation in saying that his preference would be for me." A few weeks later, Clay publicly threw his support to Adams and the election appeared to be concluded.[14]

Jackson was livid. He believed that a bargain had been struck between the two of them to steal what he characterized as "my election." Adams would be president now; once in office, Jackson believed, Adams would appoint Clay his secretary of state, the office from which James Madison, James Monroe, and John Quincy Adams himself had ascended to the presidency. Any kind of agreement along those lines would have been completely inappropriate, even by the political standards of the day.[15]

To Jackson and his supporters, the "corrupt bargain," as it became known, symbolized a low point in American politics in that it suggested a decline of the founding ideals of democracy by creating a line of succession to the presidency through the office of the secretary of state. In a public letter that channeled Jefferson, Jackson alleged that the bargain had placed "the pure principles of our Republican institutions" in mortal peril. "If at this early period of the experiment of our Republic, men are found base & corrupt enough to barter the rights of the people for preferred [*sic*] office, what may we not expect from the spread of this corruption hereafter?" Jackson asked.[16]

His supporters were livid as well. Even before the election had been resolved in the House, Adams began receiving hate mail that threatened "organized opposition and civil war" if Jackson did not become president. In private, an emissary of John C. Calhoun warned Adams that going ahead with the choice of Clay for secretary of state would create "a determined opposition" that "would use the name of General Jackson as its head."[17]

"I am at least forewarned," Adams responded, before going ahead with the plan. After the House settled upon Adams as its choice, notably in just one vote, Adams announced a few weeks later his intention to nominate Clay as secretary of state.[18]

But he shortly realized his mistake. Between the vote of the House and the inauguration, Jackson and his supporters mounted a devastating press assault that charged Adams with stealing the election, betraying true principle, and conniving to take the nation down the path to autocracy. By the time Adams was supposed to take the oath of office, he was struggling under a cloud of illegitimacy that already threatened his presidency. He needed some way to rescue himself.

Adams decided to use his inaugural to drape himself and his administration in the Founders, one of whom was, literally, his father. He had to acknowledge that his presidency marked a break in personnel from the founding generation. But he wished to make clear that his election did not represent a break in principles. To prove his point, Adams spent more than half his inaugural recounting the political history of the nation up until his election. Downplaying any conflict in the founding generation, Adams told a heroic narrative in which the devotion to principle had created American greatness. "At the close of that generation by which it was formed," Adams told the crowd, the nation has "been crowned with success equal to the most sanguine expectations of its founders." Now that the first political generation had "passed away," he promised to regard the Founders' legacy as "a precious inheritance."[19]

Clay followed his boss's lead. After the inauguration, he wrote a letter to the people of his congressional district (and, by extension, to the nation) to explain how he came to support Adams. In his telling, he was guided only by conscience, not corrupt motives. After all, the goal of the election, as Clay understood it, "was not to impair, but to preserve from all danger, the purity of our republican institutions" at a critical time of transition. To that end, Clay looked to the Founders to arrive at his decision. Jefferson, Madison, and Monroe, he pointed out, had each served as secretary of state at some point before taking office. In fact, Madison and Monroe had been elevated into the presidency directly from that office. Clay reasoned that because Adams had served as secretary of state under Monroe, his election offered "conformity to the safe precedents which had been established" by the founding generation itself.[20]

Adams and his allies also sought to line up support from the important Founders who were still alive. John Adams obviously supported his son. Monroe had given his private blessing. But neither Jefferson nor Madison had spoken. So, three days after the inauguration, an Adams ally made a trip to Virginia to visit them both. After a couple of months' wait, Adams got word of semi-good news. James Madison "appeared cordially disposed to this Administration," Adams was told. Jefferson was less excited, but his major reservations were "particularly with regard to Mr. Clay," which at least meant that Jefferson did not oppose Adams himself. The messaging strategy appeared to be safe, at least for now.[21]

But it was also, quite clearly, merely a political strategy. When they were not speaking for public consumption, neither Clay nor Adams cared much about the Founders. Adams, in particular, had little affinity for Jefferson, calling his political career "one tissue of inconsistency." Their private writings barely mentioned the Founders—and in Clay's case, most of the references to Jefferson and Madison came in letters addressed to him.

Yet those incoming letters suggested the real dynamic. The electorate revered the Founders. Clay and Adams understood that, when facing political criticism, the best rhetorical tool in order to justify their choices and to diffuse political pressure was to drape themselves in the supposed founding principles.

At the same time, doing so put them in something of an iron cage, as Adams recognized. His goal upon entering government service had been to use the government to transform American life. That was why he had been a Federalist in the beginning. Now, though, he had been backed into a corner. If all policy decisions had to be justified by reference to the Founders, the range of available possibilities narrowed considerably and did so at a time in which the rapidly changing world would require governing suppleness.

So, in November 1825, just about eight months after taking office, Adams decided to adjust his rhetorical posture. When he sat down to draft his annual message to Congress, his goal, he decided, would be to clear away the detritus of past political pieties. He would manipulate the Jeffersonian tradition to find operating room for himself by reconceiving of his relationship to the founding era.[22]

The resulting draft was bold. In the coming session of Congress, he urged a robust system of national improvements—not just roads, a national bank, and a system of tariffs, but also a national university, a national bankruptcy law, a national militia law, a national astronomical observatory, a national system of weights and measures. The list went on and on. Using Jeffersonian rhetoric about liberty to what appeared to be Hamiltonian ends about the role of government, he wrote in his draft: "Let us not be unmindful that liberty is power; that the nation blessed with the largest portion of liberty must in proportion to its numbers be the most powerful nation upon earth." That new maxim, according to Adams, helped them confront the realities of their time. They could not distrust government in order to preserve liberty and they should not be "palsied by the will of our constituents" who might fear governmental action. If they continued to worry about such past political debates, he warned, the nation would languish and drift. His message was a clarion call to a different form of politics that sought to overcome the debates of the past.[23]

But when he presented the draft to his cabinet, they were greatly concerned. Secretary of War James Barbour, Secretary of State Henry Clay, Secretary of the Treasury Richard Rush, and Secretary of the Navy Samuel L. Southard all listened for an hour and a half as Adams read the message to them. As soon as he finished, Barbour immediately objected "to the whole concluding recommendations on the subject of internal improvements." Clay concurred, arguing that Barbour had "much force in his remarks." Yet before they could get too far, Adams postponed the entire discussion.[24]

The following day they gathered for what turned out to be a four-hour meeting. Back then presidents did not give a speech. They simply sent along a prepared statement that was reprinted in newspapers and entered into the congressional journals. Wording and message, rather than delivery, were everything. So while Adams again read the message, paragraph by paragraph, the group made small changes throughout to achieve the right effect.

Finally, toward the end of the session they came to the problematic issue that Adams kept postponing. Barbour wanted all discussion of internal improvements "suppressed." He feared that it took on too much and would derail the entire message.

Clay again agreed partially. He wanted to strip the talk of a national university and perhaps a few other things. But his main concern was that Adams recommend "nothing which, from its unpopularity, would be unlikely to succeed." That would be a critical loss of political capital that Adams could ill afford.

In response, Barbour again jumped in and urged Adams not to discuss anything "so popular that it might be carried without [Adams's] recommendation." To do so would make the message unfocused.

Adams complained that he was "like the man with his two wives—one plucking out his black hairs, and the other the white, till none were left."

Though the discussion was genial, they were unable to come to a conclusion and adjourned again until the next day, when they could discuss the issue more thoroughly.[25]

In the final meeting, the real issues came out. Adams desperately wanted to keep these recommendations. They went to the core of his vision for his presidency. He believed that unless the Jeffersonian tradition became more elastic, governance would not be possible and the nation would sink into dependency and inferiority. But he was, as he realized, still in a delicate position. He needed to get beyond a fruitless debate over founding principles if he were to accomplish what he wanted. And yet the manner of his election made him into an object of contempt for many people. He did not want to further set back his administration with another self-inflicted wound.

Barbour and Clay focused on the risks given the political situation, while Adams remained committed to articulating his vision. Adams agreed with Clay that "no projects absolutely impracticable ought to be recommended." But he had a different definition of practicable. He sought to change the tradition of American political culture so that what was not possible now might be practicable later. "I would look to a practicability of a longer range than a simple session of Congress," he told them. And he could not expand the boundaries of the possible if he had to continually pay obeisance to the Founders, as though all the answers to the future were to be found in the past.

Clay recognized the logic, but kept pushing Adams on the specifics. The general principles were fine, he believed, when not paired with specifics that might get Adams into trouble. He picked out, as an example, Adams's recommendation of a new Executive Department. Clay supported the recommendation in theory, but, he noted, "there would not be twenty votes for it in the House." So why recommend it? he wondered.

"I may not be destined to send another message," Adams replied. He could die. He might be impeached. Anything was possible. He might as well put everything that he wanted in this one message, rather than wait for some other, more opportune occasion.

Faced with Adams's intransigence, Clay finally seemed to bend. After all, he fully believed in the necessity of these policy recommendations, many of which were extensions of his own American System. If Congress did not act on many of them, Clay told the cabinet, "there would be a dissolution of the Union." But he was still not sure that it was wise to put everything into one message.

In the end, Adams convinced his cabinet to go along with him. Barbour "very reluctantly" acceded to Adams's instinct. Clay agreed with the general principle but "scrupled great part of the details." Rush "approved nearly the whole." And Southard sat mostly mute, neither supporting nor criticizing. "Thus situated, the perilous experiment must be made," Adams wrote in his diary before he released the message to Congress. "Let me make it with full deliberation, and be prepared for the consequences."[26]

Unfortunately for Adams, his advisers turned out to be correct. The message was seen, even by a nationalist like John C. Calhoun, as an attempt by Adams to wipe clean the slate of the past—"to bring into discredit all, that immediately preceed[ed] [*sic*]," he complained to Monroe. Calhoun was so disturbed by Adams's message that he came to believe everyone ought "to re-ëxamine his new position, and reapply principles."[27]

Others came to the same conclusion. Word came back to Adams of letters in the Richmond, Virginia, newspapers that had begun quoting Jefferson and Madison against the administration. A general wave of disapprobation began to emerge from other parts of the Union.

Even before it crested, the Adams administration began to founder. Rather than changing the conversation, and rather than putting the endless dispute over first principles behind him, Adams's message had simply confirmed the public's suspicion of him. In trying to move beyond the familiar rhetorical pattern set down by Jefferson, he discovered that politics in the United States had become a game of political exegesis. All proposals must align—or be made to align—with the alleged founding principles. "Nearly one year of this service has already passed," Adams was forced to admit a couple of months later, "with little change of the public opinion or feelings" toward his presidency.[28]

THE PRINCIPLES OF '98

Jackson could barely contain his glee. He had formerly believed, he told Calhoun, that Adams had "a tolerable share of common sense." But the annual message seemed to suggest otherwise. Now the opposition could claim, with some degree of accuracy, that Adams wanted to depart from Jeffersonian principles. And in doing so, Jackson predicted, the opposition could "revive the asperity which marked the struggle of [17]98," when Jefferson and Madison wrote the Virginia and Kentucky Resolutions to protest the Alien and Sedition Acts. Just as that political moment revitalized the Jeffersonian movement and catapulted Jefferson to victory in 1800, Jackson began to hope that a similar movement would do the same for him in 1828.[29]

But he also did more than hope. In October 1825, he resigned his seat in the Senate and followed the Jeffersonian script of developing machinery for an opposition party, which he called the Democratic Republicans, while in supposed retirement at the Hermitage, his Tennessee manor. Meanwhile, he and his allies began buying newspapers to appeal directly to the electorate—which was just then expanding as white male suffrage became the norm and as election rules changed so that membership in the Electoral College was decided on the basis of the popular vote, rather than through a vote in the state legislature. Jackson then used the newspapers to publicize his narrative that the corrupt bargain endangered "the pure principles of Republicanism."[30]

Not satisfied with stoking the public, Jackson's Democratic Party also began to develop a legislative caucus in the existing Congress. This was a step beyond what many politicians had thought proper. It suggested the return of the party spirit that Jefferson's victory had abolished. But here, too, Jackson had a politically justifying rationale. As he explained to James K. Polk in 1826, Democratic opposition "will bring every member to the true constitutional point—we will see the republicans of 98—and those who have sailed under false colours."[31]

The campaign was very effective. Those supporting Adams, now calling themselves National Republicans, had no choice but to capitulate to the playing field of first principles the Jacksonians had laid out. Adams needed to write himself back into the Jeffersonian tradition.

In response to Jackson's criticism, in 1827 Adams and his allies began pointing to a nearly decade-old letter in which Jefferson confessed his early error in rejecting manufacturing. "We must now place the manufacturer by the side of the agriculturalist," Jefferson admitted back then, which echoed similar statements that he made in his eighth annual message. Connect that changed position on manufacturing with both his Louisiana Purchase and his enthusiasm for national expansion, they argued, and Jefferson became the first promoter of the American System.[32]

That was not a bad argument, but the Adams administration was fighting a rearguard action. They needed something more powerful, ideally something from the man himself. Jefferson had died the previous year, so that precluded a direct statement. But in the summer of 1827, as the campaign for the presidency was heating up, National Republicans began circulating a claim that Jackson never had Jefferson's approval in his bid for the presidency. Apparently Jefferson had been heard to say, as one paper reported, "that Gen. Jackson's extraordinary run was an evidence [*sic*] that the Republic would not stand long."[33]

Given the stakes of the argument over Jefferson's legacy, Jackson could not simply ignore the attack. Yet he was initially uncertain how to respond. He offered the newspapers a letter of congratulations that Jefferson had sent to Jackson after a military victory. But that letter did not say that Jefferson approved of the general's presidential bid.

While Jackson pondered what to do, his investigators eventually traced the newspaper's source back to Edward Coles, who was then the governor of Illinois but had served as Jefferson's private secretary while he was president. When confronted, Coles told them that Jefferson had indeed said what the newspapers were reporting. Jefferson had also specifically criticized Jackson's "qualifications for the office." Jackson's skills were so lamentable, Cole continued, that in Jefferson's opinion there were "one hundred men in Albemarle County [Virginia, where Jefferson lived] better qualified for the Presidency."[34]

On his own it is likely that Jackson would have lashed out. But his advisers suggested otherwise. "Remember the Immortal Jefferson, in '98," one correspondent advised. He had been "accused of every crime, and his friends libeled in every possible way, yet who slanders Jefferson now? [W]ho dares abuse his friends?" So it would be if Jackson held his peace. The immediate controversy would die down, but the public would not soon forget who was on the side of Jefferson in upholding founding principles, and who wanted to move beyond founding principles.[35]

His advisers' strategy, it turned out, was a path to electoral success. Jackson thumped Adams in the presidential election and his party took both houses of Congress. Eighteen twenty-eight became the new 1800. Just as Jefferson came into office vowing to reverse the degeneracy of the Federalists, Jackson and the Democrats received a mandate to roll back governing arrangements so that they aligned with "the pure principles of republicanism."

CONTRADICTIONS OF REFORM

Yet for all his determination to reverse the heresies of Adams, Jackson came into office without a substantial policy platform. His own election was to be the first step in reform of the political system, he believed. Beyond a proposal for Indian removal, he had not felt much need to speak specifically about what he would do once elected. Into the breach stepped his vice president, John C. Calhoun, who had decided that Jackson needed to move in one particular direction.

Over the course of the Adams presidency, Calhoun had come to believe that the American System represented a union of the North and the West against the South. The other parts of the country got money from the government for economic development, while the South paid for it through the tariff that created retaliatory taxes on the South's exports to other nations. The arrangement contradicted, according to Calhoun, the Founders' purposes in forming a Union, in that it favored one section over another and featured an ever-growing centralization of federal power. Reform, Calhoun believed, meant changing the political system to address, as Calhoun explained to an ally, "the great agricultural interest of the South."[36]

That task became especially urgent when Congress passed, just before the election, another tariff in the summer of 1828 that further raised rates. Calhoun's fellow South Carolinians called it the Tariff of Abominations, an absolute corruption of the political system that signaled a fundamental decline. Firebrands in the state began to demand immediate repeal if the North did not want to risk disunion.

As southern agitation heated up, Jackson initially seemed disposed to act in South Carolina's interests. When asked about the controversy, he echoed Jefferson's and Madison's arguments from the Virginia and Kentucky Resolutions. "The State governments hold in check the federal," he responded, "& must ever hold it in check." Only if the "sovereign states" maintained their prerogatives would the system be preserved.[37]

But to ensure swift action on his part, South Carolina state leaders began making plans to force Jackson's hand. The best way forward, they decided, was to issue an official report that explicitly warned of disunion if nothing was done. The obvious man to write such a report was none other than the sitting vice president, John C. Calhoun, who just happened to have begun developing a theory of American federalism that could justify South Carolina's actions.

According to Calhoun's new line of thinking, any state that disliked a federal law could call a sovereign convention of the people for the purpose of vetoing or nullifying that law. Only this threat of nullification could hold back the power of the federal government, Calhoun believed. That was why, he claimed, Jefferson had originally proposed the idea during the debate over the Alien and Sedition Acts. Just as 1798 represented a threat to founding principles, Calhoun argued, so now they were entering a similar time when nullification became appropriate. But the goal, Calhoun reminded his allies, was "reformation, and not revolution."[38]

Calhoun's authorship of the eventual report, which was published as the South Carolina *Exposition,* was kept secret. In addition to the report itself, the South Carolina legislative committee appended a formal letter of *Protest* addressed directly to the federal government. In keeping with Calhoun's broader theory, the *Exposition* and *Protest* objected not merely to the tariff but to the entire trend in American constitutional and political development. Any departure from the Founders' system tended toward degeneracy, the documents asserted.[39]

The timing was perfect. Both the *Exposition* and *Protest* were published just a few weeks after Jackson's election but before he had been sworn in. They further stirred controversy and focused attention to the South Carolinian cause. And the strategy seemed to show early signs of success when Jackson promised, in his inaugural address, immediate attention to "the task of *reform*." Calhoun and his allies believed that their complaint had been heard.[40]

But Calhoun's feeling of success quickly faded. When it came time to pick his cabinet, Jackson's choices were disturbing. The president had appointed a remarkably common set of people. Perhaps more important, Calhoun complained, "General Jackson formed it without consulting his prominent friends." Still, Calhoun sought to keep a smiling face while hoping for the best.[41]

Six months into Jackson's first term, Calhoun was even more concerned. Jackson had done nothing about the tariff. "That he [Jackson] is in principle true to the grounds on which he was elected I do not doubt," Calhoun explained to a friend, "but that he may by the arts and intrigue . . . be lead [*sic*] to act in opposition to the principles, on which he has been promoted, is not at all improbable."[42]

Calhoun decided that it was time to do to Jackson what the president had done to Adams—stoke the popular perception against him by suggesting that he had betrayed the Founders' intentions. Working with allies in Congress, Calhoun bided his time waiting for an opening.

Finally, in early 1830, he found a vehicle. During a debate over western land that was implicitly bound up with the debate over the American System, Calhoun's ally Senator Robert Y. Hayne of South Carolina rose to complain about the federal government's tendency to support one section of the nation over another. Such action had occurred repeatedly, Hayne argued, in both western land policy and the tariff of 1828. Unless the trend stopped, Hayne believed, the federal government would simply consolidate all power and subvert the Founders' intentions.[43]

Hayne's complaint was actually tangential to the question at hand. It was, after all, a desperate attempt to raise attention to the South Carolina cause by making the debate about something more than western land. Because the American System had become such a controversial subject, speeches touching on it were widely reprinted. Calhoun and his cohort believed that their opponents, the National Republicans, would feel compelled to respond, if only to ensure that their arguments were represented in the newspapers later on. And if they did, the door would be open to a media event that went beyond both western land policy and the tariff of 1828 to a discussion of the consolidation of federal power.[44]

Their opponents took the bait. When Daniel Webster, the golden-mouthed orator from Massachusetts and a leader of the nationalists, rose to decipher the underlying issues, the result was one of the great exchanges of the antebellum era: the Webster-Hayne debate. Over several days in the Senate, Webster and Hayne clearly articulated, for the first time in several years, many of the issues in the new dispute over the Founders.

That dispute, Webster explained to his colleagues (and, by extension, the nation), was not a small one. It turned on the theory of union and the purposes of the Founders in adopting the Constitution. Hayne believed that the Founders had created a limited national government that favored the states. Webster believed that the constitutional framers had sought to strengthen national bonds that had been weak under the Articles. The framers' point had been, Webster argued, "neither more nor less than strengthening the Union itself." The Constitution was essentially a nationalist project, according to Webster. It created an empowered federal government to bring the United States into being as a real nation. For that reason, a person could not tout a fanatical version of states' rights and claim to support the Founders' vision, as Hayne did, without risking intellectual incoherence. "This, sir, is General Washington's consolidation," Webster said of the trend toward federal power. "This is the true constitutional consolidation."[45]

Webster's response was completely defensible and cogent. But it allowed Hayne's fundamental assumption that it was a reasonable political task to work through contemporary problems by reference to the Founders. Rather than keeping the debate on the specifics of policy, an arena in which people could presumably disagree, it allowed the conversation to become a heated exchange about first principles in which disagreement became harder to tolerate.

Hayne seized the opportunity to criticize Webster's entire constitutional understanding. The purpose of the Constitution, Hayne responded, "was not to draw power from the States, in order to transfer it to a great National Government." Such an understanding came not from the framers, he said, but from the Federalists (never mind that many framers were Federalists), who had inaugurated a trend toward national aggrandizement that required a constant vigilance to restrain. Jefferson and Madison's 1798 Virginia and Kentucky Resolutions were the first skirmish in that struggle, Hayne noted. And since Jefferson's secret authorship of the Kentucky Resolutions had leaked out in 1821, Hayne further sought to draw upon the authority of Jefferson for his wider theory. "The revolution of '98 restored the Constitution," Hayne said, "and in the emphatic language of Mr. Jefferson, 'saved the constitution at its last gasp.'" By 1830, Hayne believed, the nation was at a similar point.[46]

Webster, of course, was not persuaded. After Hayne sat down, Webster rose again to show what was at stake. Each side believed that the other sought innovations in constitutional structure that were not countenanced by the Founders. But in justifying his theory, Webster said, Hayne drew upon weak evidence that was both unpersuasive and dangerous. To cite Madison and Jefferson's words in the Virginia and Kentucky Resolutions proved nothing because their language was, Webster warned, "not a little indefinite." What was clear was nullification's probable effect if carried out. It would lead to a collision between the state and federal governments. It would ultimately create civil war. Nothing could be further from the Founders' intention than that, Webster maintained. The Founders were nationalists who understood that liberty from Great Britain required a national union, according to Webster. It was this insight that Hayne lacked. "Liberty *and* Union," he declared. These were "the true principles of the constitution."[47]

While their debate was taking place, Jackson was at the White House receiving reports. "How is Webster getting on?" Jackson asked his political confidant, William Lewis, after Lewis returned from the Capitol.

"He is delivering a most powerful speech," Lewis informed Jackson. "I am afraid he's demolishing our friend Hayne."

"I expected it," Jackson responded.[48]

But still he held his silence. Jackson did not particularly believe that nullification would gain any traction in the South. He also did not want to alienate any southern support, which had been critical for his election. And he knew—after the Adams presidency—that foundational arguments about the Founders' intentions could be a palpable weapon to criticize the incumbent. Silence meant that neither side could attack him.

But the nullifiers were determined to get him on their side in order to control his reform agenda. Shortly after the Webster-Hayne debate, they began to plan a Jefferson birthday celebration in mid-April 1830. Because both Jackson and Calhoun would be in attendance, it seemed a perfect occasion to draw Jackson onto their team by asserting their commitment to Jefferson and reform. As one correspondent assured Calhoun, honoring Jefferson as "the great Apostle of Liberty and founder of the Democratic Party" would inevitably make Jackson declare for nullification. It would enlist public opinion and the reverence for Jefferson's name "to bring us back to correct principals [*sic*]."[49]

The day before the event, a newspaper friendly to Jackson published the program. When he saw that it was filled with nullifiers, he knew he had a dilemma. The organizers, he realized, sought to make him declare for nullification right then and there. The program consisted of twenty-four toasts, many of them to be given by avowed supporters of nullification. After the scheduled toasts, according to custom, the president would offer the first volunteer toast.[50]

Jackson planned carefully. When the event arrived, the president, the vice president, the cabinet, more than a hundred congressmen, and several high-ranking officers in the army and the navy were in attendance. The toasts began and all but six or seven referred to Jefferson, the Virginia and Kentucky Resolutions, and the principles of states' rights as the foundation of the Constitution and Jefferson's Republican Party.

Jackson grew increasingly disturbed by the toasts—many were borderline seditious. Finally, his turn came. All eyes regarded him expectantly. Jackson rose and said, "Our Union: *It must be preserved.*"

Silence settled over the crows. A stricken Hayne rushed around to Jackson and begged him to say, "Our *federal* Union," so that it would be published that way in the papers the following day. Jackson relented, explaining that he had inadvertently left that word out. But a pall had settled over the dinner as, in Martin Van Buren's words, "The veil was rent—the incantations of the night were exposed to the light of day."

It got only more tense from there. Next in the toast order came John C. Calhoun. He was in a difficult situation. He supported nullification, but he worked in Jackson's administration and had kept his authorship of the South Carolina *Exposition* secret. Calhoun decided to reveal where he stood. When he rose, he said loudly, "The Union: Next to our liberty, most dear: may we all remember that it can only be preserved by respecting the rights of the States, and distributing equally the benefit and burden of the Union."[51]

THE PRINCIPLES OF '98, PART 2

The split between the president and the vice president had finally cracked open. But in that split Calhoun had the upper hand. Jackson had spent years crafting a Jeffersonian narrative and making himself the defender of Jeffersonian principle. Jefferson had asserted the primacy of states over the national government in the Kentucky Resolutions. And Jackson had invoked those resolutions as a political position that he sought to uphold. Now the South Carolinians were taking that narrative to justify positions that Jackson could not defend. But he could not simply walk away from the narrative he had created, because his legitimacy before the public was at stake. With no good options, he turned on Calhoun, accusing him of undermining the administration and perverting the republican cause.

In letter after letter, he complained that Calhoun was a

purveyor of "double dealing" and "secrete intrigue," a man "actuated alone by selfish ambition" who had departed from "the true faith" and become "one of the basest and most dangerous men living." Sometimes he referred to him—with contempt—as "the great *nullifyer*."[52]

But Calhoun refused to let up. Even after Monroe wrote to say that Calhoun's public invocation of the Founders caused "great concern & distress" about what he was doing to the political system, Calhoun still did not listen.[53]

By February 1832, John Quincy Adams began to fear the worst. "This federative Union was to last for ages," he wrote in his diary. "I now disbelieve its duration for twenty years, and doubt its continuance for five."[54]

Others questioned the terms of debate. In a rare moment of political clarity rooted in exasperation, for example, a writer for *Niles' Weekly Register* observed: "*What* principle in the political ethics of our country might not be *sustained* AND *refuted* by the writings of MR. JEFFERSON?" His political principles were hardly consistent enough to construct a theory of nullification—or to critique it. The entire debate was rotten.[55]

Jackson tried to contain the situation. In the summer of 1832, word started trickling into the White House that South Carolina's leaders were approaching officers of the army and the navy in order to achieve cooperation should things come to conflict. "The idea is, that by the treachery of our officers, to get possession of our Forts, and thereby prevent a blockade," Jackson wrote to Levi Woodbury, the secretary of the navy. "*This must be guarded against, and prevented.*"[56]

Meanwhile, all sides began to prepare for a state election in South Carolina that would, many believed, sweep nullifiers into a majority and make way for a nullification convention. Jackson began receiving intelligence from Joel R. Poinsett, a Union and anti-nullification man in the state, who pleaded with him to act. "The impression on the minds of the Nullifiers undoubtedly is that no measures will be taken against them," Poinsett warned, "and that they will be left to carry out their designs with impunity." They must be disabused of that notion, Poinsett believed, because "on the issue of this contest between the federal government and a faction in this State depends the permanency of the Union and the future character of this nation."[57]

In response, Jackson placed all the forts in South Carolina on alert and warned his secretary of war that they might be surprised into action. He also sent men, arms, and ships to South Carolina. Jackson then reported his actions to Poinsett and told him to remind the nullifiers that they were not the saviors but the destroyers of the Founders' Union: "They should recollect that perpetuity is stamped upon the constitution by the blood of our Fathers—by those who atcheived [sic] as well as those who improved our system of free Government."[58]

Jackson's goal, he reported to Martin Van Buren, was "peaceably to nullify the nullifyers." But he was willing to go to any measure necessary to sustain the Fathers' system. "I will die with the union," he promised.[59]

His threats were not enough. In November 1832, after calling a sovereign state convention, nullifiers gathered and declared the Tariff Acts of 1828 and 1832 null and void. The Nullification Ordinance would go into effect February 1, 1833.[60]

The dueling invocations of the Founders had now come to constitutional crisis.

Jackson did not dither in his response. He saw South Carolina's actions as a fundamental challenge to the Union. He wanted to leave no room for misunderstanding should South Carolina go ahead with its plans. In December 1832, Jackson issued the Nullification Proclamation (a proclamation "Respecting the Nullifying

Laws of South Carolina"), which again claimed the principles of 1798. South Carolina betrayed those principles, he asserted, by taking the Founders' ideas in unforeseen directions. "Our Constitution does not contain the absurdity of giving power to make laws and another to resist them," Jackson fumed. "The sages whose memory will always be reverenced have given us a practical and, as they hoped, a permanent constitutional compact. The Father of his Country did not affix his revered name to so palpable an absurdity."[61]

In Jackson's view, the doctrine of nullification sought to claim the Founders' authority by playing on words. It started with the notion of state interposition, which could be found in the Virginia Resolutions. It then added nullification, which was found in the legislative version of the Kentucky Resolutions. And then it built an elaborate doctrine around the latter word, *nullification*, which was unknown to the Founders. "But be not deceived by names," Jackson warned. "Disunion by armed force is *treason*."[62]

The forcefulness of Jackson's response surprised many, even some of his supporters. But Jackson did not back down. If the nullifiers were correct, he told Van Buren, "such a union would be like a bag of sand with both ends open—the least pressure and it runs out. . . . It is an insult to the understanding of the sages who formed it, to believe that such a union was ever intended—it could not last a month." Van Buren responded that the Proclamation, with its stark affirmation of the supremacy of the Union, could perhaps be read as a heresy to the republican faith. But Jackson regarded nullification itself as the heresy. After Van Buren continued to balk, Jackson curtly informed him in another letter, "[Nullification] is repudiated by Mr. Madison." Then he instructed Van Buren to do more to defuse the crisis.[63]

A month later, Jackson forwarded a copy of his Nullification Proclamation to Congress and asked for authorization to use military force in South Carolina. This further ratcheted up pressure. But he also continued his war of words over the Founders by grounding his request for force in their legacy: "The rich inheritance bequeathed by our fathers has devolved upon us the sacred obligation of preserving it by the same virtues which conducted them through the eventful scenes of the Revolution." Those martial virtues and dedication to republican values justified Jackson's use of force.[64]

The situation was increasingly dangerous. Finally, with the president and South Carolina locked into a standoff, Henry Clay sensed the time for his intervention was right. He avoided the rhetorical brinkmanship over founding principles that both sides were displaying. Instead, he calmly drove a compromise tariff bill through the House. The new law lowered rates gradually and would, by 1842, do away with the principle of protection in tariff policy. Clay also supported the Force Bill, which gave Jackson permission to coerce South Carolina if it resisted the law. His proposals offered a carrot and a stick, reducing South Carolina's major complaint while rejecting nullification and promising military confrontation if the state continued its recalcitrance. After both bills cleared Congress, Jackson signed them into law on March 2, 1833.

With that, controversy fizzled and all sides claimed victory. South Carolina happily rescinded its Nullification Ordinance, though it still claimed the right to nullify and even went ahead and nullified the Force Bill. The president ignored South Carolina's final provocation and claimed credit for preserving the Union. And Clay confirmed his reputation as the Great Compromiser.[65]

FOUNDERS, FOUNDERS EVERYWHERE!

Unfortunately, the nullification crisis was a beginning, not an end. The controversy grew out of the long-standing constitutional disagreement that began with the Founders themselves. Jefferson had claimed, at least once, that states could void federal law. At other times, he rejected that opinion. Both Jefferson and Madison upheld states' rights, at least some of the time, but other Founders claimed that their particular conception of states' rights perverted the Constitution. The people who drafted the document had themselves disagreed on the exact purposes of the Constitution and the scope of federal power.

But by the 1830s no one seemed to acknowledge the differences among the Founders and the disagreement that had long existed over first principles. All sides instead claimed a stable body of founding principle, fed through Thomas Jefferson, to justify their own positions. Jefferson's victory had established this pattern in American politics, when the emergence of a single-party system with him at its head had promised to mediate the disagreements that he overcame. And yet even this simplification and consolidation of founding principle failed to clarify political debate. The partisans of Jefferson turned on themselves, unable to agree about Jefferson's ideals but also unable to break away from the pattern of argument that he had laid down.

After the nullification crisis, the pattern continued and even intensified. Jackson had spent nearly his entire time in office responding to the initiatives of others. His own agenda had been derailed. So once nullification was settled, he returned to his own political program. In the process, his actions would bring into existence the second party system, in which each party claimed to represent the true legacy of the Founding Fathers.

Jackson's goal, he had long claimed, was to bring the political system back to "the construction of the Constitution set up in 1798." That meant something very particular to him. Jackson was, above all, a democrat. Although he had sided with the nationalists during the nullification crisis, he was far from agreement with their policies. The American System, according to Jackson, contravened the Founders' democratic intentions.[66]

To understand why, we have to separate ourselves from contemporary assumptions. Today, Democrats arguing for economic justice and in the name of workingmen tend to call for the federal government to intervene in the economy. They assume that governmental intervention in the economy will regulate against abuse and ensure a fair distribution of wealth. But in the 1830s, many did not think this way. Jackson and his supporters believed that a connection between government and the economy always aided the rich. The rich were able to use their economic clout to pervert the political system in a way that denied justice to the masses. In order to preserve the political power of the common folk, economic justice required the separation of the government from the economy, Jacksonians thought, a first step to maintain what they saw as the Founders' egalitarian republic of white men. What that meant in practice was that the government needed to end its financial relationship with merchants that had been made possible by the Bank of the United States. Resisting the bank became a way of resisting the entire process of government-sponsored capitalism.[67]

Once the nullification crisis ended, Jackson was finally able to get back to this prong of his agenda. Arguing that republican government still required "a recurrence to first principles," Jackson decided to use his political capital accumulated during the crisis in order to strike a blow against the bank. But unfortunately for Jackson, the bank's charter was not set to expire until 1836. And it still had U.S. funds. Rather than waiting any longer, Jackson decided to act immediately, removing existing governmental deposits on a gradual basis and, on October 1, 1833, placing all new deposits into seven state banks chosen by the administration. The Bank of the United States might still be allowed to exist, but it would cease to be, in any functional way, the bank of the United States. His action, Jackson declared to the public, was a first step in returning the system to those principles "which distinguished the sages of the Revolution and the fathers of our Union."[68]

But Clay's allies in Congress had a different view. From their perspective Jackson was trampling on congressional authority, since Congress had created the bank and had determined that its mandate was not to expire for four more years. Jackson's actions, they said, constituted a violation of the system of checks and balances, a fundamental perversion of the Founders' system that he sought to justify with specious references to the founding principles.[69]

Yet because Jackson seemed to have a lock on Jefferson, the anti-Jacksonians decided to form a new party, which they called the Whigs. Their name suggested that they stood, just as the revolutionary generation had stood, against executive usurpation and its Tory supporters. If the Whigs were the Revolutionary Patriots, then Andrew Jackson became King George III. During the revolutionary era, Clay explained in a speech before Congress in which he introduced a censure against the president, the Whigs had been against tyranny and for liberty and independence. "And what is the present," he asked, "but the same contest in another form?"[70]

It was here that the new reality in American political debate became most apparent. Clay had earlier noted the dangers of feeding all contemporary political problems through the lens of the founding generation. It tended "to make all Mr. Jefferson[']s opinions the articles of faith of the new Church." But now the Whigs had to concede that rhetoric about the Founders was the new medium of debate. Daniel Webster, Clay's Whig ally, even felt the need to invoke Jefferson. In a letter published in the *National Intelligencer* in which he defended the formation of the

Whig Party, Webster quoted the Kentucky Resolutions: "'An elective despotism,' said Mr. Jefferson, 'is not the government we fought for.' "[71]

But their gamble did not pay off. The Whigs were never able to arrive at a compelling political narrative other than their shared antipathy to Andrew Jackson. And their invocation of the Founders only ceded the rhetorical ground to Jackson's strength. While Whigs beat vainly against his encroaching political power—raging against his imperious agenda, his political innovations, his betrayal of founding principles and the Constitution—Jackson spent the rest of his term acting pretty much as he wished. He removed the deposits from the Bank of the United States, required hard currency for land transactions, and continued to look for ways to break the power of the money interest. Congress was practically powerless to resist his initiatives.[72]

The Whigs' failure showed the strangeness of politics in the period. Real dilemmas had emerged since the Founders' era: the growing divide over slavery, the existence of class struggle in the early Industrial Revolution, the ongoing social transformation prompted by immigration, urbanization, and western expansion. The United States was, in this period, one of the most dynamic, exciting, and forward-looking nations in the world. And yet the politics of the period continually harked back to the past. Although the Founders came from an earlier, already obsolete era—a period of deferential politics that nursed suspicions of political parties, democracy, and organized political conflict—antebellum politicians summoned the Founders to provide legitimacy in a vastly different cultural and political milieu.

These many invocations of the Founders did not really provide solutions to the problems facing the nation. Jackson, Calhoun, and others rarely acknowledged the vast social transformation between the Founders' era and their generation. And

because their analysis of emerging problems obscured or simpli-
fied the issues at stake by making them, above all, a struggle over
founding principle, they were strangely unable to address those
issues in a way that suggested nuance, strategy, or self-awareness.

The irony is that Jackson, like Jefferson, was a political innovator of the highest degree. In an era marked by massive social
change, he led a similar transformation in government. He rejected the Founders' deferential politics. He legitimated political
parties, organized political conflict, and the principle of democracy in the American political system, all contrary to many of
the Founders' sensibilities. But, like Jefferson, he did this while
claiming to restore the principles of the past.

Unfortunately, Jackson never did act to address the biggest
issue of all: the divide over slavery. Clay had believed that the
American System would bridge the emerging divide. He offered
his policy vision as a forthright attempt to mitigate the realities
facing the nation. But the Bank of the United States never returned after Jackson abolished it. And as the bank went, so did
the rest of the American System.

We will never know whether Clay was correct in arguing that
a tighter economic connection would mitigate the threat to the
Union that he first saw in the Missouri crisis. But we do know
the consequences of the dispute over the Founders, which ultimately undermined Clay's proposal. By the end of Jackson's
second term, the Founders had become ciphers, even avatars, of
different kinds of political principle that antebellum politicians
wished to maintain. They became the symbolic representatives of
mutually exclusive visions for the nation that reflected but did not
always acknowledge the underlying interests at stake. This form
of argument did not encourage a straightforward policy debate. It
fostered a form of politics that, because it reflected and reinforced
existing societal divides, would prove disastrously inadequate to

its political moment. Rather than facing the dangers or proposing a different set of policies to mitigate the growing division, politicians after Jackson continued to argue about what the Founders would do. As they did so, the divides only grew.

By the time Abraham Lincoln came onto the scene, the entire situation had become truly dangerous.

CHAPTER THREE

Conservative Intentions

Abraham Lincoln was worried. As he looked out over the Union in 1852, he saw ominous signs. The nation was drifting into sectional blocs. The political system, divided twenty years earlier between the Democrats and the Whigs, was breaking down. The fanaticism, in particular, disturbed Lincoln. Though he had been out of politics since 1849, he had long been a proponent of moderation in the tradition of Henry Clay, his idol. In a eulogy for Clay given in 1852, Lincoln praised Clay's ability "as a politician or statesman . . . to avoid all sectional ground." "Whatever he did, he did for the whole country," Lincoln believed.[1]

By contrast, Lincoln saw factions springing up on all sides. Some abolitionists, led by the radical William Lloyd Garrison, had begun to call for disunion. Garrison even burned a copy of the Constitution, complaining that it was "a covenant with death, and an agreement with hell." Meanwhile, the growing proslavery faction argued that any attempt to limit the spread of slavery perverted the Founders' original intentions. Both sides, according to Lincoln, spoke for section rather than for the nation as a whole.[2]

The process, as Lincoln saw it, began after the Mexican-American War of 1845–48, when most of the American Southwest came into the United States. Seeing the vast new tracts of land, southern partisans had risen up to extend their slave empire from the Atlantic to the Pacific. Northern abolitionists objected to the extension of slavery anywhere. The dispute, which involved increasingly believable threats of civil war, was bitter. Although the sides had compromised—through the help of Henry Clay—the factions had only hardened, which was why Lincoln was worried.

But he grew even more concerned in 1854, when Stephen Douglas, a senator from Lincoln's home state of Illinois, proposed an infrastructural improvement bill to complete the transcontinental railroad. Douglas's proposal was in keeping with the long pattern of federal support for infrastructural improvements that had become the norm since the time of Hamilton and Jefferson. As a youngish senator whose oratorical skills and backroom talent had turned him into a rising star, Douglas had ambitions for the presidency. And as a Democrat, he needed to appeal to the South in order to get to the highest office.

He used the bill to accomplish a couple of things at once. First, he wanted the transcontinental railroad to go through Chicago in his home state. That shored up his base. But, second, he offered a concession to the southerners who wished to expand slavery. He proposed that what was then known as the Nebraska Territory be organized into two parts, Kansas and Nebraska. Each territory would then decide for itself whether or not slavery would be admitted.

Given the increasingly bitter politics of the period, his proposal was a dangerous one. Because the Nebraska Territory had originally been part of the Louisiana Purchase, slavery had been prohibited there by the Missouri Compromise of 1820. Douglas proposed to repeal the compromise. But he did not betray any worry that the plan might destabilize the political system. He believed that the territories would prove uncongenial to slavery. And he objected theoretically to what he saw as the artificial limitation of the Missouri Compromise, in contrast to the Founders' intentions. "The bill rests upon, and proposes to carry into effect, the great fundamental principle of self-government upon which our republican institutions are predicated," he claimed. The Missouri Compromise acted as a check on the rights of the sovereign people and rejected the Founders' commitment to state-based self-government.[3]

Abraham Lincoln watched Douglas from the sidelines with an escalating sense of outrage. Though he had left Congress after one term in 1849 with an intention to remain in private life, Lincoln grew particularly disturbed that a northern senator from his own state had acted in the obvious interests of southern partisans. That Douglas had been supported by a legislative majority was even more incredible. After turning it over in his mind, Lincoln became convinced that a nefarious, proslavery conspiracy was afoot.

His concern eventually led him to reenter political debate. The Kansas-Nebraska Act, Lincoln began to argue, was the culmination of a growing southern militancy that threatened the Union by undermining one of its fundamental principles: the assertion found in the Declaration of Independence that all men are created equal. Many southerners had argued that whatever the Founders' claims in the Declaration, the proclamation of equality could not have applied to slaves because that would make the Founders rank hypocrites. That had been the southern argument during the Missouri controversy. It had only become more common over time.

But Lincoln did not buy it. He argued that the Founders were political realists who, nevertheless, remained theoretically opposed to slavery. They recognized that slavery could not be done away with immediately, because too much wealth had been sunk into slaves and too many interests were involved. But they hoped to eliminate the institution at some point in the future. Their goal, Lincoln concluded, had been to contain slavery, to not let it spread, and from there to let it pass peacefully into extinction.[4]

Stephen Douglas and his southern backers had forgotten the position of the Founders, Lincoln claimed. "That *perfect* liberty they sigh for—the liberty of making slaves of other people— Jefferson never thought of; their own father never thought of; they never thought of themselves, a year ago," Lincoln told an audience in Peoria, Illinois, in 1854. The South now refused to recognize that slavery was an aberration to founding principles that needed to be limited. They went so far as to argue that the ability to hold slaves was fundamental to liberty as the Founders understood it. And southern interests had taken such hold of the political system that even those not attached to slavery were nevertheless under slave power. The Founders' Union, Lincoln feared, was headed toward corruption.

In making his argument, Lincoln wanted to be sure to represent a voice of moderation in the mold of Henry Clay. But in many ways it did not quite work as he wished. Lincoln's rhetoric about the Founders hardly encouraged moderation. He did not simply criticize the Kansas-Nebraska Act as a dumb idea, or one that would not work as Douglas had promised, or even as a plan that courted violence. His rhetoric turned a policy debate over slavery into a fundamental debate about the character and beliefs of the nation—which, in a way, it was. Either the spirit of the revolution would be revived, he argued, or it would perish under the influence of slave power. In Peoria he posed the issue in the starkest of terms: "Let no one be deceived. The spirit of seventy-six and the spirit of Nebraska, are utter antagonisms; and the former is being rapidly displaced by the latter." He even called his audience to a renewal that evoked Jefferson and Jackson before him, a reformation of the nation's political creed: "Our republican robe is soiled, and trailed in the dust. Let us repurify it. Let us turn and wash it white, in the spirit, if not the blood, of the Revolution. . . . Let us re-adopt the Declaration of Independence, and with it, the practices, and policy, which harmonize with it."[5]

Yet the poetry of his words obscured the degree to which he reflected, rather than moderated, the heightened antagonism of political debate as the Jacksonian political system began to come apart. In the aftermath of the Kansas-Nebraska Act, the Whig Party was destroyed by the various sectional antagonisms toward slavery that the debate provoked. The measure cleaved the Democratic Party as well, as moderate northern Democrats balked in the face of what seemed to be the continually growing strength in the southern bloc. As northerners began to withdraw from the Whig Party, southern Whigs emigrated into the Democratic fold en masse. That allowed southern hard-liners an even greater share of control over the Democratic Party after 1854. And it left moderates and antislavery advocates without a political home.[6]

Lincoln despaired. "I think, that there is no peaceful extinction of slavery in prospect for us," he wrote to one friend. But rather than prompt a milder political rhetoric, his distress only increased his own militancy and his fear that southern partisans were undermining the founding principles. Men like Jefferson had combined a sense of political realism with an idealism that had made them great, Lincoln believed. But "that spirit which desired the peaceful extinction of slavery, has itself become extinct, with the *occasion,* and the *men of* the Revolution," he wrote to his friend. Now the increased antagonism had left only one question: "Can we, as a nation, continue together *permanently—forever—* half slave, and half free?"[7]

As Lincoln pondered that question, the Kansas Territory

began to slide into civil war. The Kansas-Nebraska Act had proclaimed that the people of each territory were "perfectly free to form and regulate their own domestic institutions in their own way, subject only to the Constitution of the United States." But in 1855, in an election for the territorial legislature, several thousand Missouri residents crossed the border and cast illegal, proslavery ballots. The territorial governor, facing threats on his life, condemned the fraud but did not suspend the election results.[8]

Lincoln again watched the process with alarm, seeing the emerging guerrilla war as keeping with the nation's departure from founding principles. "Our progress in degeneracy appears to me to be pretty rapid," he wrote to his friend Joshua Speed. But Lincoln was still not quite sure where that left him. "I am a whig," he believed, but he admitted that "others say there are no whigs." He was now uncertain of his loyalties, though he had begun to believe that his most important political principle was his opposition to slavery's extension. Where that led politically he could not say.[9]

Others did not share his uncertainty. As Lincoln waffled between moderation and radicalism, many former moderates decided that the time for compromise had ended. In order to resist what they saw as southern tyranny, former Whigs and free-soil Democrats created a new Republican Party in 1854. The name, which emerged almost spontaneously, harked back to Jefferson. It conjured the now-familiar Jeffersonian rhetorical pattern as well. The Democrats, Republicans claimed, had departed from the Founders' faith in the rights of the people and become ensnared in the trap of slave power. The opposing party was now solely a party of the South and a vehicle through which the South could control national politics. To resist the domination of a slave-based aristocracy, the Republicans sought to restore, as their platform explained, "the action of the Federal Government to the principles of Washington and Jefferson."[10]

The Democrats, by contrast, doubled down on the states' rights theories of Jefferson, while rejecting the notion that Jefferson could be in any way opposed to slavery. Their platform promised "that the Democratic party will faithfully abide by and uphold, the principles laid down in the Kentucky and Virginia Resolutions of 1798, and in the report of Mr. Madison to the Virginia Legislature in 1799; that it adopts those principles as constituting one of the main foundations of its political creed, and is resolved to carry them out in their obvious meaning and import." The "obvious meaning" of the Virginia and Kentucky Resolutions was the absolute right of states to slavery and its expansion. If that right was not honored, the Democratic Party implicitly threatened the breakup of the Union.[11]

Lincoln, surveying the political scene, decided the time had come for him to switch parties. But his campaigning on behalf of the Republican presidential nominee, John C. Frémont, could not overcome Democratic strength. Once Democrat James Buchanan won the election, the political system began to come apart at the seams.

Kansas led the way. By the inauguration, Kansas had dueling state governments: a "free state" governor and legislature operating out of Topeka and a "slave state" governor and legislature operating out of Lecompton. The Lecompton government was the officially recognized government of the state, but in practice each had zones of sovereignty depending on the political sentiments of the citizens in a given area. As the dueling governments drifted into deadlock, both sides began to arm.[12]

Yet Buchanan's inaugural address kept with party orthodoxy and maintained a Panglossian tone. He betrayed an almost willful refusal to acknowledge the violence and instead cast the struggle in Kansas as a necessary one. As partisans from around the nation sent guns to the territory, Buchanan assured the nation that with the passage of the Kansas-Nebraska Act, "no other question remains for adjustment." "What a happy conception, then, was it for Congress to apply this simple rule, that the will of the majority shall govern," he exclaimed. "May we not, then, hope that the long agitation on this subject is approaching its end," he wondered, "and that the geographical parties to which it has given birth, so much dreaded by the Father of his Country, will speedily become extinct?"[13]

But his hope was in vain, as he must have known.

The day after Buchanan's inauguration, another blow fell: the Supreme Court handed down a decision in the case of Dred Scott, a slave suing for his freedom after being taken by his owner first into the free state of Illinois and then into the free territory of Minnesota. Claiming that his residency in a free territory had set him free—an argument supported by Republicans who believed that slavery could not exist in the territories—his suit directly raised many of the most sensitive issues being debated in the political arena. But the Court dismissed his suit, saying that Scott lacked standing in the federal courts because no descendants of slaves, even if they were free, could be U.S. citizens.[14]

The dismissal might not have been terribly surprising—though the Court's decision did radically contract citizenship in a way that was truly astounding. But the Court could not content itself with just dismissing the case. In justifying his opinion, Chief Justice Roger B. Taney decided to elaborate a view of the Founders' intentions that plunged directly into the boiling political controversies over slavery, the Declaration of Independence, and the nation's fundamental creed. Taney simply denied that slaves had ever been considered part of the political order of the United States or within the Founders' declaration of equality. "[Slaves] had for more than a century before been regarded as beings of an inferior order, and altogether unfit to associate with the white race, either in social or political relations," Taney wrote for the Court. Slaves were, in fact, "so far inferior, that they had no rights which the white man was bound to respect." Given their place in the nation, the Court declared, it was "too clear for dispute" that slaves had not been included in the Declaration of Independence and were not part of the "We the People" who had formed the Constitution.[15]

They were property. No more, no less. And because they were property, the federal government could not simply set them free from their owners when they happened to be brought into free territory. That would violate the Fifth Amendment's due process provision, which prohibited the government from removing property without the due process of law. Nor could the federal government prohibit slavery from the territories, the Court ruled, for the same reason. In fact, the Constitution protected slavery in the territories, the Court asserted. Any slave owner who wished to move with his slaves to any territory had that right. Taney was essentially parroting the most radical states' rights argument that had first emerged in the Missouri debates.

The opinion stirred northern antislavery activists into a frenzy. It suggested to Lincoln the growing audacity and aggressiveness of slave power. In the time of the Founders, he told a crowd in Springfield, Illinois, "our Declaration of Independence was held sacred by all, and thought to include all; but now, to aid in making the bondage of the negro universal and eternal, it is assailed, and sneered at, and construed, and hawked at, and torn, till, if its framers could rise from their graves, they could not at all recognize it." The Court, speaking in its capacity as the final interpreter of the law, Lincoln believed, had shown just how far the nation had fallen.[16]

But after the *Dred Scott* decision, Lincoln realized that he needed to hone his argument. It was undeniable that slaves, as slaves, did not have any place in the political order of the United States at the time of the founding. They were, as the Court declared, property, not citizens. Yet Lincoln still believed that the Founders were committed to the abstract ideal of equality and countenanced slaves as within that abstract ideal. The fact that the Founders never declared slaves as citizens or did much to effect their equality really did not affect his argument one way or another. After all, he pointed out, the Founders "did not at once, *or ever afterwards,* actually place all white people on an equality with one another either." No one would, in Lincoln's day, declare that white people were not equal because the Founders did not make it so. The same ought to be true of slavery. The Founders "meant simply to declare the *right*" of equality that could be enforced at some point in the future. "They meant to set up a standard maxim for free society," he maintained, "which should be familiar to all, and revered by all; constantly looked to, constantly labored for, and even though never perfectly attained, constantly approximated, and thereby constantly spreading and deepening its influence, and augmenting the happiness and value of life to all people of all colors everywhere." But now the Court threatened to undermine even the principle, making the realization of that principle impossible to achieve.[17]

Lincoln's argument was tricky. He believed that the Founders had laid down a set of principles that needed to be maintained, a posture toward the founding that was close to Jefferson's and was shared by nearly everyone in the political system. (The exception was the radical band led by William Lloyd Garrison, who rejected what they saw as the Founders' "covenant with death" and were calling for disunion.) But unlike Jefferson—though like Henry Clay and John Quincy Adams—Lincoln also believed that the

Founders had begun a tradition that was living and expanding beyond even what the Founders themselves might have recognized.

Those two commitments were in some tension with one another. They raised the question of how far the tradition could depart from founding intentions and still be considered within the
orbit of the Founders. And beyond that, his commitment to a
living tradition caused concern in southerners and their allies that,
regardless of what he said, he really wanted to do away with the
existing system of slavery.

That tension became especially clear when, in 1858, Lincoln
decided to challenge the man that he most blamed for the mess,
Stephen Douglas. Lincoln's decision was calculated and savvy.
Unlike in Jackson's day, by the 1850s candidates could speak on
their own behalf. Because Lincoln had a clear gift for oratory, he
could use his speechcraft to drive debate. And his speeches would
be reprinted and quoted in the print media system, which had
seen explosive growth since Jackson's time. The combined effect,
then, of a good speech and its wide distribution meant that a tran-
scendent political figure, as Lincoln would become, could reach
the masses, build a name for himself, and frame the issues in just
the way he wished.

But Douglas at first declined to engage Lincoln, seeing him
as a somewhat self-righteous protest candidate who ought not to
be taken seriously. To get his attention, Lincoln began following
Douglas around the state, giving speeches in the same town a day
or so after Douglas had left. As Lincoln always followed Douglas
into town, he always got the last word, which was damning. Lincoln's main argument in nearly every speech was that Douglas had
ceased to represent the state of Illinois and had become instead a
servant of slave power, a tool of the South that sought to subvert
the Founder's intentions for the South's own perverse gain.[18]

After several months, as his tactics began to cause Douglas

some concern, Lincoln made his move. He proposed a series of debates in which they traded off the last word. The proposal would ensure a fair exchange of ideas, which appealed to Douglas, but it would also mean that Douglas would have to answer Lincoln's arguments, which appealed to Lincoln. When Douglas agreed, the debates were on.

Lincoln continued his basic argument, though the instability of his position caused him some problems. At the beginning of his campaign, he had described his view of the future by using a passage from scripture: "A house divided against itself cannot stand." That sentiment was equally true of the United States, Lincoln claimed. "I believe this government cannot endure, permanently half *slave* and half *free*," he told his audience. "I do not expect the Union to be *dissolved*—I do not expect the house to *fall*—but I *do* expect it will cease to be divided. It will become *all* one thing, or *all* the other. Either the *opponents* of slavery, will arrest the future spread of it, and place it where the public mind shall rest in the belief that it is in course of ultimate extinction; or its *advocates* will push it forward, till it shall become alike lawful in *all* the States, *old* as well as *new*,—*North* as well as *South*."[19]

The radical overtones of the statement seemed to place Lincoln among the abolitionists. But at the beginning of his debates with Douglas, Lincoln adjusted his position to try to reclaim a more moderate ground. "I will say here," he said in the first debate, "that I have no purpose directly or indirectly to interfere with the institution of slavery in the States where it exists. I believe I have no lawful right to do so, and I have no inclination to do so. I have no purpose to introduce political and social equality between the white and black races." This was a startling step down. He believed that the Founders proclaimed an equality that would someday be achieved. And he asserted that departing from this belief in equality was degeneracy. But he did not have any intention of trying to bring about this equality himself.[20]

His moderation did not mean that he took anything back, at least according to him. To make sense of the semi-contradiction, Lincoln returned to the idea that the Declaration contained a seed principle that might at some point be brought into effect. It could only happen, he asserted, if slavery were kept in "the position in which our fathers originally placed it—restricting it from the Territories where it had not gone, and legislating to cut off its source by the abrogation of the slave trade, thus putting the seal of legislation *against its spread.*" Once slavery was contained, the idea of equality could grow and slavery would die a natural death.[21]

But Douglas found Lincoln's argument historically specious, intellectually self-contradictory, and ultimately dewy-eyed. On a factual level, Douglas observed, Lincoln offered a partial, even tendentious, reading of the Founders' intentions and their Declaration. The Founders had allowed several slave states into the Union even after the Constitution was ratified. And, unlike Lincoln, many of the Founders, led by Jefferson himself, had abhorred all dispute over the issue of slavery as outside the province of the federal government.

While constantly referring to "the Black Republican party"— a race-baiting phrase that suggested Lincoln was captive to black interests—Douglas also dismissed the claim that the Declaration applied to black and white alike. "I believe this government was made on the white basis," he insisted. "I believe it was made by white men, for the benefit of white men and their posterity for ever, and I am in favor of confining citizenship to white men, for the benefit of white men, men of European birth and descent, instead of conferring it upon negroes, Indians and other inferior races."[22]

From there he went on. Because he claimed that the nation's

Founders supported white supremacy, Douglas necessarily rejected Lincoln's argument that the Founders had placed slavery on a path to extinction. Nor could he see why the nation would ever have to choose between slavery and freedom, as Lincoln had claimed in his "House Divided" speech.

"Why can it not exist divided into free and slave States?" Douglas asked. "Washington, Jefferson, Franklin, Madison, Hamilton, Jay, and the great men of that day, made this Government divided into free States and slave States. . . . Why can it not exist on the same principles on which our fathers made it?"

The fact that Lincoln seemed unwilling to trust the Founders, in Douglas's estimation, suggested that his program was "revolutionary and destructive of the existence of this Government."[23]

But since neither side had convinced the other, or really even understood the other, the issue kept coming back up.

"Why should we not act as our fathers who made the government?" Douglas complained again in the third debate after Lincoln argued against the Kansas-Nebraska Act and the idea that local territorial governments could determine whether or not to allow slavery.

"That is the exact difficulty between us," Lincoln responded. "I say that Judge Douglas and his friends have changed . . . from the position in which our fathers originally placed it [slavery]."[24]

In the fifth debate, Douglas returned to the issue of the Declaration, reaffirming that it only countenanced white men.

"I see a gentleman there in the crowd shaking his head," he said. "Let me remind him that when Thomas Jefferson wrote that document he was the owner, and so continued until his death, of a large number of slaves. Did he intend to say in that Declaration that his negro slaves, which he held and treated as property, were created his equals by Divine law, and that he was violating the law of God every day of his life by holding them as slaves?"[25]

Lincoln thought he saw an opening. "I will remind Judge Douglas and this audience," Lincoln said, "that while Mr. Jefferson was the owner of slaves, as undoubtedly he was, in speaking upon this very subject, he used the strong language that 'he trembled for his country when he remembered that God was just.'" By contrast, Lincoln argued, Douglas had never, "in all his life," said anything "akin to that of Jefferson."[26]

In the next debate, Douglas returned to what he called the Founders' principle of states' rights and popular sovereignty. "If we stand by that principle," he repeated, "then Mr. Lincoln will find that this republic can exist forever divided into free and slave States, as our fathers made it and the people of each State have decided."[27]

But now Lincoln accused Douglas of historical dishonesty: "I insist that our fathers *did not* make this nation half slave and half free, or part slave and part free. . . . I insist that they found the institution of slavery existing here. They did not make it so, but they left it so because they knew of no way to get rid of it at that time." According to Lincoln, the fact that the Founders left slavery in place did not mean that at some future time they did not intend to be rid of it. "When the fathers of the government cut off the source of slavery by the abolition of the slave trade, and adopted a system of restricting it from the new Territories where it had not existed," he maintained, "they placed it where they understood, and all sensible men understood, it was in the course of ultimate extinction."[28]

By the time the debates had finished, both men were exhausted and neither had scored a knockout punch. Yet the clash had been revealing on a number of levels. As they went round and round over the Founders' political ideals, they had layers of assumptions that they rarely bothered to unravel. Both believed that the Founders established principles that must be upheld, come what may. But both also had the sense that the application of their principles might take on surprising forms, such as, in Douglas's case, the repeal of the Missouri Compromise, or, in Lincoln's case, the eventual achievement of black political and social equality and the elimination of slavery. Because they never quite elaborated their different interpretive postures to explain how they got to those positions, they kept speaking past one another all the while believing that the other was nefarious and represented an existential threat to the United States.

Douglas wound up winning the seat by a narrow margin, much narrower than he would have expected at the beginning of the contest. But neither believed that the senator from Illinois would change the direction of the nation. Both had bigger ambitions. So almost immediately after Douglas won the seat, both turned their attention to the upcoming presidential race. The outcome of the presidential contest, nearly everyone believed, would have momentous consequences for the future.[29]

CONSERVATIVES, ALL!

Lincoln had surprised Douglas during the Senate race with his eloquence and the strength of his challenge. That would not happen again. Because it was now apparent what the issue of the election would be, Douglas needed to ensure his electoral success by perfecting his narrative before the campaign began in earnest. In January 1859, just a few months after he had won reelection, Douglas crafted a more careful appeal in a speech at Independence Hall in Philadelphia.

In the imaginative tapestry of American politics, he had chosen his venue perfectly. "In this hall we find the pictures, and we feel the influence of the spirit, of those sages and patriots to whom we owe our independence and our constitutional form of government," Douglas told his crowd. The symbolic atmosphere reinforced his larger point that he alone supported the principles of the Founders. But he got more specific in this speech than he had been during the Lincoln-Douglas debates. With Lincoln arguing that the principle of equality was a living ideal to be realized over time, Douglas now put forward his countervision. The Founders handed down a political tradition, he believed, that would look different over time but not because it grew in a specific direction. Instead, the Founders' central political insight, he told the crowd in Philadelphia, had been to uphold "the right of the people of all the States . . . and of every community, to regulate its own domestic concerns and internal affairs in its own way." Self-government and popular sovereignty—the central political ideas of the Founders, according to Douglas—would of necessity lead to different arrangements in different times and places. But the ideals themselves remained stable. If these "constitutional, conservative principles of liberty" were upheld, he asserted, the nation would be fine, just as the Founders had intended.[30]

He continued to push his interpretation a few months later in a long piece that he published in *Harper's* magazine, which offered less theory and more history to connect the Founders' era to the 1850s. Rejecting again Lincoln's claim that the Founders fought the Revolution for equality, Douglas argued that the revolutionary fathers contended only "for the inestimable right of Local Self-Government under the British Constitution." That right of local government had been enshrined in the Constitution and had kept the issue of slavery from threatening the Founders' Union for the sixty-plus years of the nation's existence. It had been essential to crafting the Compromise of 1850, which relied on the principle of popular sovereignty to decide whether slavery could exist in formerly Mexican lands after the Mexican War. California had been admitted as a free state, by its own choice, and the other potential states would soon decide what to do about slavery. It had also been key, Douglas pointed out, to the Kansas-Nebraska Act of 1854, which, of course, Douglas had pushed through. Since both legislative accomplishments sought to further the Founders' vision of popular sovereignty, Douglas argued, they represented a truly conservative solution that would save the Union.[31]

As Lincoln watched Douglas roll out his messaging, he was unimpressed. Since he blamed Douglas for the crisis facing the nation after Kansas-Nebraska, to see him strike a posture of moderation was too much. While Lincoln geared up for his own campaign, he decided to hammer on Douglas's professed conservatism while claiming a conservatism of his own. He sought a way to face both forward and backward at the same time.

Nowhere was that strategy more apparent than in February 1860 in a speech that Lincoln gave at the recently opened Cooper Institute (present-day Cooper Union) in New York City. The speech could not have been more significant. Many of the important Republican decision makers were to be in attendance and, because of its location, the speech was guaranteed to reach a national audience. To appeal to the Republican base while simultaneously reaching the wider electorate, Lincoln used the entirety of the address to show that the Republican Party, not Douglas, followed the Founders.

As the crowd quietly listened, Lincoln began the speech by adding some specificity to the discussion. Counting up the constitutional framers, he noted that twenty-one of them, "a clear majority of the whole 'thirty-nine,'" had acted to limit or otherwise interfere with slavery in the territories at one time or another. The remaining sixteen had left no record of their opinion. This fact suggested to Lincoln that the Founders, in the most limited sense of those who framed the Constitution, clearly favored the restriction of slavery.[32]

It was perhaps a surprising start to an important speech: dry, patient, and fact based. But Lincoln continued from there. Those who had not framed the Constitution, but who had been part of the wider political process of the time, also seemed to favor slavery's limitation, he said. The 1787 Congress had passed the Northwest Ordinance, which prohibited slavery from the Northwest Territory. And Jefferson himself, who had not drafted the Constitution, had provided the original language for the Northwest Ordinance, Lincoln reported. The legislative history of the ordinance suggested an even wider agreement to limit slavery that was shared by almost the entirety of the first political generation.

As Lincoln slowly added fact upon fact, the speech took on the characteristic of a building avalanche that exposed what the party faithful saw as the underlying perversity of Douglas's position. Douglas had sought to portray himself as a conservative, Lincoln acknowledged, but in fact Republicans were the true conservatives since they upheld the consensus position of the Founders. *"This is all Republicans ask—all Republicans desire— in relation to slavery,"* Lincoln emphatically concluded. *"As those fathers marked it, so let it be marked again, as an evil not to be extended, but to be tolerated and protected only because of and so far as its actual presence among us makes that toleration and protection a necessity."*[33]

Yet Lincoln was not finished. In the second half of his speech, he shifted to addressing the South directly. "You say you are conservative—eminently conservative—while we are revolutionary, destructive, or something of that sort," Lincoln complained. "What is conservatism?" he asked. "Is it not adherence to the old and tried, against the new and untried? We stick to, contend for, the identical old policy on that point in controversy which was adopted by 'our fathers who framed the Government under which we live;' while you with one accord reject, and scout, and spit upon that old policy, and insist upon substituting something new." The purpose of the South, Lincoln predicted, was in fact to destroy the government and the nation as a whole, unless they were allowed to do as they pleased. But Lincoln again promised to stand firm in his conservative reliance on the Founders, and he called upon his fellow Republicans to do the same, regardless of southern threats.[34]

The Cooper Institute speech could not have been a greater success. Though he became more passionate as he spoke, he exhibited a patient and lawyerly approach that claimed the mantle of conservatism while rejecting compromise. He masterfully positioned himself both as the moderate voice in his party and as the conservative voice on the issue of slavery. Even his oratorical skills accented this balance: as he slowly moved through the issues, painting his political opponents as charlatans, hypocrites, and cowards, Lincoln never really much raised his voice. Lincoln's calm delivery electrified his audience and dazzled the press corps. His speech was nothing like the demagoguery of Douglas or much else in nineteenth-century political oratory. It rejected the Republican tendency toward moral outrage and self-righteousness. Its tone was measured, reasonable, and unbending, exactly the kind of thing, his supporters believed, that was most needed in a crisis. It claimed, with the calm and compelling accumulation of facts, a vision of the Founders that devastated all other claimants to their legacy. And in time, that was enough to catapult him to the Republican Party nomination and eventually to the presidency.[35]

But as it became more likely that he would become president, the South showed signs of bolting. Though Lincoln tried to soothe them, he could not overcome the polarizing dynamic that the debate over the Founders had created. He tried to make clear that, though he would not countenance slavery in the territories and regarded the institution in general as a moral evil, he would not interfere with slavery where it already existed.

Still, on the eve of the election, moderate southerners were uncertain where Lincoln stood. They believed that his defense of equality was more radical than he let on, and that the uncompromising posture would eventually mean the end of slavery. Lincoln was frustrated that somehow he could not make himself understood. After one acquaintance wrote asking Lincoln to do more to reassure the South, he responded: "Would it do any good? If I were to labor a month, I could not express my conservative views and intentions more clearly and strongly, than they are expressed in our plat-form [*sic*], and in my many speeches already in print, and before the public."[36]

Once Lincoln's election was confirmed, the cascade of southern secession began. South Carolina seceded on December 20, 1860. By early February, Mississippi, Florida, Alabama, Georgia, Louisiana, and Texas had joined the secession movement. A couple of weeks later, the southern states had approved a provisional constitution and elected Jefferson Davis as president and Alexander H. Stephens as vice president of the new Confederate States of America.

The dispute over the Founders had again come to constitutional crisis.

A brief standoff ensued. Lincoln had not yet entered office and would not until March 4, 1861. President Buchanan dithered, condemning secession while doing nothing to stop it or to contain it. Meanwhile, a kind of war of words began as each side sought the moral and political high ground through the Founders.

Jefferson Davis fired the first verbal volley in his inaugural address on February 18. Before the election, Davis had dismissed the Republican Party as a channel of "radicalism," with a "revolutionary tendency" that betrayed true "conservatism." Once the secession movement began, though, he changed his tune. Davis admitted that the South was leading a revolution. "Our present political position has been achieved in a manner unprecedented in the history of nations," he told the audience at his inauguration. "It illustrates the American idea that governments rest on the consent of the governed, and that it is the right of the people to alter or abolish them at will whenever they become destructive of the ends for which they were established."[37]

But unlike other revolutions, Davis claimed, their revolution was in no way radical. The Confederates sought only to preserve and to conserve the founding vision in the face of Republican degeneracy. "We have changed the constituent parts, but not the system of government" that the Founders established, Davis asserted. "The Constitution framed by our fathers is that of these Confederate States. In their exposition of it, and in the judicial construction it has received, we have a light that reveals its true meaning."[38]

Not everyone agreed. A month after Davis's inauguration, Alexander H. Stephens gave a speech at the opening of the first Confederate Congress that went in a slightly different direction. Stephens agreed with Davis that the Confederates had led a revolution, and he even agreed that it was a conservative one. But he admitted that the latter-day revolutionaries had thrown off a certain amount of inhibiting error that they had inherited from the founding generation. Stephens acknowledged Lincoln's point that the founding generation had thought slavery a social, moral, and political evil. And he agreed with Lincoln that the Founders had created the government "upon the assumption of the equality of races." "Those ideas, however, were fundamentally wrong," Stephens suggested. His generation now knew better. The Confederacy had corrected the error. "Our new government is founded upon exactly the opposite idea," Stephens proudly announced. "Its foundations are laid, its corner-stone rests upon the great truth, that the negro is not equal to the white man; that slavery—subordination to the superior race—is his natural and normal condition."[39]

Finally, in March 1861, Lincoln responded to these historical claims during his inaugural address. He had remained largely silent on the secession controversy prior to that point, but having slipped into the capital facing threats against his life, he knew on a personal level the dangers that the nation faced. He again prepared carefully. His resulting inaugural was a total departure from all that had come before him. Lincoln's chief purpose was, yet again, to assure the South of his moderation toward slavery where it existed, while also projecting a fierce refusal to contemplate secession as legitimate in any form.

"It is seventy-two years since the first inauguration of a President under our national constitution," he told his audience. The nation had endured all that time, he said, but the continuity with the Founders was now put in danger by people who claimed the Founders' authority. The Confederates' argument was specious, according to Lincoln, because the Founders who formed the Union had made it "perpetual." The secessionists could exercise "their *revolutionary* right to dismember it, or overthrow it," he admitted, but they could not also claim founding authority while they did so. And, in any case, he was not willing to let the revolution happen. Since the Union was perpetual, it was even then "unbroken." He promised to take whatever measures necessary to ensure that it would remain so.[40]

Yet Lincoln did not want war to happen. "We are not enemies, but friends," Lincoln assured the South. Rising to the height of his rhetorical power, Lincoln predicted, more in hope than in belief, that "the mystic chords of memory, stretching from every battle-field, and patriot grave, to every living heart and hearthstone, all over this broad land, will yet swell the chorus of the

Union, when again touched, as they surely will be, by the better angels of our nature."[41]

But the poetry of Lincoln's words could not solve the crisis. As the impasse stretched into April, Lincoln began to receive entreaties from moderate unionists who wanted him to negotiate for peace. Lincoln refused, again taking refuge with the Founders. As he said in response to one plea for negotiation, "There is no Washington in that—no Jackson in that—no manhood nor honor in that."[42]

And so, at dawn on April 12, 1861, Confederate artillery shells began to rain down on Fort Sumter, South Carolina. The American Civil War had begun.

THE CIVIL WAR AND THE SECOND FOUNDING

The Civil War is the great tragedy of American history. More than 600,000 Americans died, nearly 2 percent of the population. In today's numbers that would equate to about 5.1 million dead Americans. This loss of life was only the most egregious loss. The damage to property was also grave. The South was so physically devastated that its economic and industrial development, already behind the North and the West, would continue to suffer into the better part of the twentieth century. And added to the loss of life and property was the political and constitutional loss. The war left the constitutional regime of the framers in shambles and its Union changed forever.

At the outset, all the damage was not apparent. When the actual fighting began, the radicals on both sides predicted a quick end to the conflict and patted themselves on the back that they were the true defenders of founding ideals.

Lincoln, though, continued to worry. He took every opportunity to tell the Confederates that if they stopped fighting, the hostilities would cease and the Union would continue as before—with slavery protected where it existed. As late as December 1861, in his first annual message to Congress, Lincoln still affirmed his basically conservative purposes. As much as he admitted that "all indispensable means must be employed" to maintain the Union, he rejected "radical and extreme measures" such as the abolition of slavery until they became absolutely necessary.[43]

Slowly, Lincoln began to move in more consciously radical directions. In March 1862, he sent a message to Congress proposing a compensated emancipation scheme in the border states—the five slave states that had stuck with the Union. His idea was to buy out the slave owners in those states so that the Confederates would see "that in no event, will the former ever join the latter, in their proposed confederacy." That would, in effect, signal to the Confederates that they had lost the war because they lacked the resources, manpower, and wealth of the combined Union states.[44]

When the proposal failed, Lincoln had to turn to other measures. He still carefully preserved his conservative stance. Though radicals continually pressed him to abolish slavery, he resisted by delineating his goals. As he said in a letter to Horace Greeley, the editor of the *New York Tribune*, "I would save the Union. I would save it in the shortest way under the Constitution. The sooner the national authority can be restored; the nearer the Union will be 'the Union as it was.'" If he had to emancipate slaves to do that, he would, he told Greeley. If he did not have to emancipate slaves to preserve the Union, he would not. Emancipation, as such, was not germane to the purpose of the war, in Lincoln's opinion. And although he freely acknowledged, as he would say a few weeks later, that slavery was "the root of the rebellion, or at least its *sine qua non*," that fact did not require the elimination of slavery to be his goal. Only the victorious end of the war was his goal.[45]

Yet his responses were the work of a crafty politician. Even as he wrote to Greeley, he had already decided to abolish slavery on a limited basis. He waited only for a sufficient Union victory to proclaim emancipation so that it did not look like an act of desperation. As he prepared the political ground, Lincoln did not want to be seen as caving to radical interests in a way that would embolden conservative critics.[46]

Finally, on September 22, 1862, after the Battle of Antietam, in which the Army of Northern Virginia was forced out of Union territory, Lincoln issued his preliminary emancipation proclamation, which threatened to free all slaves in enemy hands. Through his war power as commander in chief, Lincoln claimed the authority to issue the emancipation in an attempt to weaken the southern enemy. As such, the emancipation would not apply to slaves in the border states, which never left the Union, or to those slaves already captured and in Union hands. If the Confederates laid down their arms before January 1, 1863, the emancipation would not be carried into effect, he said. The Union would go on as before. But if not, he promised to issue another proclamation on the first day of the new year immediately emancipating the slaves. That proclamation would, he vowed, be good even after the war was won, so the other side would need to give careful thought to their response. When the Confederates refused to lay down their arms, on January 1 Lincoln issued the actual Emancipation Proclamation.[47]

For Lincoln and for the nation, the proclamation was a major step in the transformation of the United States, though a casual observer might be excused for missing its significance based on the document itself. The emancipation was highly technical, even lawyerly in nature. Richard Hofstadter once said that it "had all the moral grandeur of a bill of lading." He had a point. It began: "Now, therefore I, Abraham Lincoln, President of the United

States, by virtue of the power in me vested as Commander-in-Chief, of the Army and Navy of the United States in time of actual armed rebellion against the authority and government of the United States, and as a fit and necessary war measure for suppressing said rebellion, do, on this first day of January, in the year of our Lord one thousand eight hundred and sixty three . . . order and designate as the States and parts of States wherein the people thereof respectively, are this day in rebellion against the United States, the following . . . ." It was so carefully constrained in its language that it nearly masked its own importance. But finally Lincoln got to the main idea. "I do order and declare," he wrote, "that all persons held as slaves within said designated States, and parts of States, are, and henceforward shall be free."[48]

Liberation for the slaves had come, at last. And for Lincoln, it was a liberation as well. No longer did he need to suggest that he sought the conservative restoration of the Fathers' Union. He was not bound to unite the Founders' political world with his own. "The dogmas of the quiet past, are inadequate to the stormy present," he told Congress in December 1862, just before his full proclamation went into effect. "We must think anew, and act anew."[49]

But even as he became more radical, he still sought to show himself in continuity with the Founders. Now that he had abolished slavery in the Confederacy, he wanted it understood that the Founders had first declared the principle of equality that he now sought to establish throughout the nation. As he said in his Gettysburg Address, "Four score and seven years ago our fathers brought forth on this continent, a new nation, conceived in Liberty, and dedicated to the proposition that all men are created equal." The Civil War was testing that proposition, but Lincoln called on the nation to persevere. The goal—"the great task remaining before us"—was not merely the preservation or even the conservative restoration of the Union. It was much more, "a new birth of freedom," he told his audience. That new birth would ensure "that government of the people, by the people, for the people, shall not perish from the earth."[50]

Even at this height of moral grandeur, Lincoln struggled to grasp how revolutionary the Civil War was. The war was too messy, too destructive, and too transformative to allow much to remain of the Founders' Union. Yes, elections still took place for the entire war. Yes, Congress still passed laws. Yes, the U.S. Supreme Court still met. But the Founders' Union had died, never to return. Lincoln's radical allies saw this better than he did. Looking to the end of the war, they argued that the Union would need to be remade entirely. "The foundations of our Republic are to be laid anew," said Aaron Cragin, a Republican congressman from New Hampshire.[51]

The war itself had made a second founding necessary. How was it to be ended otherwise? There was no going back, no return to the original situation. In a fundamental sense, the Founders' Union had failed. Constitutions are supposed to keep citizens from killing one another. In a constitutional democracy, citizens are supposed to solve their disagreements by voting. But Americans killed Americans on a spectacular scale in the Civil War. And the Founders had left little guidance on what to do about it. As one observer admitted in 1866 — and he was not a radical — "For the control of rebellious States, the fathers left no rules; for the conduct of our treasury in civil war, they laid down no system of finance; for diplomatic dealings with foreign powers, while our government was threatened with disruption, they provided no precedent." The foundation of the nation had come apart in the Civil War. The formerly *United* States were awash in blood.[52]

Despite that fact, Lincoln clung to his notion of the Founders as visionaries of principle whose Union was perpetual and remained unbroken. Certain individuals had taken up arms, he admitted. When they laid down those arms, according to Lincoln, the war would be over. But Lincoln did acknowledge that there were some intellectual difficulties. Would the secessionists be allowed to immediately elect representatives? Would the Union, after four years of bloody war, simply accept the traitors back and continue on as before? Had the South not decisively proven that it needed to be reconstructed along different lines, political, economic, and cultural? "We all agree that the seceded States, so called, are out of their proper practical relation with the Union," Lincoln said in his last public address as he responded to such concerns. "The sole object of the government, civil and military, in regard to those States," he continued, "is to again get them into that proper practical relation."[53]

As it turned out, Lincoln would not have a chance to explain what he meant. His assassination in 1865 led to two years of bumbling from Andrew Johnson, Lincoln's vice president, who ascended into the highest office after Lincoln's death. In 1867 Radical Republicans seized control of Reconstruction in order to remake the nation. This constitutional transformation came through the cumulative effect of three constitutional amendments—the Thirteenth, the Fourteenth, and the Fifteenth—that Radical Republicans used to reorder the American polity in a way that would have made it unrecognizable to the Founders. The Thirteenth Amendment abolished slavery. The Fourteenth Amendment nationalized citizenship and made the federal government into the guarantor of American rights. And the Fifteenth Amendment gave all men the right to vote. Though it would take time to work out the implications of these changes, the total effect was a profound reorientation of American government—a revolution of national purposes and constitutional design—not simply a restoration of the Founders' Union.[54]

"Candor compels me to declare," Andrew Johnson complained after the radicals assumed control, "that at this time there is no Union as our fathers understood the term, and as they meant it to be understood by us."[55]

As a result, the Founders lost their potency in mainstream political discourse after the Civil War. They did continue to haunt the backwaters and the margins of the southern psyche, but the southern vision had been discredited in war. The more unreconstructed southerners nursed their wounds and bitterly asserted that the war represented the triumph of federal tyranny over states' rights, a struggle that had begun between Jefferson and Hamilton. Jefferson Davis and Alexander Stephens each wrote fat volumes rehearsing arguments about the origins of the war and its radical effect. And in their shame at their lost cause, they tried to write slavery out of the story by invoking the Founders' abstract ideas of liberty and states' rights, divorced from the right to own slaves.[56]

But within the mainstream, the long tradition of discerning the Founders' purposes simply did not have the same degree of urgency that it had had. The chasm of the Civil War was too great to cross for those seeking a return to some primeval moment of national creation. As President Ulysses S. Grant said of the war, "The fact is the constitution did not apply to any such contingency as the one existing from 1861 to 1865." Had the Founders been able to foresee the war, he conceded, they might have supported the right of states to secede rather than risk brothers shedding blood. But Grant dismissed the relevance of the Founders to his present. When the Founders first created the Constitution they lived in an age of sail and horse. Grant's generation now used steam, the telegraph, the iron ship, and a thousand other things that the Founders could have never dreamed of. The "immaterial circumstances" of the age, Grant asserted, "had changed as greatly as [the] material ones." That radically different intellectual and physical world meant that the Founders were no longer relevant. Speaking for nearly an entire generation that would come after the war, he argued, "We could not and ought not to be rigidly bound by the rules laid down under circumstances so different. . . . It is preposterous to suppose that the people of one generation can lay down the best and only rules of government for all who are to come after them."[57]

And so began a long period of quiescence in the battle for the Founders' legacy.

CHAPTER FOUR

The Interregnum

In 1875, a visitor to Washington, D.C., would have encountered an odd sight. On one end of what is today the National Mall, the U.S. Capitol Building stood in a stately splendor, newly completed in 1868. The dome rose to great heights. Its gleaming whiteness emphasized its elegance and proportion. It projected an image of strength and of national renewal. But its beauty was perhaps marred by what sat across from it, over a broad expanse of patchy grass. There, rising out of the mud, was a stumpy white column, much like a huge industrial chimney, that ended abruptly in a makeshift roof. On one side, at its base, sat a group of shacks propped up from various angles by boards that were braced against the ground. Pigs, cows, and sheep dozed in and around the buildings, while the remnants of a decaying scaffold encircled what was supposed to have been the Washington Monument. It had sat unfinished since 1854, when the group paying for construction ran out of money. Though the government would soon be forced to assume responsibility for the shrine, in 1875 a sadder memorial would be difficult to imagine.[1]

And yet, for all its squalor, the partially completed monument was an appropriate symbol of the postwar neglect of the Founders. The nation's fathers appeared part of a bygone political era, now obliterated. The nation itself had been fundamentally changed by war. Capital networks had grown extensively during the conflict. The industrial economy became primed for takeoff. Large corporations began to dominate American life. Labor unrest became an everyday phenomenon. Immigration soared with people from all over the world arriving in large numbers on the nation's shores. The nation's cities swelled into giant metropolises. Modern America, in other words, came into existence following the war.

Because the Founders had little obvious place in a postwar world dominated by machines and corporations, the politics of the era showed little effort to make them relevant. A Republican like Rutherford B. Hayes might invoke the Founders in passing to support civil service reform. Or a Democrat like Grover Cleveland might use them to support his tariff policy. But for the most part the invocations of the Founders became minor, halting, and largely irrelevant. These small-scale fights over civil service reform or the tariff hardly amounted to a large-scale debate over the Founders' intentions and purposes, which had been such a prominent part of antebellum political life.[2]

Even the most sustained effort to discuss the Founders, led by the Populists at the end of the nineteenth century, came up short. William Jennings Bryan, the 1896 Populist and Democratic Party candidate, referred constantly to Jefferson as a man who understood their movement and therefore justified their policies. But even among the Populists there were those who doubted that Jefferson would have supported such causes as the public ownership of railroads, the creation of an income tax, and the beginning of stronger financial oversight by the federal government in the economy. As one Populist judge remarked, "Jeffersonian simplicity" could not work in the complex industrialized society of the late nineteenth century. Jefferson's "extreme individualism" made no sense given the way in which the railroad, the telegraph, and the modern corporation had embedded the individual into wider patterns of social interdependency and connection.[3]

And in any case, Bryan lost. After the election, President William McKinley unsurprisingly neglected to mention the Founders in his inaugural address.

Even historians of the period began to assert the irrelevance of the Founders to the contemporary moment. Books began appearing with titles like *The True George Washington* (1896) and *The True Benjamin Franklin* (1899). The new historical work sought to cut down the mythos of the Founders that still existed among the American citizenry. And it did not shy away from depicting what one historian, John Bach McMaster, called "the political depravity of the Fathers." As he explained in an 1896 essay by the same name, "A very little study . . . will suffice to show that in filibustering and gerrymandering, in stealing governorships and legislatures, in using force at the polls, in colonizing and distributing patronage to whom patronage is due, in all the frauds and tricks that go to make up the worst form of practical politics, the men who founded our State and national governments were always our equals, and often our masters."[4]

By the early twentieth century, an overtly critical attitude toward the Founders also became apparent in the era's politics, which often assumed that the Founders were part of a past that needed to be overcome. That attitude was especially apparent after McKinley's assassination in 1901, when his vice president, Theodore Roosevelt, ascended into the nation's highest office. Roosevelt was not a man much committed to the Founders. As a historically minded politician who would later serve as the president of the American Historical Association, he knew too much about the past to worship it. Instead, Roosevelt continued what he saw as Lincoln's project: the revitalization of the Republican Party by expanding the administrative apparatus of the government, using the presidency as a bully pulpit to create and promote national policy, and connecting the presidency with the management of the private sector unions and big business.[5]

In doing so, Roosevelt self-consciously rejected what he took to be the Founders' vision of government. As he explained in his inaugural address in 1905, "Our forefathers faced certain perils which we have outgrown. We now face other perils, the very existence of which it was impossible that they should foresee. Modern life is both complex and intense, and the tremendous changes wrought by the extraordinary industrial development of the last half century are felt in every fiber of our social and political being." To the extent that the Founders still mattered, it was, Roosevelt explained, their example of "self-government." But in all other ways, Roosevelt believed, "the problems are new," and "the tasks before us differ from the tasks set before our fathers."[6]

The mutually reinforcing dynamic between critical historians and politicians continued through the Progressive Era. It did not always manifest itself as a rejection of the Founders. In 1908, the historian and political scientist Woodrow Wilson, who was then the president of Princeton University, published a groundbreaking new book called *Constitutional Government in the United States,* which took as its starting point the fundamentally anachronistic character of the Founders' government. "Our life has undergone radical changes since 1787," he wrote, "and almost every change has operated to draw the nation together, to give it the common consciousness, the common interests, the common standards of conduct, the habit of concerted action, which will eventually impart to it in many more respects the character of a single community." The new industrial concentration meant that many aspects of the Founders' system, since it was so decentralized, could no longer work. Federalism would need to be rethought, Wilson believed. The system of checks and balances would need to be modified to allow for quicker executive action. "Fortunately," he observed, "the definitions and prescriptions of our constitutional law . . . are sufficiently broad and elastic to allow for the play of life and circumstance." Wilson assumed, with Lincoln and even Clay and Adams before him, that the Constitution was in some sense living and could be adapted to the new circumstances of the nation.[7]

Wilson remade the Founders themselves in a similar fashion. When asked to give an address on any particular Founder, he generally said the same thing. In 1906, while giving an address on Washington, he took as his theme "George Washington as an ideal American." But rather than glorifying Washington the individual, Wilson held up Washington as an expression of the innate genius of the United States, which always embraced change and growth. Or as he said in another address that same year, "One of the most characteristic marks of an American is his power of adaptability. The most typical American of his time, Benjamin Franklin, is our great model." The next month he turned to Jefferson, whom he called "a typical American of his region and generation." While stressing that no common problems could unite the nation of the Founders' era and the nation of the present, he still believed a certain connection was possible so long as one distinguished between policies and ideals. Even though Jefferson's policies were wholly inadequate to cure "the present maladies of our politics," Wilson thought that Jefferson's ideals of freedom and self-government still had resonance if interpreted in a new way.[8]

Others did reject the Founders root and branch. Led by

Charles Beard, a prominent historian at Columbia University and a leader in the progressive trend in historical writing that would soon sweep the academy, many progressives argued that the Founders were white, property-owning elitists who set up the government under the Constitution to protect their own interests. Beard's own arguments called into question any defense of the Founders by suggesting that their political system reinforced elite privilege and needed to be modified significantly, if not completely replaced.[9]

That spirit of skepticism toward the Founders and their government grew the following year, when a group of young intellectuals formed a new political magazine, the *New Republic,* whose name gestured to the progressive aspirations of the endeavor. As a group, Herbert Croly, Walter Lippmann, and Walter Weyl saw progressivism as "an idea" that promised to "emancipate" Americans from the dead political past. That emancipation was necessary, they believed, because only by overcoming the "political heirlooms of revered—but dead—ancestors" could the nation's political system be brought in line with the new realities of their age. They also recognized, with Beard, that the new progressive movement would require massive change in the nation's system of governance. But there was some disagreement over just what that meant. Lippmann argued that they needed to replace the Founders' "naïve faith" in checks and balances and their "machine philosophy," which trusted the system over the people, with a politics that was more centralized, more planned, and more nationalist in its orientation. Weyl sided with Beard in urging a new constitution entirely. And Croly engaged the Founders in specific terms by urging the use of Hamiltonian means (centralization of government) to effect what he saw as Jeffersonian ends (the achievement of democracy).[10]

Together, Croly, Weyl, and Lippmann made the *New Republic*

into the premier liberal-progressive magazine of the era and influenced a generation of American politicians. If any of their political statements sounded like Theodore Roosevelt, that was not accidental. Although Roosevelt had left the White House to go on safari in 1909, he shortly returned to the United States unhappy with his successor and convinced that he needed to do more. As he surveyed the political system, he came to the dispiriting conclusion that it was becoming dystopic. Money had swamped the political affairs of the nation. The little guy was being squeezed. Roosevelt now believed that only a truly invigorated national government could achieve the democratic ideal. "We must have progress," he said in 1910, "and our public men must be genuinely progressive." In that progressive era, they could not be bound in any rigid and dead-lettered way by the past. As he said a few years later, "I do not for a moment believe that the Americanism of today should be a mere submission to the American ideas of the period of the Declaration of Independence. Such action would be not only to stand still, but to go back."[11]

All of this intellectual activity—in spite of the various disagreements—created a progressive moment during the 1912 election in which three of the four presidential candidates ran as progressives. Roosevelt, after failing to win the Republican nomination, bolted to start the new Progressive Party, predicated on a new vision for national life. Wilson, the Democratic candidate, trumped his own progressive bona fides by continuing his belief that the American political tradition was one in which old ideas could be adapted to new realities, even if that required massive change in policy. The Socialist candidate Eugene V. Debs ran as the progressive leader of a new socialist future. Only the incumbent, William Howard Taft, ran as a conservative defender of the status quo. But even he declined to talk about the Founders. His status quo proposed the continuation of the policies of McKinley and the early Roosevelt. He did not propose taking the nation back to the 1790s.

When Wilson won the election, his victory carried the progressive moment into governance. By 1912, progressives had come to the conclusion that if a gap existed between the Founders' era and the twentieth century, then the government also needed to be changed even beyond what had occurred after the Civil War. Since the Founders were clearly elitists in a deferential age, their political system needed to be modified to allow greater democratic participation. And given the power of money and corporations in American society, the progressives believed that a more activist government would need to remake society into what Herbert Croly called an "industrial democracy."[12]

A number of changes followed. Through constitutional modifications on the state level, progressives introduced such new measures as the ballot initiative and referendum and the party primary system run by state governments, both measures designed to allow greater democratic participation in governance. Through congressional legislation, progressives established the Federal Reserve to regulate the nation's money supply and to provide a toolbox to control the nation's economy as a whole. Through federal constitutional amendments, progressives modified the system of constitutional governance. The Sixteenth Amendment (ratified in 1913) allowed for an income tax—a more progressive form of taxation than the tariff that it partially replaced. The Seventeenth Amendment (also ratified in 1913) provided for the direct election of U.S. senators, rather than the Founders' more elitist system of election by the state legislatures. The Eighteenth Amendment (ratified in 1919) began Prohibition, a disastrous experiment and not entirely a progressive one but a clear departure from the alcohol-soaked culture of the founding era. And the Nineteenth Amendment (ratified in 1920) finally granted women's suffrage, broadening the ability to vote to the majority of American citizens over a certain age. Together these amendments significantly modified the Founders' system of governance—making it more democratic and allowing for a stricter regulation and oversight of American economic life to create the actual conditions of equality. When combined with the three post–Civil War amendments and the modifications on the state level, the Founders' government was deeply altered.

This interregnum was not a perfectly progressive era. The postwar period saw the failure of Reconstruction, the rise of segregation, and the beginnings of a vicious class conflict that lasted into the 1920s. But the character of politics was considerably different than before the war. Though political disputes were quite deep, politicians and political activists did not assume the same level of consensus in the founding era and did not connect that consensus with the maintenance of their political system. As a result, they did not feature the same endless argument over the supposed ideas of the Founders that characterized the prewar period. They rejected the notion that only those who held to that consensus, however defined, were safely within the orbit of political legitimacy. Instead, they plunged into remaking the system according to the new realities of their era.

But the changes were not universally embraced. After Wilson's two terms, a renewed commitment to the Founders' government, at least as it was then understood, began to emerge within the Republican Party. In 1920, the Republican nominee for president, Warren G. Harding, focused his entire campaign on a promise of "return to normalcy." Though his slogan sought in part to overcome the disruptions of World War I, his gauzy vision of the past went hand in hand with a belief that the Founders would have supported big business and rejected progressive politics. It was Harding, in fact, who had invented the phrase "Founding

Fathers" in a speech before the Republican National Convention four years earlier. In his campaign, he sought to renew the founding adoration for a new generation.[13]

It was a great success. When he won the 1920 election in a landslide, he returned to the Founders in his inaugural address. "Standing in this presence, mindful of the solemnity of the occasion, feeling the emotions which no one may know until he senses the great weight of responsibility for himself," Harding told the crowd, "I must utter my belief in the divine inspiration of the founding fathers." The sum of his address suggested that the last several years of innovation had been a disaster. The war, and the consequent change of governmental life, had led the nation astray. The United States now needed to return to the tried-and-true path, the old patterns given by the Founders. "Our supreme task is the resumption of our onward, normal way," he said. Only by following their timeless principles, which in Harding's case meant policies that helped big business, could the nation return to what it once was.[14]

To really establish that narrative, though, he needed to overcome the sense that the Civil War was a chasm too great to cross. He returned to the issue in 1922 at the dedication of the Lincoln Memorial. The flagging progressive fortunes and the renewed attention to the Founders could perhaps be seen most clearly here. Unlike the Washington Monument's dedication in 1884, at which President Chester Arthur gave a perfunctory speech lasting no more than five minutes, the dedication of the Lincoln Memorial was a comparatively lavish affair attended by a host of dignitaries. Harding spoke at length of the greatness of the Founders and elaborated on the architectural narrative embedded in the placement of the twin memorials. The Washington Monument honored the Founder of the Nation. The Lincoln Memorial honored the savior of the nation. As Harding saw it, Lincoln did not oversee a second founding. "He treasured the inheritance handed down by the founding fathers, the ark of the covenant wrought through their heroic sacrifices," Harding told the crowd. In that way Lincoln proved "the wisdom of Washington and Jefferson and Hamilton and Franklin" in preserving their system of constitutional government. Republicans of today, Harding implied, sought to do the same.[15]

As progressive momentum began to flag, sympathetic writers sought to renew the political moment by redoubling their criticism of the Founders. These "debunkers," as many of the writers were then called, often complained that the hagiographers of the founding generation and the politicians who followed them lacked any proper sense of history. After all, as the debunker William E. Woodward pointed out, a clear-eyed view of the Founders did not always inspire admiration. His own attempt to debunk the founding myth, published in 1926 as *George Washington, the Image and the Man*, offered a quintessential example of the debunkers' method. It was not so much critical as casually snide.

"George Washington came of a family that must be called undistinguished," the book began, "unless a persistent mediocrity, enduring many generations, is in itself a distinction." That derisive tone continued throughout the book as Woodward extended the mediocrity of Washington's family to Washington himself, and in the end indicted not only Washington but also the American character. "He has been considered the least understood of our great men," Woodward observed, "when in truth he is the best understood."

> People have thought that they did not understand him because they could not see in him anything that was not in themselves. It was just in that quality that his greatness lay. He was the American common denominator,

the average man deified and raised to the *n*th power. His preoccupations were with material success, with practical habits, with money, land, authority . . . and these are the preoccupations of the average American.

Other debunkers spoke in similar fashion, trying to antagonize what the *New Republic* called the "oldish and reactionary men" who happened to be in power at the moment.[16]

Yet the debunkers could not slow down Republican dominance through the 1920s. After Harding's one term in office, Calvin Coolidge came to power determined to continue a probusiness agenda. Four years later, he was succeeded by a self-identified progressive, Herbert Hoover, who nevertheless continued the same Republican policies.[17]

But in 1929, after a decade of conservative governance, the beginning of an economic downturn quickly provided the greatest argument for progressivism ever mounted. The Great Depression proved to be a catastrophe in the nation's economic and cultural life. The economy, so good during the 1920s, quickly came apart. Whole industries basically ceased to function. U.S. Steel, at one time the world's most valuable company, slashed full-time employees from 225,000 in 1929 to zero on the first day of April 1933. By March 1933, more than 15 million workers nationwide had lost their jobs. As people lost work, consumer demand dried up, which caused more people to lose their jobs, which further lowered consumer demand, in a seemingly endless cycle. On American farms, dropping demand meant a fall in prices, which required farmers to grow more food and raise more livestock to meet their fixed costs, which then further lowered prices as the glut in agricultural commodities grew, in yet another vicious cycle. On top of all that, the nation's commercial and credit infrastructure continually seized up as millions of dollars vanished with the collapse of the stock market and banks tottered on the edge of insolvency. For many people the cumulative effect of the Depression called into question the sustainability of capitalism itself.[18]

But not for the man at the top. President Herbert Hoover, in thrall to the businessman's ideology of the Republican Party, re-sisted any innovation in the nation's political structure that might help combat the Depression. Even though there was plenty of food and necessaries to sustain the population, he rejected rad-ical proposals to use governmental power to overcome the pa-ralysis of the market. To do so, he warned, would "destroy the very foundations of the American system." Even as the Depres-sion deepened and people lost their homes and faced starvation, he continued to suggest that the natural laws of the market would eventually right the ship. By the end of his term, when he cre-ated the Reconstruction Finance Corporation to make direct gov-ernment loans to businesses—a governmental incursion into the market that contradicted his ideology—he did so only with the greatest reluctance.[19]

By contrast, his Democratic rival in the 1932 presidential elec-tion had no such compunction. Franklin Delano Roosevelt was by disposition an optimist and by belief a progressive. As he sur-veyed the past, unlike Hoover he did not find much to praise. "We cannot review carefully the history of our industrial advance," he told an audience in Atlanta in May 1932, "without being struck with its haphazardness, the gigantic waste with which it has been accomplished, the superfluous duplication of productive facilities, the continual scrapping of still useful equipment, the tremendous mortality in industrial and commercial undertakings, the thou-sands of dead-end trails into which enterprise has been lured, the profligate waste of natural resources." According to Roosevelt, the chaos of the Depression was merely the culmination of several inadequacies that had long plagued the economic system and that had been enabled by those in government. Their dedication to obsolete ideas about government and a businessman's creed of the self-correcting power of markets had paralyzed state forces at the exact moment when the government had become most necessary.[20]

So unlike Hoover, Roosevelt premised his entire campaign on a rejection of the outmoded ideas of the past. The problems of the present were "so complex, so widely distributed," he told the crowd in Atlanta, that only the federal government could engage in the necessary "social planning" to address the Depression. Using Progressive Era language he promised "bold, persistent experimentation" to counter the drift that had overtaken the nation's economic and political life. Roosevelt had progressivism's view of the Founders as well. He did not dismiss them or their relevance, but the subject never really came up. He instead continually drove home his campaign theme of a break from the past in order to renovate and reconstruct government.[21]

Roosevelt turned out to be a brilliant campaigner. After he received the Democratic nomination for the presidency in July, he took the unprecedented step of telegraphing party leaders to hold the convention in session while he flew to Chicago—this at a time when plane travel was still rare—in order to accept the nomination in person. When he arrived at the convention, he told the tired but electrified crowd, "Let it also be symbolic that . . . I broke traditions." He believed that the times demanded a rejection of outmoded practices and worn ideas that no longer made sense. He was not, he told them, one of those "who squint at the future with their faces turned toward the past, and who feel no responsibility to the demands of the new time." Quite the opposite. "I pledge to you, I pledge myself, to a new deal for the American people," he concluded. "Let us all here assembled constitute ourselves prophets of a new order."[22]

As the waves of approbation greeted the conclusion of his speech, the United States seemed on the verge of just such a new political order. Hoover had lost all legitimacy. By November 1932, Roosevelt's election was a foregone conclusion. His eventual victory with 57 percent of the popular vote (and an Electoral College triumph of 472 delegates to 59) served as an utter repudiation of Hoover's philosophy. The crisis of the Depression had delivered a leader so steeped in progressivism that the Founders neared total eclipse.

But even for a politician as skilled as Roosevelt, the American political tradition of invoking the Founders could not be so decisively rejected. The pattern of argumentation proved too useful, too alluring a weapon. As he began to ramp up his program, his critics, though few, would soon make effective use of the Founders to try to block his agenda. And when they did, Roosevelt would have to decide how to respond. In the process, he began the modern fight over the Founding Fathers.

CHAPTER FIVE

A Moral and Emotional Purpose

They say that a crisis is a terrible thing to waste, which was certainly how Roosevelt saw it. Leading up to his inauguration, all signs pointed to a crisis of epic proportions. Although Hoover had been utterly repudiated, he had to helm the government for a full four months until Roosevelt could take the oath of office in early March. Under the stewardship of both a lame-duck Congress and a lame-duck president, the economy worsened through the winter of 1932. Many people verged on starvation as their jobs vanished, their money ran out, and their homes were taken by banks or landlords. If the private suffering were not enough, a wave of bank failures, begun at the end of 1930 and continuing steadily since then, began to crest. As confidence dropped, depositors rushed to their banks to withdraw as much as they could, which caused banks to collect the loans that they had made to other banks, which caused even more banks to fail. The financial order, already strained, began to approach systemic collapse. "[The] world [is] literally rocking beneath our feet," a financial official in Hoover's administration wrote as inauguration day approached. "The history of H's administration is Greek in its fatality."[1]

Though the financial system was still intact when Roosevelt stood on the dais of the Capitol, the slightest tremor would bring it down. He needed to act fast. "First of all," Roosevelt told the crowd at his inauguration, "let me assert my firm belief that the only thing we have to fear is fear itself." The normally smiling and ebullient president was grim. The nation lay in near-total paralysis, but it was not a paralysis caused by the usual suspects. The United States, he explained, had experienced no failure in its productive capacities. Plenty for all lay within easy reach. But the unregulated market system had broken down. Food and the necessaries filled warehouses while the people starved. Roosevelt blamed the bankers—"the unscrupulous money changers," he called them. His language was the prophetic one of the Scriptures. Taking the mantle not of the Founders but of Jesus, Roosevelt observed, "The money changers have fled from their high seats in the temple of our civilization. We may now restore that temple to the ancient truths."[2]

As millions listened to his address on the radio, Roosevelt promised an aggressive program working on three tracks. He would restore the credit system, put people back to work by rehabilitating the industrial economy, and save the nation's farms. In that effort he hoped to maintain "the normal balance of Executive and legislative authority." But he also believed that the crisis might require special latitude for his ability to act. If so, he saw no problem with the Constitution. The Founders, he told his audience, had created a practical instrument that made it "possible always to meet extraordinary needs by changes in emphasis and arrangement without loss of essential form."[3]

Roosevelt's messaging was simple and effective—and essentially Wilsonian in its treatment of the Constitution. He believed that the government was powerful enough to accomplish his aims, and that the Constitution would provide no real constraint because its principles could be applied in new ways given the different circumstances. But in carrying through his promise of vigorous governmental action, he knew that public confidence would be the key to his success. He needed not just to govern effectively, but also to message effectively.

So he worked on two fronts. Although his first act in office was to declare a bank holiday—forcing closure of all banks so that no more could fail—almost the very next thing he did was to hold a press conference. Because Roosevelt knew the power of print media to shape opinion, he did away with his predecessor's requirement that reporters pre-submit written questions. But at the same time he laid down rules that would help him maintain a consistent message.

"I do not want to be directly quoted, unless direct quotations are given out . . . in writing," he told the assembled press corps. In lieu of offering quotable statements he would talk to them in two ways. He would offer them information on background that could be used by reporters on their own authority but not attributed to the White House. And he would offer confidential information that he wanted the reporters not to repeat to anyone—not even their editors. That information was solely to give them a fuller picture.[4]

Predictably, and according to plan, a clubby relationship developed almost instantly between the press and Roosevelt. The twice-weekly press conferences placed the White House at the center of governmental action, and the newspapermen wrote story after story about the White House response to events and the president's legislative efforts. Critics would later complain that Roosevelt planted stories and used the press conference as a publicity arm of the administration—charges Roosevelt denied—but it was certainly true that his strategy could generate positive coverage. Within the year even Theodore G. Joslin, Hoover's old press secretary, admitted his admiration for Roosevelt. "The comradery between him and the press . . . augurs well for the future," Joslin wrote. "Mr. Roosevelt talks with amazing freedom. There have been times when he has said little of consequence, but he has talked—and remember, that is the one thing the press wants the President to do." The fact that most of his comments were on background worked to his advantage. The reporters would use his information without quoting him directly but in a way that inevitably shaped their stories.[5]

That messaging worked in tandem with his legislative program. After calling Congress into a special session, Roosevelt proposed a bill to recapitalize the major lending institutions in order to slowly reopen banks while restoring public confidence. Once Congress passed the bill, he took to the airwaves for what would become his first fireside chat, a radio address that millions regularly tuned in to.

"My friends," Roosevelt spoke into the mic at the beginning of his first address, "I want to talk for a few minutes with the people of the United States about banking." He spoke slowly, patiently laying out the problems in the system and ticking off the plans that he had in place. Then, he announced that the next day the banks would begin to reopen. There was, he repeated, nothing to fear but fear. Everyone needed to trust the system, which had been fixed, he assured his audience. His entire demeanor and delivery—his slow pace, his assumption of intimacy, and his clear explanation of the problems and the solutions—calmed nerves and created confidence. When the banks reopened, millions of people redeposited their money. The banking crisis was over.[6]

Roosevelt's masterful handling of the crisis suggested the extraordinary program to come. As his first one hundred days unfolded, the president continued to operate on multiple fronts. Under his direction, Congress enacted sweeping rules that promoted government regulation of industry, enacted price supports and subsidies for farmers, put people back to work by offering them a government job, and established regulations for banks while insuring small depositors. It was an unprecedented array of legislative programs. And the whole time it was unfolding, he messaged the story with the press and continued to speak directly to the American people.[7]

In that messaging, Roosevelt's justification for his program continued to be a progressive one. For the first year that rhetorical posture was successful. His threefold initiatives in industry, agriculture, and the credit system got the nation through the winter of 1933. By the following spring the economic situation seemed to be looking up.

But as the sense of crisis faded, critics began to emerge. Discontent focused especially on the National Recovery Administration (NRA), which Roosevelt considered the centerpiece of his reconstructive efforts. The NRA consisted of a series of industrial guilds that were allowed to set industry-wide price controls, production quotas, and employment contracts. But the complaints were many. Consumers resented the price floors that the administration set. Workers complained that their wages were being unilaterally determined by a conspiracy of businessmen. Small businesses objected to codes that often favored larger corporations. And big businessmen itched to escape the bounds of their self-imposed regulation in order to destroy their business competitors.[8]

Big business's increasing uneasiness, in particular, suggested a problem within the Roosevelt coalition. Businessmen had taken credit for the economic boom of the 1920s. And Republicans, who controlled the government during that decade, lauded the genius of American business for its stewardship of the nation. But once the Depression set in, public opinion swung strongly against business, and Roosevelt, as much as he sought to incorporate businessmen into the New Deal coalition, did not stop railing against the "money changers." Businessmen began to fear that Roosevelt sought a fundamental reordering of the American political economy that would, inevitably, require a loss of their power and profits. That concern grew after a series of strikes, led by labor radicals, in the summer of 1934. The new pressure from the left, businessmen worried, would give Roosevelt an excuse to undo American capitalism.[9]

"It must have now become clear to every thinking man," Irénée du Pont, of the DuPont Company, wrote to a confidant, "that the so-called 'New Deal,' advocated by the Administration, is nothing more or less than the Socialistic doctrine called by another name." The trend toward governmental control, du Pont feared, would eventually culminate in income redistribution that would sap the work ethic and entrepreneurial drive of the nation. In order to meet that threat, Irénée du Pont enlisted his two brothers, Pierre and Lammot II, along with several other business associates, in a like-minded businessmen's gathering in July to discuss a plan of action.[10]

The resulting meeting became a turning point in the New Deal program. In banding together, the emerging group represented a cross section of the nation's commercial, legal, and philanthropic leadership. Because the du Ponts drew upon the business elite of the nation, their combined financial power was stupendous. But the group decided that in becoming a new organization they should not refer directly to property in their advocacy—even though that was their main concern—because a property-based argument would turn off the common man suffering under the Depression. They needed, wrote the future secretary of the American Liberty

League, W. H. Stayton, "a moral or an emotional purpose" that could motivate the common man. Stayton thought he knew one that would work. Not many issues, he wrote,

> could command more support or evoke more enthusiasm among our people than the simple issue of the "Constitution." The public ignorance concerning it is dense and inexcusable, but nevertheless, there is a mighty—though vague—affection for it. The people, I believe, need merely to be led and instructed, and this affection will become almost worship and can be converted into an irresistible movement.

Stayton flatly admitted that he wished the repeal of the Sixteenth Amendment, which allowed an income tax that hurt the rich more than the poor, but for the moment he believed it would be better to act as though, in Stayton's words, "the Constitution is perfect." Their posture needed to project an attitude of infinite reverence: "We do not seek to change it, or to add to or to subtract from it; we seek to rescue it from those who misunderstand it, misuse and mistreat it." "And we should remember," he concluded, "that he who takes the 'Constitution' for his battle cry, has as his allies, the Fathers of old. It will be of inestimable aid to quote Washington, Franklin, Hamilton, Adams, Jefferson, Madison, Monroe and other mighty men of the past."[11]

Shortly thereafter, when the American Liberty League announced its incorporation, Stayton was the organization's secretary. The League followed his recommendations exactly. The Roosevelt administration, League spokesmen claimed, was "gnawing at the vitals of the Constitution," "wrecking the Constitution," undermining "Constitutional Liberty," carving out "vital portions of the Constitution by direct attack and subtle usurpation." "The issue is not whether the Constitution shall be amended," one Liberty League pamphlet claimed, "but whether it shall be destroyed."[12]

The League immediately became a sensation. It made the papers daily for almost two years straight, beginning with the 1934 press conference announcing the organization and continuing through the 1936 election. In part, its ability to attract coverage rested on the sympathetic owners of newspapers, many of whom were League supporters. But it also had some serious cash to throw around. *Time* magazine noted that it "takes only two members and a slogan" to create a political group, "but to keep it healthy takes money." By that standard the Liberty League was "really healthy." Its offices on the tenth floor of the National Press Building consisted of thirty-one rooms and more than fifty employees. By contrast, the national Republican headquarters consisted of twelve rooms and seventeen employees. The League used its cash to open state affiliates in twenty states. Over the course of its life it sent out more than five million pamphlets to members, newspapers, and government agencies. But it never had many members. At its peak in the summer of 1936, it boasted only 124,856 subscribers. The lack of membership proved to be a problem but the organization made up for it by an almost unlimited set of resources and the determined commitment of the nation's financial elite to defeat the New Deal.[13]

Roosevelt initially assumed a jaundiced posture toward the League. Though he was out of town for its first press conference, the White House reporters demanded a reaction on his return. "Personally, my own feeling is this," he told the press.

> When you come down to the definition of American principles you want to go the whole hog; you want to go all the way, instead of stopping short. An organization that advocates two or three out of the Ten Commandments, may be

a perfectly good organization in the sense that you couldn't object to the two or three out of the Ten Commandments, but it would have certain shortcomings in having failed to advocate the other seven or eight Commandments.

The American Liberty League, Roosevelt thought, had done the same thing with the American political tradition. But Roosevelt was not content to leave it there. He slyly asked the reporters "whether the other name for their God was not 'property.'" If so, the League could be said to have violated the most important commandment of all.[14]

Yet his amusement concealed a deeper concern. Roosevelt quickly saw the danger the League posed to his own program. As a master of the symbolic aspect of governance and the use of mass media, he realized that by capturing media attention and by using the symbolic cover of the Constitution to move its agenda, the League created a narrative that could delegitimize Roosevelt's legislative goals.

That danger became even more apparent after the U.S. Supreme Court began striking down New Deal legislation, moves by the Court that the League also encouraged. After its incorporation, League leaders quickly convened a committee of the nation's best corporate lawyers, in accordance with Stayton's plan, who produced a brief against the constitutionality of various New Deal programs. The total cost to a corporation for such a brief, considering all the billable hours and the lawyers involved, would have run at least $100,000, but the League distributed it to all manufacturers for their free use. The first print run was forty thousand copies, and it was followed quickly by another large print run. As a result, a fifty-dollar lawyer could file the brief on behalf of a manufacturer in his local court, which smoothed the way to numerous business challenges to the New Deal. When the courts

131

then struck down various programs, it reinforced the League's narrative that Roosevelt sought to destroy the Constitution.[15]

At no time was the danger clearer than May 1935, when the Court issued two devastating opinions that threatened the entire New Deal program. The first, *Retirement Board v. Alton Railroad Co.,* struck down a pension scheme that sought to regulate the railroads. The five-person majority believed, like Jefferson of old, that the government created by the Constitution was "one of enumerated powers." The commerce clause of the Constitution, which allowed the federal government to regulate interstate commerce, did not cover a pension scheme and so was "beyond the true purpose of the grant [of power]." Although the minority on the Court saw the Constitution as a relatively capacious grant of power and objected to the "unwarranted limitation" that the majority placed on the Congress, it became apparent that the New Deal allies on the Court did not have the votes.[16]

If that were not bad enough for Roosevelt, the second decision, *A.L.A. Schechter Poultry Corp. v. United States,* went much further. In a unanimous decision the justices struck down the National Recovery Administration, which Roosevelt considered the centerpiece of the New Deal. In rejecting the administration's arguments in favor of constitutionality, the Court ruled that the bill creating the NRA suffered various fatal flaws. It improperly delegated legislative power—the power of writing regulation—to the executive branch. That violated the separation of powers and tended to create too strong an executive. And those regulations applied too broadly, even to businesses that did not sell their products out of state. Without that interstate sale, the Court ruled, the commerce clause could not apply. The federal government had overstepped its authority.[17]

Roosevelt was incensed. "Well, where was Ben Cardozo?" he demanded, referring to a reliable ally on the Court. "And what about old Isaiah [Louis Brandeis]?" Roosevelt could not understand how they could support the logic of the ruling.[18]

Four days later, he gave vent to his anger at a remarkable press conference. "Suppose we make this background," he told the reporters. Then he launched into an extended tirade against the Court. Roosevelt read from telegram after telegram that denounced the decision and that pled with him to do something to save the legislation. But all of these telegrams, Roosevelt explained, missed the essential implication of the Court's ruling, which was "more important than any decision probably since the Dred Scott case." By defining interstate commerce as the transit of goods across state lines, the Court had gone back to an old and obsolete conception of commerce. Given the interconnectedness of modern markets and the interdependence of many interests in the nation, many business concerns inside a state would still affect interstate commerce—from prices to production to wages. The Court had been applying, before this latest decision, a broad definition of interstate commerce appropriate to "present-day civilization." Now it threatened to take the nation back to what Roosevelt called "the horse-and-buggy age," the age of the Founders.[19]

But the Founding Fathers, Roosevelt continued, had no understanding of the relationship between earning capacity, buying power, and national economic health. "The question of fair business practices had never been discussed" when the Constitution was drafted, because "the word was unknown in the vocabulary of the Founding Fathers." "In other words," he concluded, "the whole picture was a different one when the interstate commerce clause was put into the Constitution from what it is now." Yet the Court obtusely sought to interpret the Constitution without regard to circumstance.[20]

When his tirade came to an end, the reporters pressed him. "You referred to the *Dred Scott* decision," one asked. "That was followed by the Civil War and by at least two amendments to the Constitution." Could the administration overcome the Court "except by a Constitutional Amendment?"

"No; we haven't got to that yet," Roosevelt responded.

"Or a war?" another asked, to the general amusement of the reporters.

"Just qualifying the issue, that is all," the president told him, again ducking the question.[21]

Roosevelt recognized the difficulty of his position. Up until that point, he had made a straightforward progressive argument: The nation had changed since the time of the Founders. The old ideas no longer applied. The new interconnectedness of the industrial economy required either the new application of old ideas or, more simply, required new ideas entirely. But now he faced a business insurgency—the Liberty League—which clothed its activities in the Constitution, and a hostile Court, whose decisions seemed to buttress the League's claims. The entire New Deal was imperiled.

The trick, which he declined to reveal in the press conference, was to frame his goals in a way that did not play into his opponents' hands. He needed a better narrative that removed the symbolic covering of the Liberty League and that pressured the Court while legitimating his own actions. He needed, in short, to appropriate the Founders for himself.

THE SYMBOLS OF GOVERNMENT

That, it turned out, would be a difficult task. Roosevelt was essentially making what he saw as a rational historical argument, while the American Liberty League was demagoguing to cover their true interests. Reason and historical analysis seemed inadequate to address the threat. So what to do?

Liberal thinkers had been pondering just that issue for a while. Back in 1922, shortly after Republicans began invoking the Founders again, Walter Lippmann, who was one of the intellectuals who began the *New Republic* in 1914, had come to the dispiriting conclusion that the public was just not rational. People possessed inchoate and often contradictory mental images about themselves and the world that needed to be flattered or assuaged, he believed. Politicians needed to understand whatever irrational mental symbols existed in the public's brain so that they could frame their message not according to the canons of rationality but in a way that would maximize support among this irrational public. Mass communication could then be used to manipulate public opinion in order to achieve what Lippmann called "the manufacture of consent."[22]

The proper word for such a program is, of course, propaganda. As Harold D. Lasswell, an eminent theorist of propaganda, explained in 1927, "Every cultural group has its vested values" to which a would-be leader must appeal. If a political leader sought to create support for his plan, the initiative "must be presented, not as a menace and an obstruction, nor as despicable or absurd, but as a protector of our values, a champion of our dreams, and a model of virtue and propriety." The key to effective propaganda lay in "the management of collective attitudes by the manipulation of significant symbols," such as the Founders or the Constitution.[23]

By 1935, as the Court began striking down New Deal legislation, it appeared that the American Liberty League was winning the propaganda war. By using the Constitution as a symbol to preserve businessmen's political and social power, they had successfully set Roosevelt on his heels. And although polling proved to be not entirely accurate in this era, the polls through 1935 showed a precipitous drop in Roosevelt's approval ratings. In spring 1935, a poll for the Democratic National Committee found that Roosevelt's approval rating was at its lowest point since taking office. Going into the 1936 election cycle, the news was worrisome.[24]

As a result, Roosevelt's allies began to think even more seriously about the problem of propaganda—or as we might say, messaging. Thurman Arnold, a Yale law professor who operated as an outside consultant for the administration and would soon lead the antitrust division of the Justice Department, wrote that Roosevelt needed to realize that his appeals were not working. Because he was battling "the legal theology of the times," a rational argument only went so far. Law operated by constantly looking backward, in spite of the onward flow of time. To rail against that dynamic displayed only futile resistance to "the irrational elements of [all] institutions." So rather than resist that irrationality, Arnold believed, Roosevelt should embrace the reality of "governmental symbols" in order to "use the Constitution as a great unifying force without foregoing sensible and practical advantages on its account."[25]

The problem was how to do that. As another liberal political scientist, Edward S. Corwin, explained, the Constitution provided both an opportunity and a threat by existing as a symbol in what he called "the *mass mind*." It was—as W. H. Stayton had observed before him—pretty much an empty symbol that equated with whatever a person thought was good. And since the Founders were also revered, a self-reinforcing dynamic occurred in which, Corwin explained, "the virtues of the framers were imputed to their handiwork, as were its virtues to them." Given the popular reverence for both the Constitution and its framers, the public was liable to regard the Constitution as a closed system of perfected genius that needed to be honored without change. That attitude toward the Constitution made it into a powerful weapon of entrenched minority interests, who could appeal to some putative constitutional arrangement in order to thwart any effort for democratic reform. Slaveholders had perfected the strategy prior to the Civil War, and now, Corwin feared, big business was doing the same thing.[26]

Fortunately for his allies, Roosevelt had instinctively thought along just these lines. He loved quoting Oliver Wendell Holmes's maxim "We live by symbols." And Roosevelt was ordinarily a master manipulator of the symbolic aspects of governance. But now he felt stuck.[27]

Not sure exactly what to do, he first began to rebuild his coalition. In April 1935, he signed the Emergency Relief Appropriation Act, which created, among other things, a much-expanded jobs program under the Works Progress Administration. That June, he proposed a new series of taxes on the wealthy, called the "Soak the Rich" taxes, in order to make up the budget shortfalls. The next month he signed the National Labor Relations Act, a transparently prolabor bill that provided an enforcement mechanism to protect workers' rights to organize and to collectively bargain. Since business had begun to pull out of the New Deal effort, Roosevelt had nothing to lose by pursuing an even more aggressive antibusiness agenda. And the next month he signed the Social Security Act, which represented a sea change in governing assumptions about personal responsibility. By protecting the old, the unemployed, and the disabled from indigence, the act created a new set of social rights to be protected by the federal government.[28]

But his political warrant for pursuing these actions was muddled, at best. When he proposed the new taxes on the wealthy, he used the old progressive trope of interdependence. "The individual does not create the product of his industry with his own hands," he lectured Congress. "He utilizes the many processes and forces of mass production to meet the demands of a national and international market." But Roosevelt also introduced a new point. When he recommended new inheritance taxes, he began to speak of the Founding Fathers. Massive accumulation of wealth, Roosevelt explained, was "inconsistent with the ideals of the generation which established our Government."[29]

Though he did not elaborate on the idea, he spent the rest of 1935 trying out various messaging strategies without committing to any single one. At the approach of the New Year, he had decided on his new message, which he would roll out at the State of the Union in early January. To ensure that it would reach the widest possible radio audience, he requested the nearly unprecedented procedure of an evening address to both houses of Congress. The previous and only occasion when a president had given such an evening address was back in April 1917, when Wilson presented his War Message to Congress, just prior to American entry into World War I. Republicans complained about Roosevelt's publicity stunt, and the press immediately saw that the address would, in the words of the New York Times, "set the pattern for the administration re-election campaign."[30]

Public demand for the speech turned out to be enormous. More people requested seats than on any other occasion since Wilson's War Message, so when the evening arrived the chamber was completely packed. Roosevelt stood behind the podium, looked out over the crowded room, and began speaking into the microphones. His goal was to regain control of the narrative, and it became apparent early on that the speech would make no concessions. Roosevelt directly addressed his business opponents and, by implication, the Supreme Court, calling them an entrenched and aristocratic minority that sought to obscure their invidious goals by appropriating "the livery of great national constitutional ideals." Instead of upholding the best of American life, Roosevelt maintained, they secretly sought economic autocracy.

To the Capitol audience and the millions listening on the radio, Roosevelt promised to resist the autocrats. In doing so, he said, he would be defending America.[31]

To explain his resistance, he fully shifted his rhetorical strategies. He now no longer spoke of reconstructing and transforming American government to meet the new realities of an industrial age. His goal, he said, was primarily restorative. The battle he fought began "in the Constitutional Convention of 1787." "From time to time since then," he elaborated, "the battle has been continued, under Thomas Jefferson, Andrew Jackson, Theodore Roosevelt and Woodrow Wilson." Roosevelt stood in this tradition and had fought the battle for the past thirty-four months. Now, he believed, the work of restoration was nearly complete. But "a power-seeking minority" sought to block his accomplishments. "I recommend that we advance," he told the crowd, "we do not retreat."[32]

It was perhaps a subtle shift, but it turned out to be a decisive one. His partisans were electrified. His opponents were outraged. In turning to the Founders, he now put forward an almost cyclical view of history in which the founding ideals came under threat and had to be reformed back to their original intentions. It was fully Jeffersonian in its rhetorical posture toward the founding era. "Permeated with a fighting spirit," the *New York Times* reported the next day, "the message was even more than the partisan critics of tonight's spectacular setting had expected in the way of a call to political battle."[33]

Unfortunately for Roosevelt, three days later the Court handed down another rebuke to the administration. In a 6–3 decision, the justices struck down the Agricultural Adjustment Act as unconstitutional. Their reasoning was, by all accounts, highly peculiar. The act had used a taxation scheme to limit agricultural production and to pay for farm subsidies. Everyone agreed that the federal government had the power to tax. But, the Court declared, "the act invades the reserved rights of the states." Even though the act used a power that everyone acknowledged Congress possessed—because it was specifically enumerated in the Constitution—the Court declared that the Agricultural Adjustment Act used a legitimate power of Congress as "but [a] means to an unconstitutional end." In other words, the Court now claimed that it could strike down an act that used a legitimate and express power of Congress, if that act infringed on the powers of the states, which were for the most part unexpressed and undefined by the Constitution. Critics of the decision thought that the Court's reasoning granted itself power to strike down almost anything that did not accord, as Roosevelt said in a memo, with "the private, social philosophy of a majority of nine appointed members of the Supreme Court itself."[34]

But in public Roosevelt kept his peace and avoided a repeat of his earlier press conference, when the Court struck down the NRA. He simply stuck to his message that he sought to preserve the Constitution of the Founders.

Two days later he gave his second national address in a week, where he sought to solidify his new narrative. At the Mayflower Hotel in Washington, Roosevelt walked out beneath a portrait of Jackson and began speaking into the microphones so that his address could be relayed to three thousand other Jackson Day dinners around the nation. Though he avoided specific discussion of the case, he continued to suggest that the Liberty League and his Court opponents were modern Tories, aristocrats who had resisted the democratizing efforts of Jefferson and then Jackson.

"Because history so often repeats itself," Roosevelt noted, "let me analyze further." Jackson faced an entrenched minority interest of the wealthiest of the nation. All the power of the nation was arrayed against him, Roosevelt said. The only thing he had on his side was the people. But that was enough to triumph. The more Roosevelt spoke about Jackson, the more it became apparent that he was really talking about himself. In case anyone missed his point, he said the same thing two more times. "History repeats— and I am becoming dimly conscious of the fact that this year we are to have a national election," he coyly observed. And again a little later: "History repeats." His point was that he, like Jackson, was a conservative defender against perennial opponents of founding ideals.[35]

But as Roosevelt rolled out his new narrative, the Liberty League did not sit idle. The Leaguers' own narrative needed to be nurtured and expanded. A couple of weeks after Roosevelt's media blitz, the League recruited Al Smith, the Democratic presidential candidate in 1928 and a four-time governor of New York, to give a national address denouncing Roosevelt. The League's speech was also slated to be at the Mayflower Hotel. Because the dinner was so obviously the League's response to Roosevelt's two earlier messages, advance media attention was all that League leaders could have wished. Breathless news coverage spoke of the dueling messages between the President and the League, which further stoked interest.[36]

On the evening of the dinner, the place was crammed with wealthy men and women in formal wear. So many people had wanted to attend that tables were placed in the main hall of the hotel in order to handle the guest list. Yet the organizers still had to turn down four thousand people who had requested tickets. As the warm-up speakers addressed the audience, Smith listened with obvious impatience for his turn. Finally, Smith stepped up to the microphones accompanied by thunderous applause. His raspy and working-class voice, obvious on the radio, was perfectly chosen to counter Roosevelt's charges that the League represented rich Republicans.

Smith presented himself only as a patriot, not as a man running for office and, in fact, as a lifelong Democrat. The present Democratic administration had begun to undermine "the fundamental principles on which this government of ours was organized," Smith claimed. That fact pained him, he said, and ultimately caused him to speak up. Then he said just what the League had wanted to hear. According to Smith, Roosevelt had abandoned "the greatest declaration of political principles that ever came from the hands of man, the Declaration of Independence and the Constitution of the United States." While professing fidelity to the Constitution and while stressing the necessity of his actions, Roosevelt had taken the nation off course and down the road to socialism and autocracy. Smith implored the members of Congress to remember their oath to support the Constitution: "I suggest from this moment on they resolve to make the Constitution again the civil bible of the United States and pay it the same civil respect and reverence that they would religiously pay the Holy Scripture." Only then could the American experiment continue to provide opportunity for the common man.[37]

To see a champion of the working class attack Roosevelt so ruthlessly was a thrill for Liberty League supporters. Smith's speech was punctuated by so much applause that Jouett Shouse, the president of the League, at one point urged silence as the radio time was "passing swiftly." But as much as Shouse was concerned with the wider audience, he failed to consider the political effect of a speech given to the nation's business elite. Newspapermen estimated that the audience's personal wealth topped $1 billion, an astounding amount in 1936. And no matter the working-class origins of Al Smith, the applause from the nation's business elite reinforced Roosevelt's entire narrative that the League consisted of a plutocracy who sought to hold back his programs while enriching themselves.[38]

Still, as much as Roosevelt sensed weakness, he worried about the financial power of the League, which could buy coverage at will. So as the administration's political team prepared for the 1936 election season, they decided to ignore the Republican Party and instead concentrate all their fire on the League and its spokesmen. It had to be portrayed as a selfish agent of aggrandizing businessmen who simply wanted to protect profits. "Ours must be a truth-telling and falsehood exposing campaign," he stressed to an adviser, "that will get into every home." Roosevelt placed himself at the center of the campaign's operation, laying down clear lines of authority and delineating specific portfolios of responsibility for his lieutenants. "I should like to glance personally at this publicity before it is decided on," he informed another manager, as he sought to control the message so that everything stayed on point.[39]

By early 1936, both sides agreed on the central issue. The election was to be a straightforward referendum on the success and constitutionality of the New Deal. And both sides worked feverishly to lock their own preferred narrative in place.

Roosevelt used the advantages of the incumbent. In speech after speech, all of which necessarily garnered widespread attention because he was president, he refined his message of constitutional fidelity. In April 1936, at a Thomas Jefferson dinner in New York City that was broadcast on national radio, Roosevelt argued that the founding era was a moment of profound nationalism. The Founders regarded the nation "as an economic unity," which is why the Constitution had been drafted in the first place. But under the pressures of slave power and various special interests, this conception of the United States had faded. Only with the Depression, he told his audience, had "the broader vision of the Founding Fathers" returned. With the "nationwide thinking, nationwide planning and nationwide action" that were characteristic of the New Deal, Roosevelt had abandoned the immediate past of Hoover to retrieve the primeval past of the Fathers.[40]

The next month, on the centenary of James Madison's death, Roosevelt sent out a greeting—again widely reprinted in newspapers—that used the Father of the Constitution to buttress support for New Deal measures. Roosevelt quoted one of Madison's most nationalist sentiments in order to demonstrate "his attachment to the Union and his fervent belief that the people of the United States constitute a Nation with common interests and a common purpose."[41]

The next month he gave a major address in Little Rock, Arkansas, that further fleshed out his story. Arkansas had been part of the Louisiana Purchase, he reminded the crowd. That starting point allowed him to begin a fable about the way that the nation emerged from the brilliant stewardship of the founding generation. Elements of his old message remained. The simplicity of the Founders' world was gone, he told the audience, "and we are each and all of us, whether we like it or not, parts of a social civilization which ever tends to greater complexity." But the founding principles remained relevant precisely because the Founders had created a constitution that offered powerful flexibility. "Under its broad purposes we intend to and we can march forward, believing, as the overwhelming majority of Americans believe, that the Constitution is intended to meet and to fit the amazing physical, economic and social requirements that confront us in this modern generation," he concluded.[42]

Meanwhile, the Liberty League tried to leverage its strength by continuing a print blitz of hundreds of thousands of tracts to the press and to governmental officials. Its messaging also sought the symbolic sheath of the Constitution and the Founders to protect the liberties of the people. With titles like "The Constitution and the New Deal," "The American Constitution—Whose

Heritage?," "The American Form of Government—Let Us Preserve It," "The Constitution—What It Means to the Man on the Street," "The Constitution: The Fortress of Liberty," "What the Constitution Means to the Citizen," "Shall We Have Constitutional Liberty or Dictatorship?," "Constitutional Heresy," and "Whose Constitution? The Dominant Issue of the Campaign," the Liberty League continued to portray itself as the Constitution's protector against the proto-socialist dictatorship of the New Deal. "The issue," according to one representative pamphlet, "is between constitutional democracy and democratic despotism."[43]

The League was helped in its campaign in late May when the Supreme Court struck down a New York minimum wage law, in the latest decision that called into question the constitutionality of New Deal policies. Court and League again seemed to be in tandem.

But Roosevelt barely missed a beat. At his next press conference, his three hundredth since taking office, a reporter asked, "In view of the Supreme Court's series of opinions about the New Deal objectives, do you see any way in which those objectives can be reached within the existing framework of the Constitution?"

"I think I shall have to reframe your question," Roosevelt responded. He did not want to concede the presumption that the Court had gotten the Constitution right.

"Have you any comment on the Supreme Court decision?" Roosevelt asked himself.

Then, having reworded the question so that it accorded with his narrative, he answered that the people of the United States "should read all three opinions" from the Court because the Court was finally beginning to make something clear. The Court had earlier struck down laws claiming that they trampled either on the prerogative of Congress or on the province of the states. Now they struck down a state law as impermissible. They were dangerously close to creating a "no-man's-land" in which no government—state or national—could interfere with the selfish profit-taking of businessmen.

"How can you meet that situation?" a reporter asked.

But Roosevelt was not interested in addressing the question. "I think that is about all there is to say on it," he responded—to the general amusement of the press. They recognized that he wanted to separate the Court from the Constitution in the mind of the public, and that his plan to "meet that situation" involved their reporting the narrative as he wished.[44]

Later that month, during his acceptance speech at the Democratic National Convention in Philadelphia, he redoubled his efforts. After he was renominated, he again decided to accept the nomination in person. But instead of arriving by plane at the last minute, he planned ahead and held the speech in the football stadium of the University of Pennsylvania. On the day of the event it rained steadily, but just as the president's train pulled into the station, the rain stopped and a glowing half-moon appeared. Half an hour later, Roosevelt stood before more than one hundred thousand people gathered under a clear sky.[45]

Bracing himself before the radio microphones, he laid down his campaign message that he had honed to perfection. His goal, he told the partisan crowd, was simply "to preserve to the United States the political and economic freedom for which Washington and Jefferson planned and fought." For that reason, the location of the convention in Philadelphia was "fitting ground." It provided the Democratic Party a symbolic space "to reaffirm the faith of our fathers; to pledge ourselves to restore to the people a wider freedom; to give to 1936 as the founders gave to 1776—an American way of life." The Founders had wiped out the political tyranny of the crown, he said. But the age of machinery, electricity, the telegraph, and the railroad had brought forward a concentration of economic power and the possibility of mass economic suffering. Now a new breed of tyrants wanted to thwart change and protect their own privilege. Roosevelt had set himself against "these economic royalists" with his New Deal program, and in doing so had channeled the Founders. Yet his opponents sought "to hide behind the Flag and the Constitution," he told the crowd. They masked their malevolence behind patriotic symbols. But he was confident that the mass of people could detect that it was the Liberty League and their Republican puppets, not Roosevelt, that represented "the resolute enemy within our gates." "Our allegiance to American institutions requires the overthrow of this kind of power," he asserted. Only by doing so could they preserve the democratic intentions of the framers.[46]

A more concise statement of his message was difficult to imagine. He believed, like Lincoln, that founding principles needed to be preserved but that they grew over time in ways that went far beyond the Founders. His opponents saw that claim as specious, a betrayal of the Founders while claiming their authority. But his partisans were thoroughly convinced and energized. After his speech, thunderous applause and cheer after cheer boomed down upon Roosevelt as he rode around the stadium. For millions listening on the radio, the issues had been defined.[47]

The American Liberty League had trouble competing on this symbolic terrain. When it first began operating in 1934, its leaders had predicted a mass movement. But by July 1936 its membership had peaked and the group was undeniably, as Roosevelt had suggested, a project of the rich. The League, in the words of the *New York Times,* represented, "either through principals or attorneys, a large portion of the capitalistic wealth of the country." But its leaders were so out of touch that they had trouble seeing just how much of a liability wealth could be in a time of depression. As one observer noted, Roosevelt did not really have to do much to refute the views of the League. He "had only to call the roll."[48]

Republican party operatives, at least, realized their dilemma. Alfred M. Landon, the 1936 Republican candidate, admitted that appearing in public or even being associated with League spokesmen was a "kiss of death." Republicans begged the League not to endorse Landon or to get involved in the election on their side in any overt way. Though the League acceded to their request, Roosevelt's earlier decision to discredit the League by ignoring the Republican Party had already worked to make a connection in the public's mind, so their restraint hardly mattered.[49]

Yet going into election night some Republicans still held out hope. Maine had voted for Landon in an early election, and it appeared that perhaps Roosevelt still might lose. But as the returns came back, it became apparent how sadly self-deceived they had been. Roosevelt won the most sweeping victory since James Monroe's unopposed election in 1820. He won every state but two. He won the popular vote with 60.8 percent to Landon's 36.5. And he carried so many Democrats with him that they had trouble fitting into the Capitol. At the beginning of the next Congress the seventy-five Democratic senators could not all squeeze into their side of the chamber. Twelve Democratic freshmen had to sit with the saving remnant of the Republicans.[50]

STORM OVER THE CONSTITUTION

But Roosevelt had still not beaten the Court. After the election in November, Roosevelt took a cruise to South America, and he brought along a book published a few months prior: Irving Brant's *Storm over the Constitution*. Brant was a journalist-turned-historian who pointed out the topsy-turvy character of the contemporary debate. Democrats—who claimed Jefferson as their progenitor—were the ones advocating centralized power in the New Deal. And Republicans—who revered Hamilton—objected to Roosevelt's use of the federal government to intervene in the economy. The debate suggested just how changed the world had become since the Founders' time and how difficult it was to seamlessly connect their thought with the Depression-era United States.[51]

Roosevelt had been mulling over exactly that problem since the Court struck down the NRA and the AAA. In fact, in pondering a way forward, many on his team had begun considering a constitutional amendment to overcome the objections of the Court. But after reading Brant's book, Roosevelt decided that he did not need a constitutional amendment to support the New Deal. He needed instead a way, in Brant's words, to convert "the liberal Supreme Court minority into a consistent majority." Roosevelt decided to achieve what Walter Weyl, a founder of the *New Republic,* had labeled "amendment by interpretation."[52]

The strategy had risks, in that it sought to ground a progressive program in the conservative rhetoric of restoration. But Roosevelt decided the other course was still more hazardous because of the time involved and the uncertainty of success. So he used his second inaugural to lay the foundation for his plan. Rather than pivoting from his campaign narrative, he locked it more firmly into place.

"This year marks the one hundred and fiftieth anniversary of the Constitutional Convention which made us a nation," Roosevelt told his audience. Instead of reflecting on the enormous changes in the nation over those one hundred and fifty years—as he might have done four years before—Roosevelt continued to draw parallels between 1787 and 1937:

> At that Convention our forefathers found the way out of the chaos which followed the Revolutionary War; they created a strong government with powers of united action

sufficient then and now to solve problems utterly beyond individual or local solution. A century and a half ago they established the Federal Government in order to promote the general welfare and secure the blessings of liberty to the American people. Today we invoke those same powers of government to achieve the same objectives.

The genius of the Constitution, according to Roosevelt, was that it transferred the power of the people to the structures of government with the caveat that the people could change their government if they did not like what it was doing. That was the central check that the Founders had created against tyranny, a democratic mechanism whereby the powerful government that the Founders created could be restrained. "The Constitution of 1787 did not make our democracy impotent," Roosevelt asserted. The Founders had wanted a government to better the lives of its citizens, he believed, which now enabled him to build "on the old foundations a more enduring structure."[53]

The question was how to get the Court to recognize Roosevelt's interpretation. He had devoted considerable thought to the issue since reading Brant's book, and at a press conference two weeks after his inauguration he revealed his plan. The administration had been reviewing the Court's caseload for a good many months, he told the White House press corps. The judiciary was stretched thin, it turned out. The Supreme Court accepted only a small fraction of the cases that came before it. Even those cases that it took required a long wait time. To address the supposed bottleneck, Roosevelt wanted to add to the number of justices on the bench. For every justice who was over seventy and a half years old, Roosevelt wanted to appoint another justice to the Supreme Court—up to a total of fifteen. The additional justices would ostensibly help overcome the more limited abilities of the older ones, who were slowing down with age. The Court would then be able to act more efficiently.[54]

Roosevelt's plan immediately became a lightning rod for criticism. Gallup polls had shown that nearly 60 percent of the public wanted the Court to change its hostility to the New Deal, but only 41 percent favored a curb on Court powers. Since his plan was pretty clearly a frontal challenge to the Court, the public did not necessarily embrace his idea. Many Americans also did not know that the number of justices was not specified in the Constitution, so they believed, contrary to his intentions, that Roosevelt sought a change in the Founders' plan of government. Meanwhile, critics drew upon the popular opposition to a tamed Supreme Court by complaining of Roosevelt's "Court-packing" scheme, a name that suggested Roosevelt's desire to overcome an independent judiciary.[55]

"Are you surprised at the reaction to your Judiciary bill?" a reporter asked Roosevelt a week after he announced the plan.

"It depends on which paper you read," Roosevelt responded, which again amused the White House press corps in its obvious evasiveness. He did not wish to acknowledge that he had made an error in political judgment, but he did explain his reasoning. On background, he told the reporters that he had been driven to the plan out of a lack of any other good options. The Court was dead set against doing anything to stop the Depression. Although he had thought about an amendment to the Constitution, he realized that it might not work well. Out of so many possible amendments, he worried that he might not get Congress to agree on one. Even if he could get one through Congress, the ratification process was no guarantee. A "thoroughly skilled and organized opposition directed at the point of least resistance"—like the American Liberty League—could easily prevent ratification in thirteen states, which was all that would be necessary to defeat the amendment.

The whole bother was not really necessary, Roosevelt believed, because his plan was undoubtedly constitutional.[56]

A month later he tried to take the message before the public in a fireside chat. In his telling, he had been working feverishly to address the Depression but—returning to his narrative—an entrenched plutocracy had resisted him at every step. Although he and his party had won three national elections and received an overwhelming popular mandate, the plutocracy had now retreated into the safe confines of the Court, where it still stymied his ability to protect the people from economic devastation. "It is a quiet crisis," he told his listeners, but no less real for that. In case anyone had any doubts, he wanted to stress that the crisis did not arise out of the Constitution. "I hope that you have re-read the Constitution of the United States in these past few weeks," he said.

> Like the Bible, it ought to be read again and again. It is an easy document to understand when you remember that it was called into being because the Articles of Confederation under which the original thirteen States tried to operate after the Revolution showed the need of a National Government with power enough to handle national problems.

Because the Court had failed to recognize the purpose of the Constitution, according to Roosevelt, it had ceased to give reasonable benefit of doubt to Congress. In doing so, it had overstepped its bounds by ceasing to be a judicial body and by taking on the apparatus of a policy-making one. "We have, therefore, reached the point as a Nation where we must take action to save the Constitution from the Court and the Court from itself," Roosevelt concluded.[57]

Still his plan went nowhere. Even for a politician of Roosevelt's skills, he could never really untangle the Court as a symbol from the Constitution as a symbol. To attack the Court was to attack the Constitution.

But it turned out not to matter. Although the Court-packing plan never emerged from Congress, in April 1937 the Court abruptly switched tacks and upheld the National Labor Relations Act as a permissible application of the commerce clause. Writing for the five-person majority, Chief Justice Charles Evans Hughes accepted Roosevelt's argument in total. "The great basic industries of the United States," the Court ruled, acted at the center of a web of economic actions "with ramifying activities affecting interstate commerce at every point." The Court now concluded that it was unreasonable to expect that old interpretations of the commerce clause could make sense in the new industrialized world, which gave the go-ahead for Roosevelt's legislative agenda and marked a major shift in the Court's jurisprudence. Roosevelt had won.[58]

"Have you any comment on the decision of the Supreme Court?" a reporter asked Roosevelt the next day.

"Off the record, and really off the record and just in the family," Roosevelt replied, "I have been chortling all morning, ever since I picked up the papers. I have been having a perfectly grand time."[59]

Though he had other political battles in the future, the decision of the Court meant that those battles would not be fought on a constitutional terrain and would no longer be about the intentions of the Founders. Roosevelt wound up instituting a constitutional revolution without a constitutional amendment. And along with that came a political transformation. After Roosevelt, the president possessed vastly expanded legislative powers. The office became the focus for government. The conception and proper role of government were greatly enlarged. Roosevelt left a legacy of anti-depression controls and regulatory mechanisms through which the government could direct business. And he liberalized the role of government in the protection of the more marginal members of society—the poor, the sick, the disabled, and the elderly. All of his activities underwrote an emerging liberal consensus that set a legislative trajectory that would hold for the next forty years.

But his victory was not entirely clean. When he initially ran for office, he spoke the frank language of progressivism. The industrial development and interdependence of the nation had rendered past political notions obsolete, he claimed. The nation needed a new vision of governance, which he promised to create. When challenged by a conservative minority, he changed his rhetorical stance. By his second term he completely dropped any mention of his desire for political reconstruction. Like the Founders, he claimed, he fought for self-determination and democracy against an entrenched elite. Sometimes his invocation of the Founders presumed a living tradition that he sought to advance. At other times, his cyclical view of history mirrored Jefferson in the belief that any departure from the founding intentions represented degeneracy.

In neither case did his rhetoric prevent creative policy solutions as it had prior to the Civil War, but the ambiguity turned out to be critical. Though Roosevelt won the debate, he did so, much like Jefferson had done over a century before, by demonizing his opponents as Tories and by presuming a founding consensus that he alone represented. In that way, he ratified the cynical argument of the American Liberty League that American politics was premised on the maintenance of a supposed founding consensus, a consensus that required constant vigilance to uphold. For Roosevelt, that consensus was the achievement of political and economic equality. For the American Liberty League, it was the defense of states' rights and the individual right of property. But both represented their politics as mirroring that of the Founders while the other side represented an existential threat to the nation's ideals.

The irony is that neither Roosevelt nor the League supporters really seemed to believe their own arguments about the absolute necessity of founding ideals. They did believe in the essential malevolence of the other side. But their Founders rhetoric was really just rhetoric for public consumption. Their respective appeals to the Founders were parts of their propaganda campaign to mobilize the masses. After the battle was over, the campaign faded for a bit or at least went semi-underground.

But slowly the rhetoric became more than just rhetoric, particularly among conservatives. Though the League had adopted a fake posture of worship toward the Constitution and its framers, their conservative successors were not so craven. Nor were they so feckless. Armed with a sense of grievance and a burden of loss, wounded businessmen and conservative grassroots activists nursed their wounds and reorganized. As Harry S. Truman sought to uphold New Deal measures, as John F. Kennedy proposed the New Frontier, and as Lyndon Johnson advocated the Great Society—all extensions of Roosevelt's political ideals that would have been inconceivable to the founding generation— New Deal opponents became truly committed to the idea that the United States was headed down the path of utter ruin. By the time of the civil rights movement and Ronald Reagan's political debut, conservatives were mobilized to create a counterrevolution. They marched under a banner of restoration.[60]

CHAPTER SIX

The Montage Effect

In the sweltering August of 1963, Washington, D.C., braced for an epic riot. Plans were for hundreds of thousands of black protesters to descend on the capital. To make sure that order was kept, no one was taking any chances. The authorities brought in two thousand police officers, two thousand National Guardsmen, and two hundred park police to patrol the single mile of National Mall between the Washington Monument and the Lincoln Memorial. An extra four thousand troops from the army and Marines were waiting in the wings, on call. The organizers themselves deployed two thousand marshals to direct the march and to discipline anyone who got out of hand.[1]

On the day of the event, swarms of immaculately dressed protesters began to gather at the Washington Monument. By 9 a.m., the police estimated the crowd, mostly black but with a surprisingly large number of white sympathizers, at 90,000. Still the people kept coming. Two hours later, the full complement of more than 200,000 was gathered. While the leaders were at the Capitol meeting with lawmakers, the crowd decided, on its own and ahead of schedule, to begin walking toward the Lincoln Memorial. The march between the memorials was quiet and without incident, eerily powerful in its slow-moving mass. For many observers it suggested an inevitability that could not be held back. The *New York Times* spoke of "the human tide that swept over the Mall." "Like every revolution, the Negro revolution is formless," *Time* observed. It sprang not from a single source that could be stopped but was, instead, "an oceanic tide of many waters."[2]

That surge of people had occurred because of recent events. The March on Washington for Jobs and Freedom was the conclusion of a summer of revolt. Rejecting the centuries of oppression, the decades of segregation, and the constant recommendation of patience from would-be white sympathizers, black leaders left the bloody conflicts earlier that summer in Birmingham, Alabama, convinced that the time for civil rights was "Now!" Organizers sought to seize on white sympathy that had emerged when Birmingham police let loose dogs and water cannons on peaceful protesters, many of whom were teenagers. That perhaps fleeting rupture in the public's usual indifference could be put to use.[3]

Simply by amassing that many people, the organizers had accomplished part of their task. "The presence of nearly a quarter of a million petitioners anywhere always makes a Senator think," the columnist James Reston observed. "He seldom ignores that many potential votes, and it did not escape the notice of Congressmen that these Negro organizations, some of which had almost as much trouble getting out a crowd as the Washington Senators several years ago, were now capable of organizing the largest demonstrating throng ever gathered in one spot in the District of Columbia."[4]

But just as important, the march combined other things that a politician would find hard to ignore. It drew on the church, which added religious sanction to the cause. It had the benefit of black singers and other celebrities, which drew further media attention.

"And it was able to invoke the principles of the founding fathers," Reston said, "to rebuke the inequalities and hypocrisies of modern American life."[5]

In fact, the entire event sought to call up the Founders, moving from the monument of the nation's first president, George Washington, to the monument of the Great Emancipator and preserver of the Union, Abraham Lincoln. Nowhere was that founding narrative more apparent than in the signal event of the day, the address by Martin Luther King Jr. in front of the Lincoln Memorial. In a speech that would instantly become his most famous, his "I Have a Dream" address, King brilliantly elaborated the visual and symbolic messaging of the march for any who missed it.

"I am happy to join with you today in what will go down in history as the greatest demonstration for freedom in the history of our nation," he began. Their protest was epic partly because it had been a long time in coming. The goal of freedom had been deferred, he explained, since the American Revolution itself. "When the architects of our republic wrote the magnificent words of the Constitution and the Declaration of Independence," King told the crowd, "they were signing a promissory note to which every American was to fall heir." But that promise had not been applied to citizens of color. First in an era of slavery, and then in an era of state-enforced segregation, black Americans had been marginalized from American life. They existed in "a lonely island of poverty in the midst of a vast ocean of material prosperity." "The Negro," he said, "is still languished in the corners of American society and finds himself in exile in his own land."[6]

King believed that the oppression had gone on long enough. It was time, he said, for the nation to "live out the true meaning of its creed." If others had different ideas, they needed to wake up to the new realities of the day. "The sweltering summer of the Negro's legitimate discontent" would continue, he promised, until justice was achieved.[7]

King's speech was powerful not least for its optimism—his repeated assertion, "I have a dream . . ."—in the midst of his jeremiad. But his use of the Founders was a calculated message. King had referred to the Founders before, but they were not among his most frequent rhetorical subjects. Reference to the Founders involved him in a semi-complicated explanation. Though many in the original generation would never have conceded the equality of black Americans, King assumed (with Lincoln) that American politics was a living tradition in which ideals derived from the past could grow over time. The march embodied this idea, with its onward flow from Washington (the founding) to Lincoln (emancipation) and then looking into the present and the future (King's dream). As march organizer A. Philip Randolph told *Newsweek,* the civil rights movement was "an inevitable outgrowth of the incompleteness of American history." The promise of 1776, even if it was not one that the Founders would have recognized, had too long languished. It was now to be achieved.[8]

Yet not everyone agreed with that sense of incompleteness in American history. Conservatives had long watched the movement with alarm. They rejected the idea that the onward flow of time had augmented founding ideals or had created any sense of historical necessity. As William F. Buckley Jr. famously put it in 1955, the conservative is one who "stands athwart history, yelling Stop, at a time when no one is inclined to do so." As such, conservatives cast a jaundiced eye on King's call for change. They rejected in particular any suggestion that the federal government ought to intervene to protect civil rights. To allow the government to mess with states would be to subvert the Founders' decision to vest power within the states. "The intentions of the founding fathers in this matter are beyond any doubt," Barry Goldwater, the conservative senator from Arizona, stated flatly. The federal government could not overturn white supremacy, he said, because the Founders had left all educational decisions to the states and all concerns about private property to its owners.[9]

The march was, in large measure, designed to break through such sentiment. By showing up in Washington, organizers hoped to pressure the Senate to enact a law to protect black civil rights in the South over the objections of a minority of southern partisans. But it was already apparent, as King stood between the Lincoln Memorial and the television cameras, that the key senators had not been entirely moved. For that, they needed something more. "Whether this will win any new votes for civil rights and economic legislation," James Reston said afterward, "will probably depend on the over-all effect of the day's events on the television audience."[10]

It turned out that the Civil Rights Act, which prohibited discrimination on the basis of color, would have to wait nearly a full year before it could be passed. Once President Kennedy was assassinated the following fall, Lyndon Johnson pushed a reluctant Congress into action by arguing that the bill would honor Kennedy's memory. Goldwater, not interested in Kennedy's memory and by then the 1964 Republican Party candidate, stuck to his principles and voted against the act.[11]

Just then a new voice appeared on the scene.

"Ladies and gentlemen," the television announcer intoned over a black-and-white shot of a theater audience, "we take pride in presenting a thoughtful address by Ronald Reagan." As the audience clapped politely, the faded B-list actor, known most recently for his decade-long stint as a spokesman for General Electric (GE) and host of *General Electric Theater,* adopted a concerned and serious mien.[12]

This was not an episode of his television show. Reagan had actually been fired two years earlier. His growing conservatism had been fine with GE bigwigs—until, that is, he began criticizing programs for which GE was a major contractor. After a series of back-and-forth exchanges about whether and to what extent Reagan could articulate his conservative ideas, GE cut him loose and canceled the show. Now unencumbered and somewhat adrift, he had decided to give this nationally televised address in support of the Barry Goldwater campaign, a week before the 1964 presidential election.[13]

"The sponsor has been identified," Reagan began, "but unlike most television programs, the performer hasn't been provided with a script." Looking earnestly out over the audience, he told the crowd that he spoke not as a politician but as a concerned citizen anxious about the upcoming election. The Democrats had asserted over and over again that the election was about the maintenance of prosperity and the promotion of a more liberal and humane social order. But Reagan had his doubts. He saw a high tax burden, large deficits, a growing national debt, creeping inflation, and the war in Vietnam as symptoms of an emerging existential threat to the United States. He feared that the nation as he knew it was on the wane. It was another jeremiad.[14]

But Reagan's jeremiad was unlike King's, though they shared certain points of view. Reagan agreed with King that American greatness began with the Founding Fathers, who had established the principles of freedom that set the United States on its course. But unlike King, he believed that the nation had actually lived up to those principles, which were what made it great. His vision of the past occluded any sense that the Founders had been short-sighted or that the American past was in any way blemished. No, the nation had done just fine, according to Reagan, until Franklin Roosevelt came into office.

In that belief Reagan found common ground with his backers. His speech had been funded by wealthy California businessmen who saw in Reagan a powerful spokesman for conservative causes. They had been looking for such a person since the American Liberty League quietly disbanded in 1940. Back then, the conservative cause fell victim to optics. Wealthy plutocrats wringing their hands about the New Deal did not inspire mass concern in a time of depression. But the businessmen who had supported the League did not abandon their belief that the emerging liberal consensus was a disaster that must be resisted. And their sons hoped still to reverse the liberal advance in order to create a more business-oriented regime.[15]

In Reagan they found a true believer. Though he had voted four times for Roosevelt, he had steadily turned conservative as the liberal agenda solidified and as he began to move in wealthier circles. While American liberalism began to address civil liberties in the late 1940s, Reagan by contrast began to worry that concern for private economic rights was going by the wayside. By the 1960s he had become a man obsessed, anxious about the future, reverential toward the past, and positively adoring of the Founding Fathers in particular. Although Reagan was not personally bigoted, in 1964 he found himself advocating for a smaller federal government at the exact moment that civil rights protesters were calling for it to expand in order to protect civil liberties.[16]

The problem, according to Reagan, was that liberalism had disregarded the tried-and-true way. Liberals sought a shortcut to the kingdom. In doing so they risked too much of the past. Liberal spokesmen talked openly about what they considered the antiquated nature of the Constitution. They decried that it limited, as one liberal congressman said, "the full power of centralized government" to achieve liberal aims like civil rights.

To Reagan, such sentiment spoke of tyranny. " 'The full power of centralized government!' " he exclaimed in outrage.

> This was the very thing the Founding Fathers sought to minimize. They knew that governments don't control things. A government can't control the economy without controlling people. And they knew when a government sets out to do that, it must use force and coercion to achieve its purpose. They also knew, these Founding Fathers, that outside its legitimate functions, government does nothing as well or as economically as the private sector of the economy.

> Precisely because the liberal establishment could not accept the Founders' vision, he continued, they sought to feed government and to buy votes by giving to people from governmental largesse. Liberals would eventually take all power from the people, as their creeping socialism and moral anarchism reached their logical conclusion in communistic totalitarianism.[17]

The next few years were the crossroads in Reagan's dystopian vision. While civil rights leaders pushed the nation to live up to its promise of equality, Reagan pushed the nation not to lose sight of the Founders' vision as he understood it. "I think it's time we ask ourselves if we still know the freedoms that were intended for us by the Founding Fathers," Reagan warned his audience. Rather than looking to a nanny state to solve all problems, Reagan believed that the Founders would have wanted the nation to uphold individual initiative and fiscal austerity. That, in any case, was what he saw as the issue of the election: whether the United States was to "abandon the American Revolution" or whether it was to reclaim the self-government necessary to preserve freedom.[18]

THE VANISHING LIBERAL CONSENSUS

Though both King and Reagan looked to the Founders to sustain their politics and to invigorate political allies, they had radically different perspectives on the past and, therefore, radically different visions for the future. Ultimately, these different ways of looking at the Founders fed an acrimonious and not entirely straightforward dispute that mirrored the fracture of American life more broadly. It is probably not too much to say that the debate over the Founders became a marker of political and social dysfunction in the late 1960s, as what Arthur Schlesinger Jr. once called "the vital center" of American politics slowly broke down.[19]

But that decay did not occur overnight. In fact, it was not readily apparent in 1964. The liberal center held. Though political observers had been intrigued by Reagan—he offered a powerful new voice in what was otherwise a dreary election season—his argument was not yet politically viable. Even as he was giving his speech, no one really believed that it would do much to elect Goldwater. It had been clear for many months that Lyndon Johnson would win a decisive victory. Reagan's speech might save Goldwater from utter humiliation. Or it might not. But it would certainly not change the fundamental dynamic, many observers believed.[20]

Johnson's eventual triumph, the largest popular landslide in American history, suggested that Reagan did not do much. Goldwater won only his home state of Arizona and the five Deep South states (Louisiana, Mississippi, Alabama, Georgia, and South Carolina) that were most concerned to uphold white supremacy. Civil rights leaders spoke of the imminent end of segregation and the beginning of a whole new era. Commentators in general lauded "the politics of consensus" that Johnson seemed to embody—essentially the liberal consensus begun under FDR with a new commitment to civil rights and poverty reduction. Everyone believed, *Newsweek* reported, that the election represented "a massive repudiation" of any attempt to alter the liberal trajectory.[21]

Given the size of the defeat, Republicans immediately began a round of soul-searching. Goldwater and Reagan had presented the election as "a choice, not an echo" of liberal policies. But many Republicans concluded, as one prominent party leader told *Newsweek* after the votes were counted, there had, in fact, been no choice: "The choice was made in 1932 [when Roosevelt was elected]. When the voters went to the polls Tuesday, they just confirmed it." Richard Nixon, who had served as vice president under Dwight Eisenhower, complained bluntly that Goldwater had "let the nuts take over." Moderate Republicans from around the nation began counseling a move back to the center in order to maintain viability as a party.[22]

But Reagan, in particular, did not back down. His advisers had seen in his speech enough to make them positive. He had the power to articulate conservative beliefs in a way that energized the base. And he had a winsomeness that could reach beyond the conservative core to make converts to the cause. Around Reagan they believed that it might be possible to create a political movement. Like the American Liberty League, they hoped to use Reagan's arguments about the Founders to rally the masses.

Reagan was certainly open to their goals. In 1966, he allowed himself to be talked into running for the California governorship. It must have seemed, at the outset, a wildly quixotic bid. But in a surprise to the liberal Democratic establishment, Reagan won a landslide victory against the incumbent, Pat Brown.[23]

As a result, Reagan was in office as sixties movement politics kicked into high gear. Campuses erupted in controversy as second-wave feminism and the peace movement challenged mid-twentieth-century mores. While protests grew over Vietnam, the National Guard began to occupy campuses around the nation in order to help keep the peace. Reagan raged against the "beatniks, radicals, and filthy speech advocates" who seemed to have taken over prominent universities.[24]

American society began to suffer. In 1965, Los Angeles went up in flames during the Watts riots. Angry black protesters raged against the hopelessness of the black ghetto and the patterns of oppression that they had endured. In subsequent years, the scene was repeated in Detroit, Newark, Chicago, Cleveland, and other cities. After Martin Luther King was assassinated in 1968, black inner cities across the nation erupted in more violence and anger. Protesters even looted and burned several blocks in Washington, D.C., a couple of miles north of the Capitol. To Reagan, it seemed that his prophecies were coming true.[25]

But still, the liberal consensus held. In 1968, when conservatives sought to woo Reagan into the presidential race, he considered just long enough to conclude that he could not win. He instead threw his support to the eventual nominee (and victor) Richard Nixon, a more moderate politician who accepted a liberal view of government.[26]

Amid the angry clamor, Nixon initially sought to move in different directions than Reagan. Claiming to speak for the "silent majority," Nixon sidestepped the debate over American foundations and represented himself as a voice of common sense and decency. As he told the nation at his inauguration, the United States had come to the end of the 1960s "rich in goods, but ragged in spirit." He believed that the nation needed a renewal, a return not to the Fathers but to civility and a feeling of brotherhood. "To lower our voices would be a simple thing," Nixon said.[27]

But the problem was never just raised voices. As Nixon

settled into office and Reagan ran for a second term as governor, the economic challenges that Reagan observed became more definite. The nation began experiencing a series of economic shocks that further eroded the liberal agreement. With the war spending from Vietnam and the growth of domestic spending from the War on Poverty, inflation took off. At about the same time, a series of energy crises, begun after the peak of U.S. oil production in the early 1970s, undermined the liberal economic program and suggested a general crisis in the nation's governance. All of that led fairly quickly to the beginning of 1970s stagflation—economic stagnation combined with high inflation, a combination that economists had previously thought impossible.[28]

Almost immediately, people began to speak of the malaise of the 1970s. A sense of bewilderment and crisis spread to the chattering classes. "What ails the American Spirit?" *Newsweek* asked for its 1970 Independence Day issue. Complaining of "the reduced Spirit of '70," the magazine blamed the "half decade or more of war, inflation, ghetto turmoil, campus uprisings and political assassination." The purpose of the issue, the editors announced, was to take stock of these and other problems.[29]

But such self-flagellation was not particularly interesting to Nixon. It failed to advance his vision of a still-vital consensus that he sought to harness. So rather than chronicling the nation's failures, he argued in his own Independence Day address, "It is time to stand up and speak about what is right about America." Only then could the nation properly orient itself. Yet in spite of Nixon's efforts, the center was slowly vanishing. The façade of consensus was becoming harder to maintain.[30]

At no time did the loss of consensus become more apparent than in planning for the bicentennial of the nation's founding. Though political leaders had many other things to concern them, the bicentennial was supposed to be a feel-good moment that would redound to the political benefit of whoever was in office. But it did not seem to be shaping up that way. In the mid-1960s, while Johnson was president, Congress had set up a commission to plan for the festivities. But given the antagonism already apparent by that time, no one could agree on how the event should be celebrated. Nothing much got done.

The issue became only more complicated once Nixon came to the presidency. Johnson's head of the commission, Richard W. Barrett, resigned almost immediately. Like the civil rights protesters before him, Barrett believed that the bicentennial offered an occasion to examine what A. Philip Randolph had called "the incompleteness of American history." "My view is that the bicentennial should be a vehicle for social change," Barrett told the *Los Angeles Times*. But Nixon was "not prepared to deal with the kinds of problems" that the bicentennial raised.[31]

Nixon responded, in turn, by appointing campaign members to the commission, which threatened to turn the celebration into a partisan vehicle. That led to jeers from those outside his party and a dawning realization that a national celebration, given the antagonisms of the late 1960s, was going to be difficult to pull off.[32]

Those problems turned out to be just a beginning. Once Nixon began putting his stamp on the commission, New Left activists opposed to the Vietnam War began making noise. At a time of war, they distrusted the overt displays of nationalism inherent in a bicentennial celebration. They objected in particular to the idea that the Founders would have supported the corporatization and militarization of American public policy that sustained the Vietnam War. Jeremy Rifkin, an antiwar protester and graduate of the Wharton School, grew so disgusted that he decided to form the People's Bicentennial Commission. "The Nixon Bicentennial is really a Tory effort," Rifkin told the *Los*

Angeles Times. "You know, 200 years ago, they would have been on the other side."[33]

Press coverage subsequently gravitated toward the People's Commission. Congress became concerned that the event was going to be hijacked. After holding hearings on the issue, investigators concluded that the official commission had failed to accomplish even a fraction of its basic mission. In spite of a large budget, it had become paralyzed by infighting and competing agendas. To save the event, Congress created a smaller but more powerful American Revolution Bicentennial Administration (ARBA).[34]

But that, too, only led to more controversy. The politics of commemoration and the competing views of the past could not be overcome. As the political gridlock became apparent, business representatives began making public pleas for action. Travel industry leaders urged the ARBA to coordinate with them, since the bicentennial was essentially a travel event to various heritage sites. Public relations and advertising executives offered their expertise in selling "America to Americans," as one open letter to Richard Nixon promised.[35]

That led Jeremy Rifkin of the People's Bicentennial to complain of the "plan, conceived by the White House and Big Business and already underway, to marshal and direct the greatest concentrated mass propaganda campaign ever conceived in the United States of America." Since that propaganda was going to be unavoidable, Rifkin sought to use the national symbols of the Founders and the founding to build "a mass revolutionary movement for a radically restructured America," in other words, "to commit revolution American style."[36]

Even Nixon got in on the debate as the remains of consensus slowly vanished. During his second inaugural address, he declared that the time for finding fault with the American past was over. "The time has come for us to renew our faith in ourselves and in America," he said. The constant criticism and self-flagellation did nothing, he believed, to move the nation forward. But he was confident that the finger-pointing would stop. In the "judgment of history," he predicted, his presidency would be one in which "the spirit and promise of America" were renewed for its "third century."[37]

It was not to be. Within a year and a half Nixon resigned in disgrace as a result of the Watergate affair. His vice president–turned-president, Gerald Ford, tried to paper over the fissures underlying the bicentennial celebration—as he did in so much else and with as little success. With the bicentennial approaching, the organizers simply threw their hands in their air. No massive world's fair–type events were planned. They instead decided to support local planners in whatever they wanted to do, which defused conflict and made a virtue out of necessity by allowing for a variety of celebrations. "We did our best" was the unintentionally pathetic headline in ARBA's final report on their work.[38]

On the day of the bicentennial, the press did its best as well. *Newsweek* declined to cover such a diffuse celebration. The editors decided instead to spend the entire issue providing short snapshots of the views of forty-six Americans, from a California death row inmate to Henry Kissinger, on their view of America at age two hundred. *Time* noted flatly that many people had a hard time coming up with much "energetic enthusiasm" for commemoration of the founding.[39]

African-Americans were particularly hostile. Said Charles Rangel, a black congressman from New York, "If the Bicentennial is some kind of self-congratulatory celebration, it is frivolous and meaningless to the black community." After the social strains of the sixties, the Founders and the founding no longer offered the symbols of unity that they once did. In the end, the event reflected the social fragmentation and the conflict that had come to characterize American society more broadly.[40]

To Reagan, such conflict was dispiriting but it also presented an opportunity. Faced with a widespread sense of malaise, Reagan came to believe that the nation was ready for his full-throated call to renewal. He decided to run for president.

Yet as Reagan began his campaign for the 1976 Republican primaries, he made a fateful choice. He still believed everything that he had been saying for the past twelve years, but it had grown a little stale. Reporters complained about "the speech," a subtle dig at Reagan's inability to move beyond his essential jeremiad, which he first presented in his Goldwater address. So to satisfy the press and to establish a new policy platform for his campaign, Reagan's advisers wrote a new speech that Reagan gave in late September. As a statement of principles and policies, it would form the intellectual centerpiece of his 1976 campaign. Top aides from Washington and Los Angeles flew in to hear the message.[41]

The nation, Reagan told his assembled supporters, had now entered its long-prophesied decline. The problem was a loss of national sanity that had come down from the Founders and from Jefferson in particular. "In his first Inaugural, nearly a century and three-quarters ago," Reagan explained, "President Thomas Jefferson defined the aims of his administration." Those aims were basically the conservative principles of limited government, fiscal austerity, and states' rights, which, Reagan reported, had guided the nation for its first one hundred fifty years.[42]

But since FDR, Reagan said, the nation had strayed from its Jeffersonian path. Liberals had embraced big government and massive spending, which had, he believed, created the economic problems of the 1970s. The high rate of taxation had reduced incentives for business and investment, thereby causing economic stagnation. The high rate of government spending had caused inflation. Stagflation, Reagan argued, was the result. Meanwhile, "Big Brother government in Washington" grew ever more powerful, presiding over a disemboweling of the federal system and threatening individual freedom. "If Jefferson could return today," Reagan told the crowd, "I doubt that he would be surprised either at what has happened in America, or at the result."[43]

But just what ought to be done? It was here, as was so often the case when Reagan tried to articulate solutions, that he stumbled. "What I propose," Reagan said, "is nothing less than a systematic transfer of authority and resources to the states—a program of creative federalism for America's third century." By giving states control over welfare, education, housing, food stamps, Medicaid, and community and regional development, among other things, Reagan believed that he could do several things at once. He would, first and foremost, be returning to the Founders' principles of states' rights and local control. But the issue was not merely ideological. That return would make other things possible. It would create efficiencies in government, as the Founders foresaw, in order to save $90 billion. That amount would, in turn, be enough to balance the federal budget, to begin to pay down the national debt, and to reduce every citizen's taxes by 23 percent, he happily reported. It would also solve inflation, prime the economy through tax cuts, and set the nation back on its upward trajectory. He could solve all the problems in one masterstroke, he claimed, if only the nation would return to the original Jeffersonian vision.[44]

Observers were amazed. Less than a decade after the civil rights movement, Reagan sought to gut the federal government and to return to a state-dominated governing structure that had been essential to the preservation of segregation. A Democrat in the general campaign would have a heyday with the ideological implications of Reagan's program. But even in the Republican primary, the speech seemed to be a gift to the other side.

The Ford campaign immediately commissioned an economic report to show how devastating Reagan's plan would be. The cut in government spending that Reagan proposed would first cause massive unemployment, as the economy contracted. That contraction would result in an eroding tax base, causing large federal deficits. As the economy further contracted, states and municipalities would be threatened with bankruptcy and would have to make up the revenue in some way, likely by raising taxes. Reagan's "grand rhetoric is completely out of touch with reality," the report concluded.[45]

Many in the press agreed. In otherwise evenhanded reports, journalists wrote that Reagan offered a "taste of pie in the sky," indulged in "bombastic" rhetoric, offered "an almost apocalyptic assault" on the government that he proposed to lead, and ultimately gave vent to "pure counter-revolutionary rage." *Time* magazine reported that his "oversimplified formulas" had caused many Republicans "to doubt his grasp of national and world affairs." The question, *Time* concluded, is whether Reagan "represents a conservative wave of the future or is just another Barry Goldwater calling on the party to mount a hopeless crusade against the 20th century."[46]

The total effect of the coverage was damning. Reagan lost the New Hampshire primary, gave Ford a brief scare by winning North Carolina, but eventually just faded away. It was a bitter defeat and the loss of what seemed a perfect political moment.[47]

But rather than second-guess his viability, Reagan immediately announced his candidacy for the 1980 election. He would need, he realized, a different kind of messaging to carry him in that campaign. The jeremiad and the constant references to the

Founders made him seem like a symptom of political dysfunction, as the press coverage suggested. And the specific policy proposals that he put forward had allowed him to be attacked from all sides. He needed to maintain his critical edge without getting himself into trouble.[48]

While he planned his next move, several developments played into his hands.

The first was the simple ineffectiveness of the other party and the final erosion of the liberal consensus. As the commentator Meg Greenfield observed, prior even to the 1976 election, "The string has pretty much run out on 40 years of liberal government and theory." Though the Democrat Jimmy Carter beat the incumbent Ford, he turned out to be unable to navigate the new political shoals. As a fiscally conservative Democrat from a southern state, he presented himself as the beginning of a new style of liberalism. But liberals objected to what they saw as his betrayal of the liberal cause. It did not help that he ran again and again into difficulties in managing the economy and in steering the ship of state. Since he claimed to be a liberal, Carter's failures fed directly into Reagan's antiliberal and antigovernment message.[49]

Carter's actions also prompted an emergent conservative movement during the 1978 midterm elections. Called the New Right, the conservative grassroots insurgency wanted, like Reagan, small government, lower taxes, and a society-wide renewal of the traditional Christian values that they believed had inspired the Founders and made the United States great. The fervent evangelicalism of New Right supporters meshed perfectly with Reagan's secular jeremiad. Because they believed that the nation's existence was at stake, they promoted a new militancy that energized the Reagan campaign. "Fight," the New Right periodical *Conservative Digest* counseled, "and if you lose, at least make the opposition pay."[50]

The new insurgency worked within a new intellectual paradigm that proved to be enormously useful to Reagan. Critics had argued during his 1976 run that his promise to balance the budget while also cutting taxes was incoherent, unless Reagan further promised a massive cut in such popular programs as Social Security, Medicare, and other entitlements. Reagan did not want to make such a cut, and did not believe that he would have to. But he could not explain his reasoning. Fortunately, as he was planning his campaign, Reagan was introduced to a new economic theory—supply-side economics—that gave him a response to his opposition.

Traditional economics, supply-siders argued, was flawed in several respects, mainly by failing to account for the effect of incentives in a tax system. In any given scenario, they maintained, there was an optimal tax rate that would maximize revenue. If the rate was too high, as Reagan believed that it was in the 1970s, the tax structure crushed incentive and stifled economic growth. But if that rate was lowered, supply-siders argued that it would prime economic growth and, because the overall economy would grow, it might actually increase governmental revenue since there was more economic activity to tax. For Reagan, supply-side economics worked with his sense of first principles and assured him that if only the nation returned to the Founders' ideas—now almost entirely equated with supply-side theory—no tough choices would have to be made.[51]

That, in any case, was what he told himself. Backed by the militant New Right and armed with a new economic theory, Reagan and his advisers turned the 1980 election into a referendum on the national character and purpose. He occasionally dog-whistled to racist southerners. For example, he began his 1980 general campaign with an address in Philadelphia, Mississippi, where three murdered civil rights workers had been found under an earthen dam sixteen years earlier, during the Freedom Summer of 1964. "I believe in states' rights," he told the Mississippians, "I believe in people doing as much as they can at the private level." He would, he pledged, "restore to states and local governments the power that properly belongs to them."[52]

His careful sublimation of racial animosities into the language of states' rights and local control was characteristic of his messaging throughout the campaign. He stayed away from the specifics that got him in trouble during the previous campaigns and stuck, mainly, with offering abstract slogans and criticizing Carter. His most explicit promises were big but few: he would reduce taxes, increase military spending, and balance the budget.[53]

Critics continued to point out the mathematical impossibility of reducing revenue through tax cuts, increasing expenditures through military spending, and somehow not running massive deficits. Reagan's rival for the Republican nomination, George H. W. Bush, even called Reagan's plan "voodoo economics." But Reagan serenely assured his critics that they were operating on false assumptions, which was part of the reason for the economic mess in the first place.[54]

He also largely stayed away from much specific use of the Founding Fathers. Listeners waited in vain for a justification of his candidacy that looked anything like 1976, much less 1964. He used instead an array of patriotic images, what critic Michael Arlen called a "montage effect" that juxtaposed his policies with the nationalist symbols that he conjured. At campaign rallies, for example, he might emerge to an instrumental rendition of "The Star-Spangled Banner" and speak behind a backdrop of a giant flag. His supporters decked themselves in red, white, and blue. But the essential jeremiad—in which the nation had departed from the wisdom of the Founders and needed to return—was carefully muted so as not to turn off independents. It was an approach perfectly calibrated to the changed nature of politics in the TV era, with its tendency toward sound bites, campaign commercials, and carefully crafted images.[55]

Unlike his earlier runs, the total effect of his 1980 campaign was masterful. In the final week before the election, the contest turned from what had been projected to be a narrow Reagan victory into a landslide. Reagan thumped Carter 489 to 49 in the Electoral College. Republicans gained twelve Senate seats and assumed the majority of the upper chamber. In the House they made significant inroads into the Democratic majority, much to the shock of the House leadership.[56]

While the Democrats reeled from their losses, Reagan sought to articulate a new political consensus. As he explained in his inaugural address, liberals in government had gotten the essential issues exactly wrong. "In this present crisis," he told the nation, "government is not the solution to our problem; government is the problem." He pledged to contain and reduce the size of the federal government, to give power back to the states, and to always keep in mind, in a neo-Confederate twist, that "the states created the Federal government" rather than the other way around. In closing he returned to the Founders—"the giants on whose shoulders we stand." While planning the inauguration, his advisers had decided to shift the ceremonies to the western front of the Capitol, which had better views. Taking advantage of those views, he concluded his address with a public tour of the various shrines laid out before him. As the TV cameras cut to take in the different monuments, he assumed the role of tour guide in chief. "Directly in front of me," he began, "the monument to a monumental man, George Washington, the father of our country . . ."[57]

CHAPTER SEVEN

Crackpot Theories

The Reagan Revolution had begun, though critics were still stunned by the turn of events. Reagan had somehow made it into office, by a landslide no less, even though he had twice been rejected in the Republican primaries as too extreme. He had gone from being a symptom of political and social dysfunction during the 1960s to being a potential cure for the problems of the late 1970s and early 1980s.

But one thing he had not done: he had not made up for the loss of a coherent national narrative with which to understand the present. The antagonisms of the sixties had wrecked that possibility. His own jeremiad about the Founders did not sell with the wider public, which is why he had stayed away from it in his 1980 campaign. He would need to advance his political revolution without getting caught up in the lingering animosities born of the 1960s.

That would prove a difficult task. What he most wanted, he told his cabinet in its first meeting, was to "reduce the size of government very drastically." He could accomplish something with a hiring freeze and with an immediate reduction in executive branch expenditures. But to truly reverse the course of taxing and spending, he would need the help of Congress.[1]

After some discussion, his advisers decided to mount a public relations offensive. The first step was an address to the nation from the Oval Office on the economy, just over two weeks after his inauguration. Speaking into the camera, Reagan argued that the liberal programs designed to help people had not worked out the way that they had been intended. Rather than helping people, he said, the programs had hurt them. Governmental growth had both created inflation (through government spending) and lowered productivity (through taxes and regulation). "The result?" Reagan asked: "Your standard of living is going down."[2]

Reagan promised his own plan soon. But the main point of his message was to clear the ground by arguing that old solutions were not working.

Two weeks later, he unveiled his new economic proposals in a nationally televised speech before a joint session of Congress. It was, in its comprehensiveness and its effect, as fully radical as his 1975 speech that tanked his earlier presidential campaign. Reagan promised spending cuts, tax cuts, deregulation ("getting the government off the back of people," in the words of Treasury secretary Don Regan), and stable monetary growth.[3]

But to avoid a repeat of the earlier debacle, the messaging was key. He could not afford to come off too revolutionary since he needed to convince a number of moderate-to-conservative southern representatives, known as the Boll Weevil Democrats, to get the plan through the House. Rather than repeating his old jeremiad, he adopted instead a cool, pragmatic, and problem-solving pose. He did say, at the very end of his address, "We've strayed from first principles. We must alter our course." But what he meant was that individuals had been unable to direct their own course with the products of their own hands. By getting inflation under control and renewing economic activity, he argued, he was honoring the will of the people and doing what they had wished when they elected him.[4]

The following day at a breakfast with newspaper and television editors, Reagan continued the posture. When an editor asked him about fears in Congress that his plan would not add up, Reagan critiqued the assumptions that led to their concern. "Every major tax cut that has been made in this century in our country has resulted in even the government getting more revenue than it did before, because the base of the economy is so broadened by doing it," he responded. But he again stayed carefully away from any hint of his old jeremiad.[5]

It looked, initially, like a moderately successful strategy. Polls showed that his messaging was working, though not decisive. Then, on March 30, Fortuna took a hand in the process. While Reagan was leaving the Hilton hotel in Washington, D.C., a mentally unstable man named John Hinckley Jr. shot Reagan in the chest with a .22-caliber revolver.

Reagan nearly died. But once it became apparent that he would make a full recovery, his advisers saw a perfect political opportunity to drive home their message.

The key point was to control debate. While he convalesced, his advisers were in contact with the Hill to see how members were leaning. Then, shortly before debate began on his budget cuts, Reagan appeared once again before another joint session of Congress for a nationally televised address. It was his return to public life from the shooting.

His heroic return inevitably shaped the debate. As he soaked up the triumphant reception at the Capitol, he told Congress that all other economic solutions had failed and the time for dallying had come to an end. His program was "the only answer . . .

left." He again avoided any specific mention of the Founders and spoke only of the practical and tangible effects of his economic plan.[6]

Democrats had trouble countering the message. "It was a very deceptive, extremely partisan and probably very effective presentation," House majority leader Jim Wright admitted.[7]

Wright's concerns were entirely justified. Within the week, the Reagan team won an initial vote by peeling off the Boll Weevil Democrats to approve a drastic cut to the budget. The victory was complete just before the July 4 recess, once the budget reconciliation process finished. Although his initial request for $47 billion in cuts had been trimmed to $35 billion in the final bill—with most of the cuts in programs for the poor, the elderly, and the disadvantaged—Reagan got substantially what he wanted.[8]

"Step 1 of the Reagan revolution in Government economic and social policy was just about accomplished," *Time* magazine declared.[9]

Democrats were bewildered and uncertain how to respond. "I've never seen anything like this," Speaker of the House Thomas "Tip" O'Neill Jr. said after the vote. "Does this mean that any time the President is interested in a piece of legislation, he merely sends it over?"[10]

Reagan had so masterfully worked the process that the Democrats had no effective way to stop him. And since Reagan claimed not an ideological agenda but a mandate from the people, even politicians who were inclined to resist had to think twice. "The people believe him," deputy Democratic House whip Bill Alexander bitterly explained, "so politicians have to."[11]

Reagan immediately moved to build on that momentum. In another live address from the Oval Office that again avoided any mention of the Founders, Reagan told the American people "to put aside any feelings of frustration or helplessness about our political institutions" and instead to lobby their representatives to pass his plan.[12]

Two days later his tax bill was approved, with the Boll Weevil Democrats again breaking ranks to join the Republicans in favor. The bill cut taxes by 5 percent on October 1, 1981, and by an additional 10 percent each of the next two years. Although the Congressional Budget Office projected the cost at $180 billion over three years, Reagan assured congressmen that the actual numbers would be an increase in revenue and balanced budgets by 1984.[13]

Observers were again amazed. Reagan had somehow taken his election, which was in fact a repudiation of his opponent, and turned it, in *Time*'s words, "into a mandate to revitalize the economy and to reverse the trend toward ever greater reliance on federal handouts." Reagan called it "the greatest pol. win in half a century."[14]

But not all his supporters were easy. "Pray [to] God it works," said Joe McDade, a GOP moderate from Pennsylvania who voted for the bill. Congress had been assured of the magic of tax cuts to increase revenue, but no one really knew for certain whether that was bluster or sound thinking. "If this economic plan doesn't jell," McDade worried, "where are we going to get the money for anything?"[15]

Unfortunately, his concerns were justified. Within two months Reagan had realized that he would not be able to make the 1982–84 budget targets that he had promised Congress.

"We'll cut," he decided. But when he asked Congress for additional reductions, they responded with outrage. The administration had explicitly said that the deep cuts already in place would be enough to balance the budget. Now congressmen's doubts came flooding back. Reagan's coalition began to break up.[16]

To rescue the plan, Reagan went back on television with another address from the Oval Office. Rather than back off his original proposals, he advocated more cuts to social services, the elimination of the Education and Energy departments, and a reduction in federal loan guarantees to students and others. The total agenda was staggering. His desire to dismantle liberal programs was beginning to come into view.

But because Congress had turned balky, he decided to use the Oval Office address to shore up his own partisans. A posture of pragmatism would no longer work and would not likely persuade the moderates anyhow. So at the end of his Oval Office message he tentatively returned to his earlier campaign rhetoric. The Founders' "spirit of voluntarism," Reagan told the nation, had been nearly snuffed out through governmental programs. But it was still alive. The flame needed merely to be rekindled. "As Tom Paine said 200 years ago," Reagan concluded, " 'We have it in our power to begin the world over again.' What are we waiting for?"[17]

Reagan's rhetoric could not keep the moment open. His promises were running into reality. And he could not summon a narrative that would motivate Congress. His plan had stalled.

The press turned remarkably confrontational. In a press conference shortly after his Oval Office address, CBS correspondent Lesley Stahl asked him bluntly what he would say to a mother who had lost eligibility for Medicaid and food stamps and was, as a result, unable to feed her children or provide them with medical care. Reagan simply had no response. "I don't believe that we're actually doing that," he said, even though that was exactly his plan, since the bulk of his budget reductions fell on social services for the poor.[18]

By the end of October, the economy began to tank. As reductions in federal spending went into effect and as Federal Reserve chairman Paul Volcker squeezed inflation out of the economy by raising interest rates, major economic indicators began to point in alarming directions. Business bankruptcies rose, housing starts stalled, and sales of consumer durables like cars and other big-ticket items fell precipitously. That slump followed a long downward trend in the stock market, with blue chips falling 20 percent between April and September. David Stockman, Reagan's budget director, began privately warning that the budget deficit could grow annually from $74 billion to $300 billion or more by the mid-1980s.[19]

Congress and pragmatists in Reagan's cabinet began pressuring him to increase taxes, close loopholes, or cut defense. But Reagan resisted all entreaties since doing so would be an admission that his assumptions were wrong, that he could not solve all problems with one stroke, that Thomas Jefferson did not offer principles that could save American society.

Just then, an article appeared in the *Atlantic,* titled "The Education of David Stockman." It turned out that while Reagan's team was waging legislative battles over tax and budget cuts, Stockman had been giving a series of interviews to William Greider, an editor from the *Washington Post,* with the understanding that Greider was to refrain from publishing anything until the legislative process was complete. Greider had honored the agreement, waiting until three months after the final votes. But when his article appeared, right as Reagan's plan began to go sour, it offered eye-opening revelations. Stockman had admitted to Greider during the budget battles that the entire supply-side theory was unproven. "The whole thing is premised on faith," Stockman said, "on a belief about how the world works."[20]

This notion about how the world works was in fact an ideology, an assertion that the world was whole and consistent so that economic planning required no trade-offs. But Stockman clothed the ideology with a robe of objective-sounding numbers that, it turned out, he had made up. In January, when the administration began planning for budget and tax cuts, Stockman had entered the cuts into the Office of Management and Budget's computers to run a forecast. But the computers returned what Stockman called an "absolutely shocking" number: federal deficits that were unprecedented outside of war and that continued as far as the eye could see, between $82 billion and $116 billion a year.[21]

Those numbers made sense according to conventional economics. And when those cuts in revenue were added to Reagan's promise to increase defense spending by 7 percent annually, adjusted for inflation—a proposal that would double the Pentagon's budget in five years—the entire plan collapsed. The numbers did not balance. But Stockman refused to question the faith. He simply reprogrammed the computers so that they gave him the desired number.[22]

Still, Stockman could not quite overcome his misgivings. Leading up to the budget battles in May, he pushed Reagan for a variety of modifications to the plan, all of which Reagan rejected. Once the administration put forward the plan, Stockman was defending the budget projections to Congress while privately admitting to Greider, "None of us really understands what's going on with all these numbers."[23]

After the Congressional Budget Office predicted a $60 billion deficit by 1984, instead of the balanced budget Reagan had promised, Stockman appeared to lose faith in supply-side theory even as he publicly assured Congress that everything would work out. He even told Greider that supply-side economics was really just Republicans' old trickle-down theory in new clothes—a way to justify giving tax cuts to the rich in a way that did not alienate the lower and middle classes of voters.[24]

Yet Stockman refused to abandon the administration's position. "Whenever there are great strains or changes in the economic system," Stockman sanguinely told Greider, "it tends to generate crackpot theories, which then find their way into legislative channels." That did not mean, Stockman insisted, that the administration was wrong to pursue its plan.[25]

To have such candid and brazen commentary from the administration's budget chief shocked Washington's elite.

Democrats, in particular, reacted with outrage. Senator Alan Cranston of California accused the administration of deception. "The matter now goes beyond David Stockman," he announced. "The country and the Congress are entitled to know who else in the executive branch knew that the budget was based on figures pulled out of thin air."[26]

Republicans were more guarded. Senate majority leader Howard H. Baker Jr. of Tennessee merely lamented that Stockman had been "indiscreet" in his commentary.[27]

Reagan exploded. "What was Stockman thinking of to have that kind of arrangement with a reporter?" he demanded of his aides. He felt betrayed and uncertain. But as his cabinet debated what to do, they confronted a painful dilemma. "Hell, he's our entire domestic policy staff," one person admitted. "What are we going to do without him?" Since no one else knew anything about the budget or economics, they slowly realized that, in spite of his revelations, he would have to stay.[28]

So after a meeting with the president, Stockman held a remarkable press conference to offer his mea culpa. Ashen-faced and trembling, he told the packed pressroom that he believed there had been some misunderstanding with Greider. Since the interviews had been taped, he could not really deny that the quotations were accurate. But he claimed that some were pulled out of context and others were perhaps indelicate or badly worded. In any case, he simply did not anticipate the tempest that the article caused, because, he said, he had been saying the same things in private and on background to reporters for the last nine months.[29]

But no one had said as much publicly, which made all the difference.

Democrats were now emboldened. The president and Congress had been in a budget standoff since Reagan had asked for more cuts. By early December the standoff had lasted so long that the federal government actually began to shut down. A last-minute funding bill kept the government temporarily open, but with the president unable to get anything through the Democrats' angry rejection of his initiatives.[30]

The year that had started out so promising for Reagan now appeared grim. Reality had collided with ideology. Now the way forward was unclear. As *Time* put it, "Problems are arising for which campaign rhetoric offers no solution. . . . Reagan himself is uncomfortable when faced with problems where instinct, experience or ideology do not provide a gut answer."[31]

Reagan had to confront the painful reality that he had begun to fail his mission. After a budget meeting on the 1983 fiscal year planning process, he sadly admitted, "We who were going to balance the budget face the biggest budget deficits ever."[32]

Many in the press began openly questioning the president's competence. Lou Cannon, a *Washington Post* correspondent who would soon publish a biography of Reagan with his cooperation, stated candidly the question that many reporters had begun to ask themselves: "Is Reagan up to the job?" High-level officials in the administration began to leak damaging accounts of Reagan's detachment, his ideological rigidity, and his intellectual obtuseness to the press. Anthony Lewis, a columnist for the *New York Times,* announced that the press corps had been watching Reagan for some time and had become "frightened by what they see," a man who acted "without real information" and who used "an anecdotal view of the world" to guide him in intricate policy decisions. Even conservative journals began wringing their hands publicly about the president's performance.[33]

When the press coverage turned, party leaders began to defect as well. Robert Packwood of Oregon, chairman of the National Republican Senatorial Committee, complained that Reagan seemed incapable of rational response to problems. If senators approached him worried about the $100 billion budget deficit, Reagan responded with an anecdotal non sequitur: "The President says, 'You know a person yesterday, a young man, went into a grocery store and he had an orange in one hand and a bottle in the other and he paid for the orange with food stamps and he took the change and paid for the vodka. That's what's wrong.'" But Reagan could not say what that had to do with the budget deficit, whether simply cutting off all welfare would solve the budget problems (it would not), or even how they had gotten to that point. Reporters then had no trouble finding congressmen and even members of the public with similar tales.[34]

Amid the negative coverage, Reagan's polling numbers began to fall. He was not immediately sure how to respond. But after some private waffling, Reagan decided to double down. He had come to Washington to pursue a revolution. Now was not the time to turn back. He needed only to regain control of the narrative. So in plotting a new messaging campaign, he decided to return to the Founding Fathers.

A REALITY GAP

His advisers entered the New Year ready to roll out a plan. He would change his messaging by stages, first in an interview with the *Los Angeles Times*, and then in the 1982 State of the Union address a week later. His goal would be to create a narrative of success that ran counter to the doom and gloom that was emerging about the economy.

In his first year in office, he told the *Times*, his administration had "started government on a different course, different than anything we've done in the last half century since Roosevelt began the New Deal." The American people had begun to see that liberal programs had distorted the government. They recognized that the relationship between the various echelons of government had grown out of whack. For that reason, the tax cuts were quite helpful, he argued, even if they were not having the immediate result that he had predicted. The loss of revenue contained the growth of government and helped "bring back the idea heralded by all our Founding Fathers . . . that government must stay within its means."[35]

He expanded on that theme during his State of the Union speech. Beginning with a review of his first year, Reagan told the nation that his presidency marked, at once, a new beginning and a renewal of "the oldest hopes of our Republic." His major economic programs were now in place, even if they were not yet having the desired effect. But in time they would live up to expectations.[36]

Meanwhile, more needed to be done in other areas in order to renew the Founders' system of federalism. To bring the nation back to their vision, Reagan announced a project to transfer federal grant programs over to the state and local governments in the form of block grants. In essence, the federal government would give to the states lump sums of money. That money would be capped, which reduced federal expenditures, but in exchange he promised to simplify the regulations governing states so long as they pursued the goals of the programs. He had privately called the plan a "drastic" reorientation. But publicly he continued a theme of conservative restoration. "This administration has faith in State and local governments," Reagan said, "and the constitutional balance envisioned by the Founding Fathers."[37]

Unfortunately, the new messaging did not have the desired effect, at least not immediately. His poll numbers continued to fall.

Critics pointed out that shifting power to the state governments less than twenty years after the civil rights movement would only empower state-level discrimination.

Reagan again refused to backtrack. Instead, he shifted toward shoring up his base. A month later, during an after-dinner address at the Conservative Political Action Conference, Reagan tried to tout the economic improvements made by his administration. He still believed that his plan would somehow cohere into a robust economy, increased tax receipts, and a balanced budget, but he implied that he would not alter course if it did not. "Our real concerns are not statistical goals or material gain," he told the crowd. He wanted a renewal of " 'the sacred fire of liberty' that President Washington spoke of two centuries ago."[38]

Reagan, the true believer, was slowly emerging. But others did not share his fervent belief. Congressional leaders, including many Republicans, wanted to retreat from the program. By the summer, Reagan decided he needed to shift the narrative still further. Rejecting that he had any responsibility for the budget mess, Reagan announced a plan to push for a balanced-budget amendment to the Constitution.

"Well, my fellow citizens," Reagan told a small crowd and a bunch of TV cameras as he stood on the West Steps of the Capitol Building, "today we come together on historic grounds to write a new chapter in the American Revolution."[39]

The backdrop of the Capitol fed his narrative that he was taking the fight to Congress in an effort to defend the nation's founding ideals—even as he pushed for a modification of the Constitution. The nation faced a crisis, he said, that would bring it down if left unchecked. Lawmakers had rejected Jefferson's belief in the immorality of deficits. In the process, the American people began looking to the government, like infants to their mother, to provide them with happiness. By adopting a balanced-budget amendment that fixed taxes at a certain ratio, Reagan believed the process might be reversed. His proposal would necessitate drastic cuts in federal programs that would reorder federalism so that states could "fulfill their mission envisioned by the Founding Fathers."[40]

Unfortunately, reality kept intruding on propaganda. Within the week David Stockman informed the cabinet that he now projected massive budget deficits that stretched to the horizon. Shortly thereafter, the administration had to announce that the 1983 deficit would hit $110–114 billion, the largest nonwartime deficit to that point. Critics immediately pointed out that the administration's numbers still had an air of fantasy because they assumed economic growth at a rate of 4.5 percent even though the economy was in recession. The actual numbers would be quite worse.[41]

Faced with such dismal figures, Reagan realized he had no choice but to give back some of his tax cuts. Called the Tax Equity and Fiscal Responsibility Act of 1982, the eventual bill eliminated nearly half the cuts passed just the year prior. Yet, as soon as he signed the bill, he began being attacked from his right flank by the partisans whom he had stoked. Some true believers in his administration resigned in disgust, while Reagan continued to worry about how to shore up his base.[42]

And the blows kept coming. On the first of October, the House voted down his proposed balanced-budget amendment in a decisive fashion.

When he got the news, Reagan immediately marched out to the White House pressroom to express "the deep, burning anger, I think, of millions of Americans."

But the reporters were having none of it.

"Sir," ABC reporter Sam Donaldson asked, "what's unfair about the Democrats' assertion that if you want a balanced budget you should submit a balanced budget?"

The question put Reagan in a tough spot. He danced around

the issue, claimed that there had to be "a time lapse" before a balanced budget could be achieved, and spoke of how the amendment would accomplish his goals.

"Sir, that wasn't my question. I mean, you've answered a question I didn't ask," Donaldson complained.

Reagan finally responded, somewhat defensively, that "after years of out-of-control and buildup" in the federal budget, he could not just present a balanced budget to Congress. It would be too wrenching a change that would wreak havoc with the economy, he explained—which was true, but also mixed messages and undercut his outrage.[43]

The next month Republicans lost twenty-six House seats in the midterm elections, sealing the Democratic majority. With their victory in hand, the Democrats rejected any more budget cuts to address the crisis. Even some Republicans began calling on the president to cut defense spending and to increase domestic spending in order to help the poor and unemployed during the recession.[44]

Reagan seemed completely at a loss. He had a hard time understanding what was going on.

Soon Stockman reported that they faced a trillion-dollar deficit over five years. But rather than coming to grips with the figures, Reagan began turning against his budget director. After another budget meeting of bad news, Reagan admitted, "I didn't understand his figures." He privately suspected that Stockman's "dismal picture . . . was designed to convince me we'd have to have tax increases."[45]

By November, Reagan began tiring of Stockman's "pessimistic projections." "This is a crisis situation!" Reagan exclaimed in one meeting. He wanted to force the hand of Congress to enact more cuts by taking his case to the people. But after nothing came of it and Stockman again came back with still more negative numbers,

Reagan sulkily complained, "I think Dave S. tells us more than we need to know for budget decisions."[46]

By January 1984, it was apparent that nothing would be accomplished until after the presidential elections. Democrats, hoping that one of their own would come into office so they would no longer have to deal with Reagan, began to frame their argument well in advance by pointing out that Reagan's budget was a fiscal disaster and that he had no coherent plan to fix it.

Liberal intellectuals and pundits published books and articles that sought to unmask what they considered Reagan's propaganda machine.[47]

Even David S. Broder, a commentator and journalist always careful to conceal his political leanings, gave vent to the common liberal view that Reagan was essentially a demagogue, though a genial one, who had become increasingly detached from reality. "The domestic policy disaster called the deficit budget," Broder believed, stood at the center of all of Reagan's shortcomings. The issue was not necessarily a conservative or a liberal matter. It was a fight between reality and nonreality. "It is apparently Reagan's belief," Broder wrote, "that words can not only cloak reality but remake it."[48]

The press in general began pounding Reagan with questions on the deficit. But his answers never really satisfied them.

In early spring, during an interview with regional newspaper journalists, one reporter noted that *BusinessWeek* had recently proposed some ways to close the budget gap. They ranged from eliminating farm supports, cutting state and city aid, cutting federal programs, reducing Social Security and Medicare benefits, and slowing the defense buildup, to even raising taxes on the middle class.

"Do you reject all of those, or do you—" the reporter started to ask, before the president burst out laughing.

"Quite a few of them, yes, I do, quite a few," Reagan finally responded, before talking vaguely about "structural reform" as the answer to the problem.[49]

At a news conference a bit later, another reporter pressed him. "Do you think that there's room in the Federal budget to cut spending so deeply that you can balance the budget that way?"

"No," the president admitted. "What we're looking forward to is the fact that as the recovery takes place, you are going to see some contributing factors to further reducing the deficit," he said, without explaining how that would work or if he had any actual projections to substantiate his claim.[50]

As the criticism mounted, Reagan, in turn, tried to shift the blame to the Democrats. "There's nothing in the Constitution that gives the President any right to spend any money," he said over and over again in his campaign speeches. The problem, he suggested, was Congress, not his budget plan.[51]

But perhaps the most important thing that he did was simply to wait. He rode out the storm of criticism in late winter and early spring, while honing his narrative for the general campaign. His team had decided to renew the theme of national values that he had sounded in 1980, but this time he draped himself again and again in the robe of the Founding Fathers. Because his project was a recovery of the founding values, he claimed that his opponents were betrayers of the American character and purpose and therefore thoroughly un-American. In order to sustain his claims, he interspersed important campaign addresses with what were essentially history lessons.

To the nation's governors, he represented himself as a defender of the Founders' federalism. "Jefferson and Adams and those other far-sighted individuals" had established what Reagan characterized as a "system of sovereign States" that was "vital to the preservation of freedom." This Calhounian vision supported his new federalism push.[52]

To evangelicals at their annual convention, he argued that "the debates over independence and the records of the Constitutional Convention make it clear that the Founding Fathers were sustained by their faith in God." This Christian revisionism supported his values politics.[53]

To the nation during the Republican convention in August, he argued that the Founders were free-market individualists who placed religious and moral ideals at the center of national life. While liberals sought a collectivist solution that denied the religious foundation of the nation and slowly crept toward communism, he promoted "the dream conceived by our Founding Fathers," which honored "individual freedom consistent with an orderly society."

"U.S.A.! U.S.A! U.S.A.!" the crowd responded.[54]

Democrats tried to counter by promoting what Walter Mondale, the Democratic candidate, called the "new realism." Rejecting the pseudo-reality that Reagan promised, Democrats talked of facts, limits, and honest dealing with the American people. At the Democratic convention Mondale even promised that he would raise taxes in order to address the deficit. He believed that any honest observer knew that taxes were going up, but he was up-front about that fact while Reagan, he believed, was not.[55]

Yet Reagan merely took the accusation as a gift and folded it into his message. Mondale's tax promise suggested not a new realism but a fundamentally different vision of America. "He sees an America in which every single day is tax day, April 15th," Reagan said in his stump speech. "We see an America in which every day is Independence Day, the Fourth of July."[56]

Ultimately, the Democrats' new realism could not compete with the Reagan messaging. As the economy improved after Volcker eased interest rates, Reagan could claim a genuine renewal of national purpose that resonated beyond Mondale's talk of limits, complexity, and realism. His election represented "a second American revolution," Reagan frequently said, one that had "just begun."[57]

Voters, it turned out, agreed. Reagan won the election by another landslide, taking 525 Electoral College votes to Mondale's 13. Republicans also picked up sixteen seats in the House, while Democrats picked up two seats in the Senate. With the opposition totally demoralized, Reagan believed that he had now received a mandate to pursue sweeping change.[58]

THE POLITICS OF ORIGINALISM

But in reality, the sweeping election did nothing to alter the budgetary problems or the political dynamic. Shortly after the celebration, Stockman presented the cabinet with a plan to bring down the deficit to 2 percent of gross domestic product by Reagan's last year in office. It would still not balance the budget, but it would be much closer.

Reagan was rattled. The plan involved what Reagan characterized as "a really draconian cut" that would eliminate huge swaths of governmental programs that even Reagan supported. "Frankly it's time to reverse the course of the last 50 yrs.," Reagan wrote in his diary, but he suspected that Stockman had "made it so tough" to force Reagan to consider a tax increase. "I won't," Reagan promised.[59]

But others saw no choice. The press in particular continued to grill Reagan on his deficit reduction strategy in a series of interviews and press conferences leading up to the inauguration.

"Mr. President, have you painted yourself into a corner with your campaign promises to raise taxes only over your dead body, not to cut Social Security, and to keep up defense spending?" one reporter asked.

"No," Reagan answered, before promising that he would shortly release his own budget that would begin deficit reduction.

"But, sir," the reporter pressed, "the consensus even within your own party seems to be that if you keep all your promises, there's no way that you can accomplish that goal."

"I just don't believe them," the president responded.[60]

"It seems likely from what David Stockman has said," another reporter asked, "that you will go out of office as a President who presided over the biggest deficits in history. Are you resigned to that?"

"Well, I almost have to be," Reagan admitted. But he denied any responsibility for the problem. "You have to realize how much this has been built in," he continued. "This increase is not anything that we created."[61]

But the skepticism of the press and the political elite hardly touched his speechcraft. His second inaugural address continued now-familiar themes. The election four years ago constituted a new beginning, he told the nation. "But in another sense, our New Beginning is a continuation of that beginning created two centuries ago." Although the system created at the founding was a perfectly crafted form of governance, "for a time," he told the crowd, "we failed the system." By turning to government for a solution to problems, the American people had become enfeebled and the American industrial machine became clogged. But in 1980 the people had awoken and decided to renew their faith. Looking forward to his second term, he now believed that the renewal would continue. "Let history say of us," he chanted, "those were golden years—when the American Revolution was reborn, when freedom gained new life, and America reached for her best."[62]

His words might have been powerful to the American public. But opposing politicians were unmoved. Within the year the government was flirting with default and a governmental shutdown as Congress refused to raise the debt ceiling, which it had already done nine times since Reagan took office. David Stockman also left the administration, realizing that his recommendations were not being heard and that Reagan would not believe that it was his tax cuts that had made a mess of the budget. By mid-November, as the government shutdown appeared imminent, Reagan negotiated a temporary increase in the debt limit. Shortly thereafter Congress put forward the Gramm-Rudman-Hollings Act, which provided for automatic spending cuts by the U.S. comptroller if the president and Congress could not agree to budget reductions before the deadline.[63]

Reagan lamented his position. "I can't let the mil[itary] budget be hacked away any more by Cong.," he wrote, "& at the same time I can't veto the Gramm, Rudman, Hollings bill—which threatens to do that." After a tortured struggle over the trade-offs, he decided to sign the bill and then essentially washed his hands of the deficit.[64]

But that did not mean that he gave up his goal of remaking government. Reagan simply turned to another arena: the courts. Back in 1981, he had chosen the path of moderation when he nominated—over the objections of his fellow conservatives—Sandra Day O'Connor to the first vacant seat.

But happily, in mid-June 1986 he got another shot when Chief Justice Warren Burger, first nominated by Nixon in 1969, decided to step down. Reagan still hoped to replace one of the liberal justices, but nominating a chief justice would be good, too. He immediately offered up Associate Justice William H. Rehnquist, the most conservative man on the Court.

Rehnquist's nomination proved to be controversial. In 1954 Rehnquist had clerked for Associate Justice Robert H. Jackson during the *Brown v. Board of Education* case. As part of Jackson's deliberations, he had requested his clerks to prepare memos arguing how he should rule. Rehnquist had rejected much of the jurisprudence emerging from the New Deal, just as he was hostile to the civil liberties turn that the courts began to take in the 1940s. The entire program was exactly backward, Rehnquist explained to Jackson. The Court ought to limit congressional interference with the economy and it ought to trust the states to protect (or not) civil liberties. But instead of doing that, the post–New Deal Court had further undermined the Founders' system of states' rights. Rehnquist believed that the trend needed to be stopped. What that meant in the immediate case was clear, Rehnquist wrote to Jackson. Allowing the southern states to do as they wished—which was to uphold segregation—was "right and should be affirmed."[65]

During his confirmation hearings, Democrats pressed Rehnquist on his earlier views. Although he distanced himself from his defense of segregation, he did not repudiate his desire to undo the broad thrust of the Court's post–New Deal decisions. The Court had made a wrong turn, he believed, and it was now time to return to a view of the Constitution that, as he wrote in 1977, interpreted it strictly in the way that "the Framers obviously meant it to apply."[66]

That doctrine, known as constitutional originalism, was even more on display with Reagan's next nomination to take Rehnquist's old seat: Antonin Scalia. Rejecting the progressive idea that the Constitution grows with the interpretation of the courts and the development of history, Scalia argued that the Constitution was fixed at the founding. As he would later say, "Words do have a limited range of meaning," so a judicial philosophy that tried to deal honestly with the Constitution served, in effect, to bind the government within set limits. For Scalia, it was up to the judge to determine what the words of the Constitution would have meant at the time that they were written in order to understand those limits. Once he did that, he decided cases accordingly.[67]

Faced with two true-blue conservatives who rejected, in essence, decades of jurisprudence, reporters began asking Reagan about just how he sought "to change the philosophy or direction of the Court." But Reagan's smiling responses dodged the issue since it was perfectly obvious what he hoped to accomplish. And although liberals were upset, they could not quite discover any smoking gun to prevent the confirmations in a Republican-controlled Senate.[68]

Reagan was delighted. At Rehnquist's and Scalia's swearing-in, he rejoiced in what he called "a time of renewal in the great constitutional system that our forefathers gave us—a good time to reflect on the inspired wisdom we call our Constitution, a time to remember that the Founding Fathers gave careful thought to the role of the Supreme Court." The Founders created the Court as part of a system of checks and balances to protect the limited government promised by the Constitution. Fortunately both of these men understood that function.[69]

The next year, Reagan got another crack at the Court when the moderate Lewis Powell resigned. But in the interim the political climate had gotten more difficult for Reagan. During the 1986 midterm elections, Republicans had lost control of the Senate even though Reagan personally campaigned for imperiled Republican senators. And liberal jurists, worried about the administration's agenda, began speaking out against the philosophy of constitutional originalism. Justice William J. Brennan complained that originalism was, in fact, "arrogance masked as humility," since it placed the judge's historical judgment over that of the judicial tradition. A few months later, Justice Thurgood Marshall, the first black Supreme Court member, went further, arguing that the celebrations of the original meaning of the Constitution were misguided because, in his view, "the wisdom, foresight, and sense of justice" that the framers exhibited were not "particularly profound." "To the contrary," he continued,

> the government they devised was defective from the start, requiring several amendments, a civil war, and momentous social transformation to attain the system of constitutional government, and its respect for individual freedoms and human rights, that we hold as fundamental today. When contemporary Americans cite "The Constitution," they invoke a concept that is vastly different from what the framers barely began to construct two centuries ago.[70]

But in spite of these challenges, purists in Reagan's administration saw the nomination as perhaps the only chance left to seal the conservative revolution. Accordingly, Reagan nominated Robert Bork, a conservative jurist to the right of even Rehnquist or Scalia and whom conservatives had been pushing since 1981. He seemed the perfect choice to decisively shift the Court.[71]

Unfortunately for the administration, Bork had a lengthy publishing record. As a faculty member at Yale Law School, he had elaborated his opinions on everything from the *Brown v. Board* decision (which he criticized even though he claimed not to be a racist) to abortion (which he deplored and thought was unconstitutional). When legislative aides and journalists surveyed Bork's public writings, it became clear that he viewed the entirety of the Court's last fifty years as a disaster that put the nation on a path of degradation and tyranny—America was "Slouching towards Gomorrah," as he titled a later book. His legal jeremiad worked hand in glove with Reagan's political one.[72]

Liberals were, accordingly, alarmed. In a preemptive attack,

Democratic senator Ted Kennedy of Massachusetts condemned Bork from the Senate floor as a knuckle-dragger who only called on the Constitution to disguise his backward aims. "Robert Bork's America is a land in which women would be forced into back-alley abortions, blacks would sit at segregated lunch counters, rogue police would break down citizens' doors in midnight raids, schoolchildren could not be taught about evolution, writers and artists could be censored at the whim of the Government, and the doors of the Federal courts would be shut on the fingers of millions of citizens," Kennedy said. Because of the harshness of his comments and the prominence of the accuser, Kennedy's charges received serious news attention and alerted civil rights activists and women's groups to mobilize in opposition to Bork's nomination.[73]

Reagan immediately tried to counter the criticism, with limited success. At a long-planned, campaign-style event at the Jefferson Memorial just prior to the July Fourth holiday, Reagan again sought to calibrate image and message by arguing that his and Bork's constitutionalism only reiterated that of Jefferson before him. The American Revolution was a philosophical one, he told the crowd, dedicated to the proposition that government had limits to ensure political freedom. The Bill of Rights had made those governmental limits explicit.

But, Reagan believed, it had unfortunately left obscure an equally important truth. Political freedoms such as freedom of speech, of the press, and of religion were "part and parcel" of economic freedoms such as the freedom to work, to profit, to own and control property, and to participate in a free market. In fact, economic freedoms were primary, because undermining economic freedom eventually led to the loss of political freedom, a process that had begun in the New Deal. The Founders had everywhere implied economic freedoms in the Constitution, Reagan argued, so it was important to choose jurists like Bork, who would honor the original vision.[74]

Reagan's increasingly strained jeremiad left the public and, ultimately, the Senate unconvinced. On October 6 the Judiciary Committee rejected Bork's nomination in a 9–5 vote. Bork insisted on a full vote of the Senate, so a couple of weeks later the Senate as a whole voted him down, 58–42. After such a stinging defeat, Reagan had to settle for a moderate conservative, Anthony Kennedy, to take Powell's seat.

With that, Reagan's domestic agenda pretty much came to an end. Scandals began engulfing the administration: the Iran-Contra affair, which threatened Reagan with impeachment; the savings-and-loan crisis of collapsing banks that had been deregulated under Reagan and that cost the federal government billions of dollars in bailouts; a scandal at the Department of Housing and Urban Development that provided a seemingly unending story of high-level corruption followed by indictments; a Pentagon procurement scandal that involved more governmental bribery and more indictments. The scandals became routine.[75]

If that were not enough, on October 19, stock markets around the world cratered. The Dow Jones Industrial Average lost 23.6 percent in one day. A Chrysler executive told the *Wall Street Journal*, "We are finally paying the piper for the seven years of profligacy by this administration." Reagan's approval rating, which had been falling since the previous year, dipped below 50 percent. Though he held an economic summit to address the deficit problems, nothing much came of it.[76]

Reagan, it was now apparent, had failed. Though his approval rating would go back up by the end of his term, he was never able to accomplish what he had wanted to do. He began his career in politics as a deficit hawk. He remained theoretically committed to balanced budgets while he pursued tax cuts. But his assumption that he could have both at the same time—and that this was somehow proven by the Founding Fathers—was disastrously wrong. The federal debt tripled during his eight years, going from $994 billion to $2.8 trillion. Over the course of his presidency, the United States went from being the world's largest creditor nation to the world's largest debtor nation, sustaining its spending by borrowing massively from abroad.[77]

He also failed to significantly lower the tax rate. In 1981, 19.4 percent of national income went toward federal taxes. By 1989, when he left office, 19.3 percent still went to paying taxes. But because many state and local governments had to raise taxes to make up for decreased federal spending on domestic programs (the increased outlays were mainly for the military), for many people the overall tax load moved somewhat higher over his two terms.

Reagan's main success was in pushing through tax cuts for the wealthy, which had the effect of placing the tax burden more squarely on the middle and lower classes while encouraging a rapidly widening income gap. But the entire program never achieved anything close to coherence because Reagan had neither the will nor the ability to cut the number of programs required to arrive at a balanced ledger.[78]

Yet in spite of his policy failings, by the end of his second term Reagan had changed the boundaries of debate and the pattern of political consensus. A reporter once asked him, in reference to his political victory: "What's happening?"

Reagan responded with a canned version of his jeremiad, claiming that the people had woken up to restore founding values.

"So, the debate's on your terms now?" the reporter asked.

"Yes," Reagan said.[79]

But the incoherence of those terms would cause all manner of problems in the future. He left office to the nearly unanimous praise of his followers, who believed his narrative of American decline and saw in Reagan the beginnings of a reversal, even though Reagan's story about the Founders and his political posturing as the defender of their ideals did not actually match reality. The cumulative effect of the Reagan years was a set of contradictory commitments and mutually exclusive political claims that sloganeering about the Founders could not resolve.

His immediate successor bore the brunt of these tensions. In 1988, when Reagan's vice president, George H. W. Bush, ran for president, he had to renounce his earlier criticisms of "voodoo economics" in order to appease the base. "The Congress will push me to raise taxes," he told the raucous crowd at the Republican National Convention, "and I'll say no, and they'll push, and I'll say no, and they'll push, and I'll say to them, 'Read my lips: no new taxes.'" The crowd went crazy. The base was completely appeased.[80]

But Bush was not a true believer, and although the clip offered a good sound bite, it made bad policy. Two years later, still concerned about the ongoing debt crisis, then-president Bush agreed to tax increases in return for caps on discretionary spending and future spending rules to stop the bleeding.[81]

Yet that, too, did not produce balanced budgets. In 1992, the billionaire Ross Perot grew so concerned about deficits that he decided to run for president as an independent. Though Perot did not necessarily determine the result, his nearly 19 percent of the vote suggested a popular sentiment toward deficit reduction that could not be ignored. But there was no obvious compromise position on how deficits ought to be addressed. The conservative base continued to believe that if only Reagan's plan had been fully implemented, whatever that would mean, the budgetary problems would go away. They were becoming more intransigent and more detached from reality.

Their recalcitrance was so great that when President Bill

Clinton, a Democrat, took office after the election, he felt trapped and unable to pursue any of his agenda because he was still fighting the result of Reagan's years in office. "I hope you're all aware we're all Eisenhower Republicans," he told his advisers. "We're all Eisenhower Republicans here, and we are fighting the Reagan Republicans. We stand for lower deficits and free trade and the bond market. Isn't that great?"[82]

Accordingly, Clinton's two terms were driven by the attempt to check Reagan's increasingly radicalized base. Clinton signed into law during his first year in office the Deficit Reduction Act of 1993, which raised taxes on corporations, the rich, and transportation fuel. Every Republican voted against it, which led to Vice President Al Gore breaking the 50–50 tie in the Senate. Conflict grew worse in 1994, after Republicans gained the House and Senate. Led by Newt Gingrich, the Republicans adopted a highly antagonistic posture toward Clinton in their attempt to install a new conservative regime. When Republicans wanted more tax cuts, Clinton resisted and had to endure two government shutdowns until Republicans finally conceded. After the shutdowns, Clinton worked with the Republican congressional leadership to pass the Welfare Reform Act of 1996, significantly curtailing federal responsibility for the poor. In 1998, after six years of narrowing deficits as the Bush and Clinton tax increases kicked in and the economy strengthened, the budget finally balanced. Clinton left office with large surpluses projected into the future.[83]

But when George W. Bush entered office in 2001, he immediately reverted to Reaganesque form by pushing large tax cuts that turned the surpluses into the largest deficits in history. He also massively increased military spending to fight two wars in Afghanistan and Iraq, while increasing domestic spending through a Medicare drug plan, outlays in transportation, and other building initiatives. By the end of his two terms, the financial system neared collapse as unregulated financial instruments exploded to start the worst economic downturn since the Great Depression. Reagan's political philosophy, now approaching total incoherence in his successor, appeared to be at an end.[84]

CHAPTER EIGHT

This Is America!

The Great Recession offered a powerful lesson in the importance of government. At a time in which the economy was in free fall, the only institutions big enough to stop the downward momentum were the U.S. Treasury and the Federal Reserve. Accordingly, they both moved on multiple fronts to contain the damage. But many conservatives were downright uneasy. Beginning with President Bush's Troubled Asset Relief Program (TARP), a massive government initiative to shore up banks, and continuing after Barack Obama's election in 2008, with a stimulus bill to prevent depression, conservatives began to believe that dark forces were conspiring to take over the nation.

"The government is promoting bad behavior!" the on-air editor for CNBC business news, Rick Santelli, shouted into the cameras from the floor of the Chicago Mercantile Exchange. Santelli was, in many ways, an unlikely person to give vent to conservative unease. In the waning days of the Bush administration, he had not objected to TARP because, like many business-minded

209

conservatives, he believed it had been necessary to prevent catastrophe.

But the stimulus was another thing altogether. "This is America!" he shouted, a land of self-reliance, rugged individualism, and good things to all who deserved them. Those feckless Americans who had taken on too much debt and now could not afford it, Santelli believed, were "losers" and not properly the government's problem. In order to preserve the capitalistic individualism at the heart of the American dream, he announced that he was going to have a tea party. Like the first one in 1773, the new tea party would protect American values and ways of life by protecting the capitalist system. And all those capitalists who were interested, he said, could show up in July at Lake Michigan, where the revolution would be renewed.

"Rick, I congratulate you on your new incarnation as a revolutionary leader," the studio anchor told him, stifling a laugh.

"Somebody needs to be one," Santelli responded. "I'll tell you what, if you read our Founding Fathers, people like Benjamin Franklin and Jefferson, what we're doing in this country now is making them roll over in their graves." With that, the studio went to a new segment.[1]

Santelli's rant turned out to be a harbinger of the future. Although it was far from coherent—he seemed to confuse the Boston Tea Party of 1773 with the Declaration of Independence in July 1776, and his invocation of Jefferson and Franklin had no real substance—Santelli's comments tapped into a widespread feeling of conservative grievance. The government, many felt, had betrayed them. The federal establishment was becoming a tyrant the way that Great Britain had been the tyrant in 1773. Only some act of resistance, some kind of determined stand, could stop the spread of tyranny.[2]

"Americans are looking for signs . . . of an alternative,"

Kathryn Jean Lopez of the *National Review* wrote the next day. "And so if a representative pops up—someone who appears to have roots and energy, folks will cheer them on in the hopes there's a candidate here. Maybe not a presidential candidate, but a leader of some sort." Lopez went so far as to predict Santelli's appearance on a 2012 ticket. But regardless of Santelli's political future, she and others believed a window had opened into the political present. It was now, in the words of the *New York Times,* "tea party time."[3]

Lopez turned out to be prophetic. Santelli's rant sparked an invigorating feeling of protest that raced through conservative ranks. Numerous Tea Party groups sprang into existence, seemingly overnight. Plans were drawn for rallies across the nation on April 15, tax day. As the weeks counted down, anticipation grew.

Something was happening.

When April 15 arrived, protesters held more than 750 rallies across the nation. Conservatives and their media allies turned out in force. American flags flew high. People held signs that read "Abolish the I.R.S.," "Less Government More Free Enterprise," "We Miss Reagan," and "Honk If You Are Upset about Your Tax Dollars Being Spent on Illegal Aliens." Many dressed in eighteenth-century regalia. Some events had the strange aura of an angry meeting of American Revolutionary reenactors. Fox News offered nearly continuous coverage. Various conservative media personalities—Neil Cavuto, Michelle Malkin, Sean Hannity—headlined events or broadcast their show from the protest locations. In Austin, Governor Rick Perry of Texas vaguely threatened secession. "If Washington continues to thumb their nose at the American people," he said, "who knows what might come out of that."[4]

Perry's address suggested what was to come. Politicians began jockeying to become leaders of the movement, pushing the revolutionary rhetoric in often extreme directions. Routine policy disagreement began to take on apocalyptic overtones. When Congress took up legislation to address climate change, Michele Bachmann, a Republican from Minnesota and an early channeler of Tea Party rage, went straight for the guns. "I want people in Minnesota armed and dangerous on this issue of the energy tax because we need to fight back," she told conservative talk show host Glenn Beck. "Thomas Jefferson told us 'having a revolution every now and then is a good thing,'" she continued, "and the people—we the people—are going to have to fight back hard if we're not going to lose our country. And I think this has the potential of changing the dynamic of freedom forever in the United States."[5]

Once the Democratic Congress turned toward health-care legislation, Tea Partiers went into a frenzy. During an angry summer recess in 2009, lawmakers were accosted at constituent events by outraged activists. Tea Party leaders believed that the health-care legislation was, practically by itself, the coming of government tyranny. In August, when Obama began pushing back on conservative outrage, people started showing up at his events with weapons. At a meeting in New Hampshire, a man stood outside the building where Obama was to speak carrying a sign. It read: "It is time to water the tree of liberty," a loose allusion to Jefferson's claim that "the tree of liberty must be refreshed from time to time with the blood of patriots and tyrants." That same day a man had been arrested in the school building in which Obama was to speak. A loaded gun was found in his car. At an event in Arizona held by Democratic representative Gabrielle Giffords, the police were called after a man dropped a gun in the middle of the crowd. Less than a week later, a man stood outside another Obama event with an AR-15 slung across his back. When asked why he had brought an assault rifle to the event, he responded: "Because I can do it. In Arizona, I still have some freedoms left."[6]

All that rhetoric left some people nervous, but it initially looked to be winning. In January 2010, Republicans shocked Democrats by winning a special election in Massachusetts to replace the recently deceased Ted Kennedy in the Senate. The victory "heralds the coming of age of the Tea Party movement," the *New York Times* announced. It was "the shot heard 'round the world," John McCain chortled, an allusion to the first exchange of gunfire that began the American Revolution.[7]

The same month polls revealed that the Tea Party was more popular than any of the major parties. Thirty-five percent of the public had a positive view of the Democrats. Twenty-eight percent had a positive view of Republicans. And 41 percent had a positive view of the Tea Party. David Brooks, a conservative columnist whose moderation made him a critic of the movement, predicted somewhat gloomily that the Tea Party would soon "become a major force in American politics." Tea Partiers wholeheartedly agreed. "America is ready for another revolution," Sarah Palin told a Tea Party convention in February. "This party that we call the Tea Party, this movement," Palin promised, "is the future of politics in America."[8]

YOU SAY YOU WANT A REVOLUTION

But what exactly did the Tea Party want? What was the goal?

Those questions turned out to be surprisingly difficult to answer. As a collection of amorphous frustrations and revolutionary rhetoric, it did not convert easily into actual policy. Some of its leaders wanted smaller government, less regulation, and less connection in general between the government and the economy. As Congressman Ron Paul said, by way of explanation for the small-government thrust of the movement, "The Founders were libertarians." But other Tea Partiers professed socially conservative, values politics. "Go back to what our founders and our founding documents meant," Sarah Palin told Fox News's Bill O'Reilly. It was clear that they, like the Tea Party movement, intended to "create laws based on the God of the Bible and the Ten Commandments."[9]

What these two factions shared was not so much a common set of issues as an interpretive posture. Tea Partiers believed that the Founders had offered a clear, simple, and even inspired explication of their thought in the Constitution. The task of political life was to read the Constitution, to understand its meaning, and to proceed accordingly. The process as a whole involved no real difficulty and no interpretive dilemmas, just a constitutional literalism that was supposed to solve all problems.[10]

To critics, the Tea Party offered a simplistic vision. As the historian and essayist Jill Lepore argued, Tea Partiers often had a fantastically vacuous conception of the past. Before the Tea Party's adoring gaze, the differences between past and present—the differences among the Founders themselves—fell irrelevantly away. Their mawkish nostalgia combined with a literalism so strict that Lepore accused the Tea Party of "historical fundamentalism." The past and present are the same, Tea Partiers believed. Time is irrelevant in the development of constitutional doctrine. All that matters is that true doctrine be upheld.[11]

Such simplicity, many worried, could become dangerous. It fostered fanaticism. It betrayed the moderation and compromise supposedly supported by the Founders. It was, as the historian Mark Lilla argued, more in accord with the Jacobins of the French Revolution than the moderates of the American one. And the Tea Party movement would have similar consequences, Lilla predicted. It was already pushing the Republican Party toward what Lilla called ever-"cruder" forms of thought and rhetoric. The more the Tea Party gained control, the more it would turn on itself, allowing no deviation from true doctrine and no room for political compromise. Given the fatal lack of sophistication, subtlety, and nuance in Tea Party thought, Lilla believed, the entire movement could only end badly.[12]

As if to prove Lilla correct, movement figures spent the 2010 campaign trying to outdo one another with outrageous statements. In Indiana, a Republican Senate candidate told a Tea Party rally that if they lost in the midterm elections, "I'm cleaning my guns and getting ready for the big show. And I'm serious about that, and I bet you are, too."[13]

Sharron Angle, a Republican Senate candidate in Nevada and a Tea Party favorite, was more explicit. "You know, our Founding Fathers, they put that Second Amendment in there for a good reason," she said, "and that was for the people to protect themselves against a tyrannical government. And in fact Thomas Jefferson said it's good for a country to have a revolution every 20 years. I hope that's not where we're going, but, you know, if this Congress keeps going the way it is, people are really looking toward those Second Amendment remedies and saying, my goodness, what can we do to turn this country around?"[14]

Others dispensed with the notion of revolution and, like Rick Perry, went straight to civil war. As one Tea Partier told the *New York Times,* "I don't see us being the ones to start it, but I would give up my life for my country." Pausing to consider her words, she continued, "Peaceful means are the best way of going about it. But sometimes you are not given a choice."[15]

Occasional undercurrents of racism also began to surface. In April 2009, the Department of Homeland Security warned that the election of the first black president and the 2008 recession "present unique drivers for rightwing radicalization." Although conservatives howled in outrage, the angry Tea Party crowds kept veering off message in a way that confirmed the early warning. In early spring 2010, as Congress was debating the Affordable Care Act, aka Obamacare, thousands of Tea Partiers rallied in front of the U.S. Capitol, where they gave vent to various expressions of bigotry. Representative Barney Frank of Massachusetts, an openly gay Democrat, was the target of antigay slurs. Three black congressmen reported hearing racial slurs shouted at them. Michigan Democrat Emanuel Cleaver, one of the black congressmen, was spat upon. "I heard people saying things today that I have not heard since March 15, 1960, when I was marching to try to get off the back of the bus," said Democrat James E. Clyburn of South Carolina. Tea Party groups continued to deny that there was racism within the movement.[16]

Four days later, when Congress passed the health-care bill, at least ten lawmakers received around-the-clock protection after receiving death threats. The mood was dire. But Republican leaders decided to wait several days before House minority leader John Boehner offered a statement. "I know many Americans are angry over this health care bill, and that Washington Democrats just aren't listening," he said. "But, as I've said, violence and threats are unacceptable. That's not the American way."[17]

Others were not so cautious. Shortly after the vote, Sarah Palin put on her Facebook page a map of vulnerable Democratic lawmakers with their districts marked in crosshairs and then tweeted: "Commonsense Conservatives & lovers of America: 'Don't Retreat, Instead—RELOAD!'" Three weeks later she continued her revolutionary efforts on Boston Common in front of a crowd of several thousand. "You're sounding the warning bell, just like what happened with that midnight run," she told the crowd.[18]

As the reality of the health-care legislation sank in, Republicans sought to channel the anger into the upcoming election. In July, Michele Bachmann applied to House leaders to form a Tea Party caucus. "This caucus would do nothing more than promote the timeless principles of our founding, principles that all members of Congress have sworn to uphold," she wrote to House Speaker Nancy Pelosi. On her website, Bachmann was more explicit in her criticism. She was forced to form the caucus precisely because "the Constitution is no longer at the forefront guiding Congress." The Tea Party represented a saving remnant to bring Congress and the nation back to original principles.[19]

Meanwhile, reporters and commentators began to figure out who the Tea Party was. Polls started to show that Tea Party supporters had more money, were better educated, and tended to be older, white, married men. They were loyal Republicans, conservative on a range of issues, and motivated not by personal circumstances such as the loss of a job but by political ideology. The ideological engine of the movement was the biggest surprise. "The story they're telling," historian Rick Perlstein said after the new survey data came out, "is that somehow the authentic, real America is being polluted."[20]

That story turned out to be Republicans' supreme weapon going into the 2010 elections. Though Democrats managed to retain control of the Senate, they lost sixty-three seats in the House as Republicans, led by Tea Party activists, took a commanding majority in the lower chamber. Republicans also picked up six governorships, moving their total to twenty-nine. They made significant gains in state legislatures as well. In a measure of Tea Party success, nearly every congressional district, even those that did not elect a Republican, moved to the political right.[21]

The Tea Party revolution was under way.

But, again, what exactly did the Tea Party want? For the moment, Republicans sought to hold that question at bay. Instead of putting forward policy proposals, the new leadership opted for a symbolic measure that accorded with the Tea Party narrative.

On the first day of the new session, the leadership decided

to read the Constitution aloud from the floor of the House, apparently for the first time. The reading dramatized their promise that each House bill would cite, just as a fundamentalist Christian offers a proof text from scripture, the portion of the Constitution that enabled that particular law.[22]

Yet controversy began even before the reading. Democrats argued that the Constitution should be read in its entirety, including the oblique references to slavery and all of the sections superseded by amendments. That would have led to the embarrassing spectacle of someone reading, for example, the three-fifths clause, which counted a slave as three-fifths of a person for the purpose of representation.

The Republican leadership decided instead to read the Constitution as amended, which left out the embarrassing texts. Democrat Jesse L. Jackson Jr. of Illinois continued the fight on the floor, objecting that Republicans were whitewashing history to uphold their simplistic constitutional vision. Noting that the Constitution was "a living document," Jackson argued that the "redacted" Republican version ignored "the blood, sweat and tears of millions of Americans from the Revolutionary War through the Civil War to even our current conflicts."[23]

The controversy continued in print for several days. Many liberals used the occasion to elaborate an expansive constitutional vision. "Reading the entire Constitution," constitutional law scholar Jack Balkin wrote, would have been "a way of engaging in proper humility about the products of flawed human beings" and also "a way of expressing faith in eventual improvement." After all, as Adam Serwer argued in the *Washington Post*, the Constitution "was not carved out of stone tablets by a finger of light at the summit of Mount Sinai." Yet the Tea Party–led Republicans seemed to believe that it was. Their entire posture left liberals baffled and frustrated. "To believe that American institutions were ever perfect," Adam Kirsch argued in the *New York Times,* "makes it too easy to believe that they are perfect now. Both assumptions, one might say, are sins against the true spirit of the Constitution, which demands that we keep reimagining our way to a more perfect union."[24]

But conservatives rejected the accusations of simple-mindedness and returned the favor. To claim a sin against the spirit of the Constitution, as Kirsch did, implied that the spirit was more important than the letter, something that conservatives would never grant. "The Constitution was read today to remind Congress of what it can and cannot legally do," Adam J. White argued in the *Weekly Standard*'s blog, "not to must about what mistakes of the Founding Fathers require subsequent correction." That was something that liberals seemed not to see. As Alana Goodman observed in *Commentary* magazine, the point of the reading was not the "academic historical exercise" that liberals wanted to make it. "The Constitution is actually *still used* on a daily basis to uphold our nation's laws," she observed. That she had to make such an elementary point showed exactly why the constitutional reading was needed.[25]

As a whole, the debate over the Constitution was a revealing moment. Liberals pointed out the changing nature of constitutional governance, while conservatives rejected change to point out the binding character of constitutionalism in the present. Liberals used the occasion to make the case for governmental action. Conservatives made an argument for governmental limitation. Both believed that they honored the Founders, though they conceived of their relationship to the Founders in different ways. Disagreements in policy were rooted in radically different interpretive practices and different postures toward the founding moment. Those differences would be hard to bridge.

WHAT WOULD JEFFERSON DO?

But it was also clear that there was an emerging disagreement among conservatives, one that grew out of differing dispositions, if not principle. The Tea Party movement possessed an almost centrifugal force in which ideas gravitated from the center to the margins. On the anti-intellectual fringe, the narrative about the Founders was taken up by absolutists and paranoids who supported citizen militias and the like. Yet even those not on the fringe supported the radical rhetoric. It was, in some sense, built into the movement. The logic of their argument—that conservatives were losing the country, that it had fatally departed from the Founders' intentions, that the republican experiment required periodic revolutions to renew old values—suggested that extreme and uncompromising measures were necessary to restore the nation to the old ways.

The Republican leadership, by contrast, was made up of realists. Though establishment politicians had used similar revolutionary rhetoric often enough—since at least the time of Ronald Reagan—when it came to governing they recognized the limits of their power and the importance of incremental change. But with the Tea Party revolution, the rhetoric became harder to control. The conservative base had slipped its leash. The new Tea Party activists, who rejected incremental change as part of the same old pattern that slouched toward tyranny, had begun speaking of revolution in sometimes the most literal sense.

As early as August 2009, David Frum, a speechwriter for George W. Bush, warned that conservatives were playing with fire. "All this hysterical and provocative talk invites, incites, and prepares a prefabricated justification for violence," he wrote during the angry summer recess. "It's not enough for conservatives to repudiate violence, as some are belatedly beginning to do. We have to tone down the militant and accusatory rhetoric."[26]

His warning turned out to be tragically prescient two days after the 2011 legislative session began, when Representative Gabrielle Giffords was shot in the head at a constituent event in Arizona. All told, nineteen people were shot. Six of them died, including a federal judge who was present. Reporters quickly discovered that Giffords had been on Sarah Palin's target list. The police had been called when a man dropped a gun at one of her summer events in the infamous 2009 summer recess. And she had been one of the representatives to receive police protection after her affirmative vote on Obamacare. In retrospect, it was clear that she had been in danger for some time. Now she lay in a medically induced coma with the surgeons uncertain about the extent of her injuries.

Media attention after the shooting focused on Tea Party rhetoric and paranoid behavior—Sharron Angle's talk of "second-amendment remedies," the constant references to "watering the tree of liberty," the gratuitous displaying of guns at Arizona political events. Pima County sheriff Clarence Dupnik spoke bitterly of "unbalanced people" who "respond to the vitriol that comes out of certain mouths about tearing down the government."[27]

Some commentators wondered if perhaps the Republicans had foolishly tried to ride the Tea Party tiger. It had been clear for some time that the Tea Party combined legitimate outrage over Democratic policies with more disreputable elements that tended toward extreme directions, a dialectic that the conservative columnist Matthew Continetti called "the two faces of the Tea Party." One side sought to repair various "deformities" in American politics. The other, according to Continetti, was "ready to scrap the whole thing and restore a lost Eden." One side was reformist. The other was revolutionary. One was responsible. The other was dangerous. It was really important, Continetti believed, to encourage the one side and suppress the other.[28]

But when Continetti first began worrying about how to separate the responsible side from the reactionaries, other commentators had argued that it was impossible to draw such a line. Over at the *National Review,* Jonah Goldberg suggested that these two faces were actually marching in lockstep, as they had always done. Like Goldwater and Reagan in an earlier era, the two sides were really differing dispositions. One was more strident. The other was sunnier. One sometimes drifted into apocalyptic pronouncements. The other maintained a more realistic position while offering the hope of change. But both shared a policy vision, he argued, and both rejected the twentieth-century welfare state as a betrayal of the Founders' idea of self-reliance. If the strident faction seemed to be ascendant at the moment, as it had since 2009, Goldberg was not particularly worried. Tea Party zeal would only catalyze conservative momentum that could eventually be channeled toward legislative success.[29]

But after the shooting, things looked different. With Giffords lying in a coma and half a dozen people dead, it became much more important to distinguish the hysterical faction from the responsible one. Republican leaders would need to contain the more unruly components of the Tea Party revolution, while nevertheless harnessing its energy to accomplish Republican purposes.

The question was how to do that. Even after the debate over the shooting had died down and Congress went back to its normal business, the way forward was not clear. In their zeal to fight the Obama administration, many Tea Partiers seemed to believe that their election would single-handedly reverse what they saw as governmental tyranny. But Republicans controlled only one chamber of Congress, not the Senate and not the White House. Republicans needed to find some strategic ground to accomplish their goals.[30]

Unfortunately for the Republican leadership, the Tea Party

seemed barely interested in governance. Tea Partiers wanted, above all else, a confrontation with the president regardless of the wisdom of the conflict. And because the 2010 freshman class was so large, Speaker John Boehner did not have a functional majority to pass bills without Tea Party support. That dynamic made Republican attempts to convert the posture of rage into actual policy initiatives difficult if not impossible.[31]

The problems began straightaway. By early spring, it became apparent that the U.S. debt ceiling would need to be raised, a regular occurrence since the spiraling debts under the George W. Bush administration, now exacerbated by the Great Recession and the Democrats' stimulus package to combat it. Republican leaders decided that they would resist all increases to the debt ceiling until they received sufficient concessions that would, they hoped, force a fundamental change in course.

The tactic was not new. Fights over the debt ceiling had been occasional going back to the exploding deficits of the Reagan administration. But what was new was the unbending posture of the Tea Party. In the past, when the opposition party threatened not to raise it, there was no real risk that the ceiling would not be raised. Refusing to do so was simply a way of extracting concessions. Everyone understood that actually going through with the obstruction would put the U.S. government into default—not a live option.

But what the Tea Party–led Republicans demanded—a massive cut to spending that would increase over time, a balanced-budget amendment that would permanently limit spending in the future, and the promise that these aggressive cuts would somehow balance the budget rather than creating recession and larger budget deficits—was unprecedented. There was no way that Obama could give even half of what the Tea Party faction demanded. So what would otherwise have been a routine maneuver in public bargaining became a standoff that threatened the full faith and credit of the United States. The Tea Party threatened to burn down the house in order to "save" it.[32]

As the standoff lasted through the summer, many old-guard Republicans began to grow nervous. Even those not known for their moderation began to appeal to the Tea Party faction for a sense of perspective. Under the headline "Ideals vs. Realities," the conservative pundit Thomas Sowell reminded his allies that they needed to keep in mind the course of the Founders in the American Revolution. Just as George Washington retreated from British troops to find a more strategic ground, Sowell argued, so the Tea Party might find a different place than the debt limit to begin the quest for smaller government. Or as Roger Pilon of the Cato Institute put it, "No war—and that's what we're in—was won in a day. It took 80 years for John Locke's ideas about liberty to find their way into the Declaration of Independence."[33]

But the Tea Party members remained firm. They *were* engaged in a revolution, and a revolution demanded, above all else, extreme commitment. They would continue to the bitter end. As former House majority leader Dick Armey had said at a Tea Party rally, they needed to follow the Founders and the Constitution without thought or equivocation—"This ain't no thinkin' thing," he said.[34]

Once the Treasury commenced extraordinary measures to put off default, more business-minded Republicans became frantic. The *Wall Street Journal* published an editorial denouncing the self-destructive extremism of the Tea Party faction under the title "The GOP's Reality Test." The editorial board was now convinced that the Republican Party had been taken over by a bunch of lunatics who were unhinged from the actualities of economics and governance. John McCain, having turned against his early support for the new conservatives, read from the *Wall Street Journal* editorial on the floor of the Senate in an attempt to hold back his more rabid fellow Republicans. Pressure became intense.[35]

Finally, the dam broke. Congressional leaders struck a last-minute deal to raise the debt ceiling, but only with the caveat that a special commission be set up to arrive at a budget agreement. If they failed to come to agreement, the bill provided for automatic, across-the-board spending cuts equally distributed between the domestic and the military budgets.[36]

It appeared to be a victory for the Republicans. Yet Tea Party representatives still declined to endorse the deal, which passed the House with mostly Democratic and some non–Tea Party Republican support.[37]

The future was now clear. The Tea Party movement was determined to follow their vision, even if it was self-stultifying. They professed to want to shrink government to unleash the capitalist system and they argued that not raising the debt ceiling would be a first step. But a default would have plunged the nation's economy back into recession, which would have lowered tax receipts and massively increased the debt. And the default would have further raised the cost of borrowing, which would then further increase the debt. So not raising the debt ceiling as a first step in stopping the debt cycle would have, in fact, massively increased the deficit, added enormously to the debt, and thrown the nation's economy into chaos.

As the radicalism of the new freshman class became apparent, Sam Tanenhaus of the *New York Times* wondered if perhaps the Tea Party could learn from Jefferson, their idol. Jefferson was the originator of the antistatist tradition in American politics. He had invented many of the rhetorical postures that the Tea Party now adopted. But like the Tea Party, Jefferson had found his ideology and his posturing challenged by reality, as had many antistatist politicians who crusaded to shrink government. In fact, by the measurement of actually accomplishing their goals in office, Tanenhaus wrote, "Jefferson and his heirs have been abject failures." But by learning once in office and by adjusting to the realities before him, Tanenhaus believed, Jefferson succeeded in governance.[38]

Could the Tea Party do the same? The answer was no. Unlike Jefferson, who proved to be supple in adjusting his ideology to reality, the Tea Party faction was determined to remain consistent to the bitter end. Their failure was not merely one of political thought, but grew instead out of an intellectual and rhetorical style that substituted paranoid sloganeering for actual policy analysis. Tea Partiers assumed, as Reagan, Goldwater, and others before them had done, going all the way back to Jefferson, that principles and values naturally cohered without trade-offs. Those principles had been handed down from the Founders, were betrayed at some point in the past, and now needed to be reapplied or else the people would find themselves under a federal despot. Given those stakes, the niceties of economics, the actual numbers by which decisions are made, and the policy considerations that guide choices and trade-offs were all beside the point. Total resistance was the only option.

It would be a long next few years.

SECESSION IS AN AMERICAN PRINCIPLE

"Is the Tea Party Over?" the columnist Bill Keller asked hopefully at the start of the 2012 election season. After the near miss with the default, Keller was not alone in wishing for a reprieve. But it was not to be.[39]

Because of Republican gerrymandering after the 2010 election, the party leadership could not abandon the Tea Party radicals. Since many conservatives were in safe seats, the only credible challenge that they could face would be from the right. To ignore the Tea Party faction or to sideline their political interests would only cause a challenge to the seat. "You have to kowtow to the Tea Party," a spokesman for Richard G. Lugar of Indiana said, summarizing the view of many Republican politicians. And because of the Tea Party's unbending radicalism, the Republican Party was, in effect, being driven by its most extreme faction.[40]

The resulting environment was not hospitable to moderate Republicans, especially coming up on a presidential election cycle. After seeing the radicalism of the moment, many viable Republican governors decided to sit out the 2012 race. Navigating the way through a Republican primary required too many bows to Tea Party orthodoxy and an almost willful detachment from basic budgetary math. As Jacob Weisberg observed, the new Republican orthodoxy expected all candidates "to hold the incoherent view that the budget should be balanced immediately, taxes cut dramatically, and the major categories of spending (the military, Social Security, Medicare) left largely intact." "There is no way to make these numbers add up," Weisberg concluded, a fact that had been pointed out numerous times by nonpartisan sources. But the Tea Party required the incoherent litmus test nevertheless, which had the effect of winnowing the field.[41]

As more responsible Republican governors bowed out of the race, the resulting crowd of candidates was filled with minor and often eccentric figures who hewed to Tea Party orthodoxy. The primary season itself unfolded with an unseemly chaos. Each Tea Party–supported candidate—Michele Bachmann, Newt Gingrich, Herman Cain, Rick Perry, Rick Santorum—took a turn in the lead before making a gaff, losing a crucial primary, or exposing his or her basic ignorance of public affairs. At that point, a new candidate would begin to rise to the top.

Yet the chaos of the race masked the real dynamic. The contest was not really between Bachmann, Gingrich, Cain, or Santorum. As the Jacobin quality of the Tea Party movement came into focus, the Republican primary season became a process to determine which wing of the party would emerge triumphant, the Republican establishment or the fanatical wing of the Tea Partiers. The real race, in other words, was between Mitt Romney, a moderate former governor of Massachusetts, and a composite figure that Bill Keller called "Not Mitt Romney." In singularly stark form, here was the contest between the Republican establishment and its fanatical Jacobins.[42]

The early results were confusing. To appease criticism of his past moderation as governor of Massachusetts, Romney spent the entire primary season tacking steadily to the right rather than maintaining his place as a business-friendly Republican moderate. A key part of that movement to the right was Romney's determined appropriation of the Tea Party language and story — making the now-ritualized gestures to the Founders and promising a restoration of founding values. At a debate in South Carolina in early September, Romney even went so far as to deny that the Tea Party and the Republican establishment were at odds. "The Tea Party has at its center core a belief that government is too big. Sound familiar?" he asked. "That's what we've been saying for years and years as a Republican Party," that the nation's leaders needed "to rein back government to be what it was considered by the founders."[43]

But Tea Partiers remained cool to Romney, even after it became apparent that he was to be the nominee. To energize the base, Romney decided to add some Tea Party flair to the ticket, choosing as his running mate Paul Ryan, a Tea Party darling and architect of the 2012 Republican budget that, among other things, promised to convert Medicare into a voucher system and to cut taxes (again) on the wealthy. Ryan had strengthened his already robust Tea Party credibility when he rehearsed the standard-issue Tea Party rhetoric during his 2011 Republican response to Obama's State of the Union address. Warning that the nation was "reaching a tipping point," Ryan called the nation back to its anchor "in the wisdom of the founders; in the spirit of the Declaration of Independence; and in the words of the American Constitution."[44]

Ryan seemed the perfect choice. But it turned out that the Tea Party and the American electorate had begun to diverge. Although Ryan's place on the ticket energized Tea Party conservatives, in a time of economic stagnation the Tea Party rhetoric did not sell with the wider public. The Romney-Ryan ticket was stuck in the mud, unable to pull ahead in what many Republicans had anticipated would be an easy contest. After the late-summer conventions, polling suggested a close race. But some pollsters, most notably Nate Silver of the *New York Times,* were predicting Obama's reelection.[45]

Still, many conservatives went into election night expecting to win. "I just finished writing a victory speech," Romney told reporters on his campaign plane. And a concession speech? "I've only written one speech at this point," Romney said.[46]

Yet as the election returns came in, it became apparent how out of touch Republicans had become. Obama won in decisive fashion, 332 electoral votes to Romney's 206. Even more disturbing—at least for Republicans—was the demographic composition of those who voted from Romney versus those who voted for Obama. Romney lost nearly every important demographic with one exception: 88 percent of Romney voters were white. In a nation that was turning increasingly brown, those numbers suggested crisis.[47]

Republicans were utterly disillusioned. What could be done to save the nation? Most conservative leaders were muted in their response, at least initially. But within days of Obama's reelection, a new petition appeared on the White House website advocating secession as one possible path forward. When asked about the petition, the Tea Party favorite Ron Paul affirmed, "Secession is an American principle." Others went in similar directions. Some Republican-controlled states began to entertain state-level nullification of the Affordable Care Act and other acts of state-level resistance to Obama's agenda. In the aftermath of defeat, the fringe began to emerge again.[48]

Watching the agony unfold, Sam Tanenhaus, one of the keenest of political observers, came to a disturbing conclusion: the Tea Party–led GOP was headed to the most extreme Jeffersonian position, that of John C. Calhoun prior to the Civil War. According to Tanenhaus, Calhoun's position had been built into the conservative movement from the beginning. At William F. Buckley's *National Review*, for example, Calhoun was "the Ur-theorist of a burgeoning but outnumbered conservative movement, 'the principal philosopher of the losing side.'" Through the fervent embrace of such early conservatives, Calhoun's views on federal power and the Tenth Amendment became central in the emergence of the newly conservative politics.[49]

But problems had begun to set in by the 1990s and only intensified during the Bush administration. Although Bush was reelected, it had become obvious that the Jeffersonian-Calhounian rhetoric ceased to mobilize the electorate in the same way as the nation became less white and as conservative policy goals failed to pan out. By 2009, the conservative movement hit crisis. "In retreat," Tanenhaus argued, "the nullifying spirit has been revived as a form of governance—or, more accurately, anti-governance." Led by the Tea Party, Republicans stumbled into a series of unwinnable fights over the budget, the debt ceiling, and Obamacare, each justified, according to Tanenhaus, "not as a practical attempt to find a better answer, but as a 'Constitutional' demand for restoration of the nation to its hallowed prior self."[50]

But now that approach had come to its logical endpoint after the 2012 election. The Jeffersonian argument about maintaining founding principles had degenerated into a Calhounian vision of state-sponsored nullification and retrenchment. "Denial has always been the basis of a nullifying politics," Tanenhaus believed, but after the election it was obvious that "modernity could not be nullified."[51]

How would Republicans now respond? They could either abandon their form of antigovernance—with its genuflections toward the Founders, its simplistic solutions to complex problems, and its general tendency toward obstruction. Or the party would remain, Tanenhaus predicted, "the party of white people."[52]

FANTASY POLITICS

"O-ba-ma, O-ba-ma, O-ba-ma," the crowd began chanting at Obama's second inaugural, just after he walked to the podium. Though not so deep as his first inauguration four years earlier, the audience's enthusiasm was clearly a mark of the euphoria that Democrats felt after the election. It was a feeling that Obama shared. Strolling to the podium with a big smile on his face, he was flanked by members of Congress, people on all sides, and huge American flags covering the portico of the Capitol. Obama clearly enjoyed the scene that many politicians could only dream of. After two years of obstruction and manufactured crisis, he had soundly triumphed over his opponents. His vision had been validated. He had now, he believed, a mandate for government action.[53]

But that would happen only if the Tea Party was tamed. Republicans still controlled the House, and the Tea Party still controlled the Republicans. So, in the flush of victory, Obama decided to lay out his vision in terms that the Tea Party might understand.

He went straight for the Constitution and the Founding Fathers.

To those many Tea Partiers who viewed his election as the usurpation of constitutional government, he replied that his own election was an indication of the Constitution's staying power. "Each time we gather to inaugurate a president," he told the crowd at the beginning of his address, "we bear witness to the enduring strength of our Constitution."[54]

But of course he did not quite see the Constitution in the same way the Tea Party did, a fact that he frankly acknowledged. Whereas the Tea Party used the Founders and the Constitution as instruments of obstruction, Obama believed that fidelity to American ideals demanded not obstruction but action. Whereas the Tea Party urged complete purity and allegiance to principle in all matters, Obama pointed out that even timeless principle required different application depending on time and context. Whereas the Tea Party assumed that constitutional literalism would make governing a simple and straightforward process, Obama suggested that even the most basic questions of governance involved disagreement and compromise. In response to the Tea Party currents that had threatened to sink him, Obama returned again and again to the idea that life is a journey in which principles guide but do not dictate action. Even the idea that "all men are created equal," he argued, had not been "self-executing." "While freedom is a gift from God," he said, "it must be secured by His people here on Earth."[55]

Taking that reality to heart, Obama believed, would require a totally different form of politics, one that prized action over obstruction and conciliation over confrontation. The historical fundamentalism at the heart of Tea Party politics would have to go. "We cannot mistake absolutism for principle," Obama warned, "or substitute spectacle for politics, or treat name-calling as reasoned debate. We must act, knowing that our work will be imperfect. We must act, knowing that today's victories will only be partial and that it will be up to those who stand here in four years and 40 years and 400 years to advance the timeless spirit once conferred to us in a spare Philadelphia hall."[56]

But in this call to action, Obama was bound to be disappointed. In the new Republican Party, attracted to the most extreme form of Jeffersonian rhetoric, nothing short of full-scale revolt would satisfy the base. So rather than supporting government action, as Obama had hoped, the Tea Party–led House decided upon full-scale obstruction as a way to flesh out their constitutional vision.

The pattern was set almost immediately after the inaugural, when Congress took up the issue of gun control. After a series of mass killings in 2012—at a day spa in Atlanta; at a nursing school in Oakland; at a coffee shop in Seattle; at a movie theater in Aurora, Colorado; at a Sikh temple in Wisconsin; at an office complex in Minneapolis; and at Sandy Hook Elementary School in Newtown, Connecticut, which resulted in the deaths of six adults and twenty children, many of whom were first-graders—gun control moved off the back burner onto the front of political debate. Obama vowed action after the bloody year of violence.[57]

But gun control was a tricky issue. Democrats feared reprisals from the National Rifle Association (NRA) and other gun groups that promised to defend "the firearms tradition intended by America's Founding Fathers." And given the paranoid fantasies about armed resistance during the Obama presidency, he would have to be particularly careful.[58]

Obama's proposals were, accordingly, quite modest. He declined to push for any of the broader measures that gun control activists had long proposed—a national gun registry, limitation on secondary sales of guns, expanded background checks, and a federal waiting period in order to buy a gun—in favor of a ban on assault weapons that was filled with loopholes and a limitation on the possible size of magazines. Obama's allies also sought to reassure gun owners. Democratic senator Patrick J. Leahy of Vermont opened the gun control hearings with a promise that the Second Amendment was "secure" and would remain "protected." "No one," he said, "can or will take those rights or our guns away."[59]

Opponents were not so sure. The NRA pledged retribution for any changes to existing gun laws. And the Tea Party in particular remained fiercely opposed to Obama's proposals. They were led in their opposition by the vocal freshman senator from Texas Ted Cruz. Rather than lying low during the debate, as many Republicans opted to do out of concern over the politics of the issue, Cruz decided to use the hearings to mount a full-throated defense of what he portentously called "our foundational document . . . the Constitution."[60]

The resulting exchange during the committee meetings suggested just how difficult it would be for Congress to pass any kind of law—whether on gun control or anything else. Cruz put forward an absolutist vision of the Constitution that was far more wooden than even Jefferson and Madison in their most strictly constructionist mode. As Cruz patiently explained to the committee, the Constitution was a carefully wrought document, a purposeful expression of the Founders' will that could be understood through the careful examination of constitutional language. Nowhere was this truer than in the Bill of Rights, a part of the Constitution to which, Cruz claimed, the Founders had devoted considerable care. But rather than analyzing constitutional language and respecting the Constitution as a whole, Cruz argued, Democrats were hypocritically picking the parts of the Bill of

Rights they liked, while ignoring the parts that they did not. As proof, he asked the sponsor of the gun bill, Senator Dianne Feinstein, a Democrat from California, whether she would think it proper to regulate the First and Fourth Amendments, which protected the right of free speech and free assembly and the freedom from unreasonable search and seizure, in the same way that she proposed to regulate firearms.[61]

"I'm not a sixth grader, Senator," Feinstein responded, with anger. "I've been on this committee for 20 years. I was a mayor for nine years. I walked in, I saw people shot. I've looked at bodies that have been shot with these weapons. I've seen the bullets that implode. In Sandy Hook, youngsters were dismembered."[62]

But then she stopped short. She was not really addressing Cruz's question. Her response emphasized the practical realities of gun violence that the bill sought to address. She assumed that the Constitution was expansive enough that government could address social problems. Cruz, by contrast, had ruminated on abstract rights in a way that appealed to the conservative base and the NRA. To get at the conservative concerns, Feinstein changed tack and pointed out that her bill excluded more than two thousand weapons from the proposed regulations. She demanded to know what else "the people" required. "Do they need a bazooka?" she wondered.[63]

Cruz responded with a faux earnestness that conveyed a fairly obvious contempt. "I would ask another question of the senior senator from California," he said evenly. "I would note that she chose not to answer the question that I asked"—about whether she would limit the right of assembly or freedom from unreasonable search and seizure in ways similar to gun ownership.

"The answer is obvious," Feinstein broke in. "No."[64]

But her answer did not sit well with other Democrats on the panel because it failed to challenge Cruz's constitutional absolutism. Patrick Leahy and Dick Durbin of Illinois both tried to point out the absurdity of Cruz's position. Of course Democrats supported limitations on both First and Fourth Amendment rights, Leahy and Durbin argued, just as all reasonable people would do.

"Is child pornography protected by the First Amendment?" Durbin asked Cruz, trying to suggest the absolutist fallacy of Cruz's argument. But before Cruz could respond, Feinstein added, "It's obvious that there are different tests on different amendments."

"And is it the view of the senior senator from California," Cruz asked, ignoring Durbin's point about child pornography, "that Congress should be in the business of specifying particular books or for that matter, with respect to the Fourth Amendment, particular individuals who are not covered by the Bill of Rights?"

"Sir," Feinstein answered, "Congress is in the business of making law."

Piling on, Durbin added, "The Senator [Cruz] knows, having attended law school . . . none of these rights are absolute. None of them."[65]

But Cruz and the Tea Party did in fact believe that the right of gun ownership was absolute. It was the defense of last resort against governmental tyranny. It provided a measure of protection against governmental overreach. The fact that Congress was now considering regulations suggested, yet again, the absolute degeneration of American political rights and a loss of the political vision that was received from the Founders. Even though twenty children were mowed down in their elementary school classroom by a guy carrying a military-style assault rifle, the Tea Party Republicans vowed to prevent any change to gun laws.

By the end of the hearings, the prospects for a bill looked grim. The gun lobby began mounting an intense pressure campaign, so much so that Senate majority leader Harry Reid further stripped down the bill in the hopes of passing something, anything. But when moderate Democrats from rural states grew concerned about reelection, the legislation fell five votes short of the sixty needed to stop Senate debate. An angry Obama appeared in a press conference in the Rose Garden flanked by Gabrielle Giffords, who limped from the Oval Office to stand by Obama's side, and by families from the Newtown shooting. "All in all, this was a pretty shameful day for Washington," Obama said. But he put the blame squarely on Republicans: "Ninety percent of Democrats in the Senate voted for that idea, but it's not going to happen because 90 percent of Republicans just voted against it." It appeared that the call to action in his inaugural address would go unheeded.[66]

There was little time to ponder what to do, though, for no sooner had the gun control measure died than the latest budget crisis again came to a head. Obama had put forward a budget that congressional Republicans promptly rejected, but Congress was unable to come up with one of its own. With time running out and a shutdown looming, Democrats and the more pliable Republicans began to urge meetings between the House and Senate to draft a compromise.

Yet as in the gun control battle, Cruz and his Tea Party allies dug in, vowing no compromise or even negotiation unless Democrats made specific concessions at the outset. More moderate Republicans became alarmed at the levels of obstruction that the Tea Party was willing to support. In the Senate, John McCain took the lead in calling down Cruz and his allies, labeling them "wacko birds" and telling Cruz, "We're here to vote, not here to block things. We're here to articulate our positions on the issues and do what we can for the good of the country and let the process move forward."[67]

In response, Cruz had nothing but contempt. Republicans who

compromised in the name of governance, Cruz told a Tea Party summit, were nothing but "a bunch of squishes" who refused to follow their own principles. Only strict adherence to principle would bring the nation to the Founders' constitutional vision.[68]

Cruz's response was telling. The nearly fifty years of rhetoric about the Founders had created a movement of such fanaticism that Republican leadership was now powerless to stop it. As the philosopher Gary Gutting pointed out in the *New York Times,* to the Tea Party "disruption is necessary because the current government, like that of our 18th-century British rulers, is violating our fundamental rights and so has lost legitimacy."[69]

The result was total paralysis. Unable to come to any kind of conclusion, congressional leaders passed a continuing resolution that kept spending levels constant through the summer as a way to buy some time. By the middle of May, the government hit the debt ceiling and the Treasury began extraordinary measures—moving money around so as not to have to borrow money but in order to put off default. Political commentators spent the summer discussing Congress's spectacular inability to pass anything, a charge that Speaker Boehner rejected. He told CBS's *Face the Nation* that Congress ought to be judged not "on how many new laws we create" but on "how many laws . . . we repeal."[70]

The politics of nullification had reached its logical conclusion.

By September, it became apparent that the long-awaited budget apocalypse was nigh. The Tea Party branch was driving the debate, and the Republican leadership had long since lost control. Ross Douthat, a moderate Republican columnist, began wringing his hands over the "reckless, pointless budget brinkmanship, which creates a perpetual cycle of outrage and disillusionment among conservatives and leaves Washington lurching from one manufactured crisis to the next."[71]

But there was nothing to be done. The Tea Party remained

firm. They wanted a showdown, and they were bound and determined to get one. Unable to corral his caucus, Boehner threw up his hands and let them have their way. By refusing to bring a Democratic spending bill to a vote—it would have certainly passed the chamber—he guaranteed that the government would run out of funding. On October 1 the federal government went into partial shutdown, with the government default looming just over two weeks later.[72]

Democrats rushed to point out the extremism of the Tea Party position. "They don't believe in government," minority leader Nancy Pelosi told reporters. "They're anti-government ideologues. It's the Tea Party shutdown of government."[73]

Moderate Republicans were apoplectic, pointing out that the shutdown was exactly what they had long feared. At the *New York Times,* Ross Douthat agonized over the self-destruction that the Tea Party was wreaking. "The House Intransigents" were engaged in "fantasy politics." They were revolting against a long-term pattern "in which first Reagan and then Gingrich and now the Tea Party wave have all failed to deliver on the promise of an actual right-wing *answer* to the big left-wing victories of the 1930s and 1960s—and now, with Obamacare, of Obama's first two years as well." But rather than stepping back, collecting themselves, and reconsidering their political vision, the Tea Party Republicans were engaged instead in a "foolish romanticism" that sought to return the nation back to an earlier time.[74]

As the shutdown dragged on, many Americans turned away in disgust. Polls had long shown a fairly dim opinion of the Tea Party faction. But by the shutdown's second week, new polls delivered devastating news for Republicans. Seventy percent of Americans said they thought Republicans were putting politics ahead of the country. By 53 percent to 31 percent, the public blamed Republicans more than Democrats for the shutdown.

And only 24 percent of the public had a favorable view of Republicans as a whole.[75]

Finally, the Republican leadership moved to reassert control. Rather than continuing the losing fight, they capitulated across the board. Their new bill included a clean continuing resolution that extended the budget deadline until mid-January. And it raised the debt ceiling through early February. That allowed four months to come to some kind of agreement. The bill passed the House 285 to 144.[76]

But the most telling thing about the bill was the lack of Republican support. Although the leadership realized that the politics of obstruction had turned into a total debacle, rank-and-file Republicans were not so sure. All of the 144 who voted no were Republicans. In total, only 87 Republicans voted to reopen the government.[77]

Tea Party politics had now come to its apotheosis. Congress was unable to fulfill its most basic responsibility of funding the government. Deep divides characterized all sides. Gridlock, obstruction, and dysfunction had reached astounding levels.

Given those ongoing realities, a cynical gloom pervaded the Washington press corps even after the crisis ended. Though a chastened Republican caucus acceded to a budget deal a few months later, Obama still had three more years in office. After five years of protest over founding principles—led by a Republican Party faction that was determined to roll back the twentieth and twenty-first centuries—it was hard to imagine a change in the fundamental dynamic.

"Mr. President," a journalist asked Obama when he announced the deal, "isn't this going to happen all over again in a few months?"

"No," Obama said flatly.

The reporters immediately broke out laughing.[78]

AFTERWORD

The historian's task," Tony Judt once said, "is to tell what is almost always an uncomfortable story and [to] explain why the discomfort is part of the truth we need to live well and live properly." That task is especially urgent in the contemporary United States. American culture and politics are awash in claims about the past. Politicians offer fables to justify their policies, to condemn their opponents, to mobilize their base, and to gain or to keep political power.[1]

But nearly all of these fables proceed from an incorrect historical assumption. The Founders were eighteenth-century revolutionaries who became politicians. Their political culture vanished even before their death. Within that culture they had a number of disagreements that permanently divided them. When politicians invoke the Founders, they call upon a querulous and divided group that did not and cannot offer the guidance that we might wish.

Because the Founders do not offer a stable reference to make sense of the present, their presence in American political debate has long been problematic. They have become icons of divergent visions of national life, repositories for political ideals, favorable institutional arrangements, and visions of citizenship that vary depending on who is invoking them. Jefferson spoke of the Founders as supporters of an agrarian ideal of liberty. John C. Calhoun made them into promoters of states' rights. Jackson used them to push political democracy. Others have gone in different directions, using the Founders for national economic development (Clay and Adams), slavery's restriction (Lincoln), popular sovereignty (Douglas), business rights (the American Liberty League), economic equality (Roosevelt), black civil rights (King), tax cuts and antigovernment retrenchment (Reagan), political moderation (Obama), and the revolutionary power of the people (the Tea Party).

That the various invocations contradict one another and change over time in no way inhibits the phenomenon. If, as the late historian Richard Hofstadter once said, it has been "our fate as a nation not to have ideologies but to be one," much the same can be said of the Founders.[2]

But this exploitation of the Founders tends to debase the political process. It reinforces ideological warfare. It disguises lack of thought behind a veil of propaganda. It dumbs down political debate by ignoring policy trade-offs and neglecting policy evaluation.

It also raises an obvious question. Would it not be better to have a more forthright political debate, one that avoided the historical inaccuracy and the blatant political propaganda that often come with an invocation of the Founders? Walter Lippmann once called on American politicians "to substitute purpose for tradition" so that they could deal with American life deliberately, "to devise its social organization, alter its tools, formulate its method, educate and control it." Now, a hundred years later, his call still seems relevant.[3]

And yet, in another sense, the process is already happening whenever the Founders are invoked. Politicians create the Founders in their own image. They make them into symbols of the kind of social and political life that various politicians desire. Though these positions are submerged beneath the veneer of traditional fidelity, the reverence does not change the fundamental fact: most citations of the Founders have nothing to do with the eighteenth century and everything to do with the present and the future. Given that reality, we might as well dispense with the talk of the Founders in order to make a straightforward case for whatever policy is under discussion. Doing so would not solve all of the problems. But it would be a first step to a better political debate.

ACKNOWLEDGMENTS

A number of people and institutions have helped me complete this book. I am grateful to the National Endowment for the Humanities, the provost's office at Georgia State University (GSU), and the History Department at GSU for financial support. Lucas Clawson at the Hagley Museum and Library and Christine A. Lutz at Princeton University's Mudd Library helped me greatly with some long-distance archival work. Steve Green, Harry Hirsch, David Hollinger, John Kasson, and Matt Sutton all aided me by reading grant proposals and writing letters of recommendation. The project got a big boost at the beginning when I gave a brown bag presentation to the GSU History Department. A number of colleagues, Michelle Brattain in particular, refocused my questions and changed my research. Marni Davis, Chris Nichols, Daniel Rodgers, Joy Rohde, Kevin Schultz, Alex Star, Isaac Weiner, and Larry Youngs helped me by reading various chapters and by talking me through various issues. Rob Baker, Andrew Hartman, Mike O'Connor, and Ben Wise were especially crucial to me.

No one was more helpful than my agent, Susan Rabiner. She got involved at an early stage, showed me how to write for a public audience, and then made me rewrite again and again until I got it right. I am grateful for her persistence and her patience. My editor, Alice Mayhew, lived up to her reputation as the best in the business. She showed an especially deft touch in helping me put a frame around the book. My copyeditor, Tom Pitoniak, saved me from several errors and infelicities.

Finally, I am grateful to my wife, Connie Moon Sehat, for everything.

NOTES

CHAPTER ONE: THE QUEST FOR UNANIMITY

1   On the ratification debate, see Pauline Maier, *Ratification: The People Debate the Constitution, 1787–1788* (New York: Simon & Schuster, 2010). The chapter title comes from Richard Hofstadter, *The Idea of a Party System: The Rise of Legitimate Opposition in the United States, 1780–1840* (Berkeley: University of California Press, 1969), 170.

2   James D. Richardson, ed., *A Compilation of the Messages and Papers of the Presidents, 1789–1897* (Washington, D.C.: U.S. Government Printing Office, 1897), 1:44.

3   Alexander Hamilton, James Madison, and John Jay, *The Federalist* (Cambridge, Mass.: Belknap Press of Harvard University Press, 2009), 137 (second through fourth quotations), 142 (first quotation). See also Sheldon S. Wolin, *The Presence of the Past: Essays on the State and the Constitution* (Baltimore: Johns Hopkins University Press, 1989), 11–13.

4   Thomas Jefferson to Madison, June 20, 1787, in Thomas

Jefferson, *The Papers of Thomas Jefferson*, ed. Julian P. Boyd (Princeton, N.J.: Princeton University Press, 1950–), 11:480 (first quotation); Jefferson to Madison, December 20, 1787, in James Madison, *The Papers of James Madison*, ed. William Thomas Hutchinson and William M. E. Rachal (Chicago: University of Chicago Press, 1962–91), 10:338 (second quotation).

5 George Washington to the Marquis de Lafayette, April 28[–May 1], 1788, in George Washington, *The Papers of George Washington: Confederation Series*, ed. W. W. Abbot and Dorothy Twohig (Charlottesville: University Press of Virginia, 1992–), 6:243.

6 Richardson, *Messages and Papers of the Presidents*, 1:44.

7 "Report Relative to a Provision for the Support of Public Credit," January 9, 1790, in Alexander Hamilton, *The Papers of Alexander Hamilton*, ed. Harold C. Syrett and Jacob E. Cooke (New York: Columbia University Press, 1961–87), 6:51–181; "First Report on the Further Provision Necessary for Establishing Public Credit," December 13, 1790, and "Second Report on the Further Provision Necessary for Establishing Public Credit (Report on a National Bank)," December 13, 1790, in ibid., 7:210–36, 236–342.

8 Mike O'Connor, *A Commercial Republic: America's Enduring Debate over Democratic Capitalism* (Lawrence: University Press of Kansas, 2014), 11–47.

9 Stanley Elkins and Eric McKitrick, *The Age of Federalism* (New York: Oxford University Press, 1993), 223–32.

10 Jefferson to the Citizens of Albemarle, February 12, 1790, in Jefferson, *Papers*, 16:179 (first quotation); Jefferson, "Opinion on the Constitutionality of the Bill for Establishing a National Bank," February 15, 1791, in ibid., 19:275–82 (second and third quotations on p. 276).

11   Hamilton, "Opinion on the Constitutionality of an Act to Establish a Bank," February 23, 1791, in Hamilton, *Papers*, 8:63–134 (quotations on p. 97).

12   U.S. Constitution, Article I, Sec. 8 (first and second quotations); Hamilton, "Opinion on the Constitutionality of an Act to Establish a Bank," in ibid., 8:102–3 (third quotation).

13   Thomas Jefferson to Edmund Pendleton, August 26, 1776, in Jefferson, *Papers*, 1:503 (first quotation); Hamilton, Madison, and Jay, *The Federalist*, 54 (third quotation), 58 (second quotation). On this rationale for the Constitution's structure, see Gordon S. Wood, *The Creation of the American Republic, 1776–1787* (Chapel Hill: University of North Carolina Press, 1969), 475–83.

14   Elkins and McKitrick, *The Age of Federalism*, 240–44.

15   Jefferson to Madison, May 9, 1791, in Jefferson, *Papers*, 20:293 (first quotation); Jefferson to Jonathan B. Smith, April 26, 1791, in ibid., 20:290 (second quotation).

16   Jefferson to Washington, May 8, 1791, in Jefferson, *Papers*, 20:291.

17   Jefferson to Benjamin Vaughn, May 11, 1791, in ibid., 20:391.

18   Hamilton, "Report on the Subject of Manufactures," December 5, 1791, in Hamilton, *Papers*, 10:1–340; Elkins and McKitrick, *The Age of Federalism*, 258–63.

19   Michael Lienesch, "Thomas Jefferson and the American Democratic Experience: The Origins of the Partisan Press, Popular Political Parties, and Public Opinion," in *Jeffersonian Legacies*, ed. Peter S. Onuf (Charlottesville: University Press of Virginia, 1993), 318–24; O'Connor, *A Commercial Republic*, 36–43.

20   Hamilton, "An American No. 1," August 4, 1792, in Hamilton, *Papers*, 12:157 (first quotation), 159 (second through fourth quotations), 159–60 (fifth quotation), 161 (sixth quotation).

21   Jefferson to Madison, June 29, 1792, in Madison, *Papers*, 14:333 (quotation); Jefferson to Washington, May 23, 1792, in George Washington, *The Papers of George Washington: Presidential Series*, ed. Dorothy Twohig and W. W. Abbot (Charlottesville: University Press of Virginia, 1987–), 10:408–14. See also Hamilton's response, Hamilton to Washington, August 18, 1792, in Hamilton, *Papers*, 12:228–58.

22   "Madison's Conversations with Washington," May 5–25, 1792; Hamilton to Washington, July 30–August 3, 1792; Edmund Randolph to Washington, August 5, 1792, in Washington, *Papers: Presidential Series*, 10:349–54, 594–96, 628–32.

23   Washington to Jefferson, August 23, 1792, in Washington, *Papers: Presidential Series*, 11:30 (first quotation); Washington to Hamilton, August 26, 1792, in Hamilton, *Papers*, 12:276 (second and third quotations). See also Washington to Randolph, August 26, 1792, in Washington, *Papers: Presidential Series*, 11:45–46.

24   Hamilton to Washington, September 9, 1792, in Hamilton, *Papers*, 12:349 (quotation); Hamilton, "Amicus," September 11, 1792, in ibid., 12:354–57.

25   Jefferson to Washington, September 9, 1792, in Washington, *Papers: Presidential Series*, 11:98 (first two quotations), 104 (third quotation).

26   Sean Wilentz, *The Rise of American Democracy: Jefferson to Lincoln* (New York: Norton, 2005), 40–42, 53–62.

27   On the difference between the Democratic-Republican societies and the nascent Republican Party, see ibid., 55.

28   Madison to Jefferson, August 27, 1793, in Madison, *Papers*, 15:75.

29   Madison to Jefferson, September 2, 1793, in ibid., 15:93.

30   Richardson, *Messages and Papers of the Presidents*, 1:116 (first two quotations), 117 (third quotation).

31   Wilentz, *The Rise of American Democracy*, 62–63.

32   Richardson, *Messages and Papers of the Presidents*, 1:121 (first quotation), 134 (second quotation); Washington to Henry Lee, August 26, 1794, in George Washington, *The Writings of George Washington*, ed. John C. Fitzpatrick (Washington, D.C.: U.S. Government Printing Office, 1931), 33:475 (third quotation), 475–76 (fourth quotation). See also Washington to Burgess Bell, September 25, 1794; and Washington to Daniel Morgan, October 8, 1794, in ibid., 33:505–7, 522–24.

33   Elkins and McKitrick, *The Age of Federalism*, 461–74.

34   Richardson, *Messages and Papers of the Presidents*, 1:158 (second quotation), 160 (first quotation).

35   Madison to Monroe, December 4, 1794, in Madison, *Papers*, 15:406.

36   Jefferson to Madison, December 28, 1794, in Jefferson, *Papers*, 28:228.

37   Sean Wilentz originally made this point about Washington's partisanship in Sean Wilentz, "The Mirage: The Long and Tragical History of Post-Partisanship, from Washington to Obama," *New Republic*, November 17, 2011, 26.

38   Richardson, *Messages and Papers of the Presidents*, 1:207 (first and second quotations), 209 (third quotation). On Hamilton's collaboration with Washington, see Hamilton to Washington, July 30, 1796; and Hamilton to Washington, August 10, 1796, in Hamilton, *Papers*, 20:264–88, 293–303.

39   Richardson, *Messages and Papers of the Presidents*, 1:209–10 (second quotation), 210 (first quotation), 211 (third and fourth quotations). On the partisan nature of the address in spite of its plea to avoid partisanship, see Hofstadter, *The Idea of a Party System*, 96–102.

40   Hamilton to Rufus King, February 15, 1797, in Hamilton, *Papers*, 20:515 (first quotation), 516 (second and third quotations).

41 Jefferson to Adams, December 28, 1796, in Jefferson, *Papers*, 29:235.

42 Jefferson to Madison, January 1, 1797, ibid., 29:248.

43 Adams to Jonathan Jackson, October 2, 1780, in John Adams, *The Works of John Adams*, ed. Charles Francis Adams (Boston: Little, Brown, 1850–56), 9:511 (first quotation); Richardson, *Messages and Papers of the Presidents*, 1:220 (second and third quotations), 221 (fourth quotation).

44 Wilentz, *The Rise of American Democracy*, 84.

45 Hofstadter, *The Idea of a Party System*, 105–11.

46 Hamilton to Rufus King, June 6, 1798, in Hamilton, *Papers*, 21:490.

47 Elkins and McKitrick, *The Age of Federalism*, 590–93.

48 Ibid., 719–26.

49 Jefferson to John Taylor, June 4, 1798, in Jefferson, *Papers*, 30:388 (first through third quotations), 389 (fourth and fifth quotations).

50 William Heth to Hamilton, January 18, 1799, in Hamilton, *Papers*, 22:423.

51 Hamilton to Theodore Sedgwick, February 2, 1799, in ibid., 22:452 (first quotation), 453 (second and third quotations).

52 Hamilton to Rufus King, January 5, 1800, in ibid., 24:168 (first and third quotations); Hamilton to Tobias Lear, January 2, 1800, in ibid., 24:155 (second quotation).

53 Richardson, *Messages and Papers of the Presidents*, 1:310.

54 Ibid., 312.

55 Jefferson to John Dickinson, March 6, 1801, in Jefferson, *Papers*, 33:196 (first quotation); Jefferson to James Monroe, March 7, 1801, in ibid., 33:208 (second and seventh quotations); Jefferson to Levi Lincoln, July 11, 1801, in ibid., 34:546 (third quotation); Jefferson to Joseph Priestley, March 21, 1801, in ibid., 33:393 (fourth and fifth quotations); Jefferson

to Horatio Gates, March 8, 1801, in ibid., 33:215 (sixth quotation); Jefferson to Levi Lincoln, October 25, 1802, in Thomas Jefferson, *The Works of Thomas Jefferson*, ed. Paul Leicester Ford (New York: G. P. Putnam's Sons, 1904–1905), 9:401 (eighth quotation); Jefferson to Walter Jones, March 31, 1801, Jefferson, *Papers*, 33:506 (ninth quotation).

56 Jefferson to Monroe, March 7, 1801, in Jefferson, *Papers*, 33:208.

57 Richardson, *Messages and Papers of the Presidents*, 1:318.

58 Jefferson to Pierre S. du Pont de Nemours, January 18, 1802, in Jefferson, *Papers*, 36:391.

59 Wilentz, *The Rise of American Democracy*, 108–11.

60 Richardson, *Messages and Papers of the Presidents*, 1:367, 397–98.

61 Wilentz, *The Rise of American Democracy*, 131–35; Hofstadter, *The Idea of a Party System*, 171–82.

62 Richardson, *Messages and Papers of the Presidents*, 1:443.

63 Jefferson to James Sullivan, June 19, 1807, in Jefferson, *Works*, 10:421.

64 Richardson, *Messages and Papers of the Presidents*, 1:567–68.

65 Ibid., 2:8 (first quotation), 10 (second quotation).

66 Jefferson to the Marquis de Lafayette, May 14, 1817, in Jefferson, *Works*, 12:62 (first and second quotations), 63 (third quotation).

CHAPTER TWO: SPECTERS OF FRACTURE

1 Sean Wilentz, *The Rise of American Democracy: Jefferson to Lincoln* (New York: Norton, 2005), 222–31.

2 Annals of Congress, 15th Congress, 2nd session, 1180 (first three quotations); 16th Congress, 1st session, 958 (fourth quotation).

3   Annals of Congress, 16th Congress, 1st session, 1005.

4   Thomas Jefferson, *Notes on the State of Virginia* (London: J. Stockdale, 1787), 270 (first quotation); Annals of Congress, 16th Congress, 1st session, 1377 (second and third quotations).

5   Annals of Congress, 16th Congress, 1st session, 269.

6   Annals of Congress, 15th Congress, 2nd session, 1436 (first two quotations), 1437 (third and fourth quotations). I have changed the quotations from the past tense of the reporter's voice to the present tense that Cobb would have used.

7   Henry Clay, "Resolution of Thanks to the Speaker," March 3, 1821, in Henry Clay, *The Papers of Henry Clay*, ed. James F. Hopkins (Lexington: University Press of Kentucky, 1959–), 3:57.

8   Annals of Congress, 18th Congress, 1st session, 1978.

9   Annals of Congress, 18th Congress, 1st session, 1962–2001 (quotation on p. 1978).

10 Annals of Congress, 18th Congress, 1st session, 1994–95.

11 On the presumption that Jackson supported improvements, see Calhoun to Joseph G. Swift, August 24, 1823, in John C. Calhoun, *The Papers of John C. Calhoun*, ed. Robert Lee Meriwether (Columbia: University of South Carolina Press for the South Caroliniana Society, 1959–2003), 8:243–44.

12 Harry L. Watson, *Liberty and Power: The Politics of Jacksonian America*, updated ed. (New York: Hill & Wang, 2006), 80–81.

13 Henry Clay to Francis Preston Blair, January 8, 1825, in Clay, *Papers*, 4:9 (first and third quotations), 10 (second quotation).

14 John Quincy Adams, *Memoirs of John Quincy Adams, Comprising Portions of His Diary from 1795 to 1848*, ed. Charles Francis Adams (Philadelphia: J. B. Lippincott, 1874–77), 6:465.

15   Andrew Jackson to John Coffee, January 6, 1825, in Andrew Jackson, *The Papers of Andrew Jackson*, ed. Sam B. Smith and Harriet Chappell Owsley (Knoxville: University of Tennessee Press, 1980–), 6:8.

16   Andrew Jackson to Samuel Swartwout, February 22, 1825, in ibid., 6:42 (second quotation); Jackson to William Berkeley Lewis, February 20, 1825, in ibid., 6:37 (third quotation).

17   Adams, *Memoirs*, 6:483 (first quotation), 506 (second and third quotations).

18   Ibid., 6:507.

19   James D. Richardson, ed., *A Compilation of the Messages and Papers of the Presidents, 1789–1897* (Washington, D.C.: U.S. Government Printing Office, 1897), 2:294 (third and fourth quotations), 295 (first and second quotations).

20   Clay, "Address to the People of the Congressional District," March 26, 1825, in Clay, *Papers*, 4:154 (second quotation), 163 (first quotation).

21   Adams, *Memoirs*, 6:527, 7:7 (quotations).

22   For an excellent explanation of Adams's position from the perspective of a political scientist, see Stephen Skowronek, *The Politics Presidents Make: Leadership from John Adams to Bill Clinton* (Cambridge, Mass.: Belknap Press of Harvard University Press, 1997), 110–27.

23   Richardson, *Messages and Papers of the Presidents*, 2:316.

24   Adams, *Memoirs*, 7:59.

25   Ibid., 7:60–61 (quotations on p. 61).

26   Ibid., 7:62–63 (quotations on p. 63).

27   John C. Calhoun to James Monroe, June 23, 1826, in Calhoun, *Papers*, 10:132–33 (first quotation), 134 (second quotation). Also see John C. Calhoun to Joseph G. Swift, December 11, 1825, in ibid., 10:56.

28   Adams, *Memoirs*, 7:98 (quotation), 105–6.

29 Jackson to John C. Calhoun, July 18, 1826, in Jackson, *Papers*, 6:187.

30 Jackson to William Pitt Martin and the Citizens of Fayetteville, Tenn., July 5, 1826, in ibid., 6:183.

31 Andrew Jackson to James K. Polk, May 3, 1826, in ibid., 6:167.

32 Jefferson to Benjamin Austin, January 9, 1816, in Thomas Jefferson, *The Works of Thomas Jefferson*, ed. Paul Leicester Ford (New York: G. P. Putnam's Sons, 1904–1905): 11:504. For more on the debate over Jefferson during the 1828 campaign, see Merrill D. Peterson, *The Jefferson Image in the American Mind* (Charlottesville, Va.: Thomas Jefferson Memorial Foundation, 1998), 21–29.

33 See editorial comments in Jackson, *Papers*, 6:340–41 (quotation on p. 341).

34 Ibid., 341.

35 Caleb Atwater to Andrew Jackson, September 4, 1827, in ibid., 6:390.

36 Calhoun to Littleton Waller Tazewell, July 1, 1827, in Calhoun, *Papers*, 10:293.

37 Jackson to James Hamilton Jr., June 29, 1828, in Jackson, *Papers*, 6:476.

38 Calhoun to Mahlon Dickerson, April 7, 1827, in Calhoun, *Papers*, 10:283; Calhoun to Littleton Waller Tazewell, August 25, 1827, in ibid., 10:300–302; Calhoun to Bartlett Young, July 16, 1828, in ibid., 10:401; Calhoun to William C. Preston, January 6, 1829, in ibid., 10:545 (quotation).

39 "South Carolina Exposition and Protest" in Calhoun, *Papers*, 10:442–539. See also Calhoun to William Campbell Preston, November 6, 1828, in ibid., 10:431–33; Calhoun to William Campbell Preston, November 21, 1828, in ibid., 10:433–34.

40 Richardson, *Messages and Papers of the Presidents*, 2:438.

41 Calhoun to Christopher Vandeventer, March 14, 1829, in Calhoun, *Papers*, 11:11.

42 Calhoun to John McLean, September 22, 1829, in ibid., 11:76.

43 Register of Debates, 21st Congress, 1st session, 31–35.

44 On the role of media in antebellum American politics, see Daniel Walker Howe, *What Hath God Wrought: The Transformation of America, 1815–1848* (Oxford: Oxford University Press, 2007), 5–7, 493–97.

45 Register of Debates, 21st Congress, 1st session, 38.

46 Register of Debates, 21st Congress, 1st session, 48 (first quotation), 50 (second and third quotations). On the revelation that Jefferson authored the Kentucky Resolutions, see Peterson, *The Jefferson Image*, 39.

47 Register of Debates, 21st Congress, 1st session, 72 (third quotation), 77 (first quotation), 80 (second quotation).

48 James Parton, *Life of Andrew Jackson* (Boston: Houghton, Mifflin, 1859), 3:282.

49 Marcus Morton to Calhoun, April 13, 1830, in Calhoun, *Papers*, 11:147.

50 Robert V. Remini, *Andrew Jackson and the Course of American Freedom, 1822–1832* (New York: Harper & Row, 1981), 233–34.

51 This account of the dinner is taken from ibid., 234–36 (first three quotations on p. 235, fourth quotation on p. 236). Remini's account closely follows Parton, *Life of Andrew Jackson*, 3:282–85.

52 Jackson to John Coffee, December 6, 1830, in Jackson, *Papers*, 8:681 (first quotation); Jackson to Coffee, December 28, 1830, in ibid., 8:718 (second and sixth quotations); Jackson to Coffee, April 24, 1831, in Andrew Jackson, *Correspondence of Andrew Jackson*, ed. John Spencer Bassett and David Maydole Matteson (Washington, D.C.: Carnegie Institution

of Washington, 1926–35), 4:269 (third quotation); Jackson to Samuel Jackson Hays, December 7, 1830, in Jackson, *Papers*, 8:681 (fourth quotation); Jackson to Coffee, May 13, 1831, in Jackson, *Correspondence*, 4:282 (fifth quotation).

53 James Monroe to John C. Calhoun, January 7, 1829, in Calhoun, *Papers*, 10:547.

54 Adams, *Memoirs*, 8:479.

55 *Niles' Weekly Register*, April 7, 1832, 92.

56 Jackson to Levi Woodbury, September 11, 1832, in Jackson, *Correspondence*, 4:474.

57 Joel R. Poinsett to Jackson, October 16, 1832, in ibid., 4:481 (first two quotations), 482 (third quotation).

58 Jackson to Poinsett, December 2, 1832, in ibid., 4:494. For Jackson's military preparations, see Jackson to Lewis Cass, October 29, 1832, in ibid., 4:483.

59 Jackson to Martin Van Buren, November 18, 1832, in Jackson, *Correspondence*, 4:489 (first quotation); Jackson to John Coffee, December 14, 1832, in ibid., 4:500 (second quotation).

60 Watson, *Liberty and Power*, 126–27.

61 Statutes at Large, 34th Congress, 1st session, 771 (first quotation); Richardson, *Messages and Papers of the Presidents*, 2:645 (subsequent quotations).

62 Ibid., 2:654.

63 Jackson to Van Buren, December 25, 1832, in Jackson, *Correspondence*, 4:506 (first quotation); Jackson to Van Buren, January 25, 1833, in ibid., 5:13 (second quotation). For Madison's repudiation of nullification, see Madison to Webster, May 27, 1830, in Daniel Webster, *The Papers of Daniel Webster*, ed. Charles M. Wiltse (Hanover, N.H.: University Press of New England, 1974–89), series 1, 3:77–78.

64 Richardson, *Messages and Papers of the Presidents*, 2:631.

65 Watson, *Liberty and Power*, 128–31.

66 Richardson, *Messages and Papers of the Presidents*, 2:487.

67 Mike O'Connor, *A Commercial Republic: America's Endur-ing Debate over Democratic Capitalism* (Lawrence: Univer-sity Press of Kansas, 2014), 48–81.

68 Richardson, *Messages and Papers of the Presidents*, 2:518 (first quotation), 590 (second quotation); Watson, *Liberty and Power*, 154–56.

69 Watson, *Liberty and Power*, 156–59.

70 Register of Debates, 23rd Congress, 1st session, 1314.

71 Clay to James F. Conover, May 1, 1830, in Clay, *Papers*, 8:200 (first quotation); Webster to Benjamin G. Welles, April 5, 1834, in Webster, *Papers*, series 1, 3:340 (second quotation).

72 On the ideological incoherence and the general dysfunction-ality of the Whig Party, see vols. 1–2 of Arthur M. Schlesinger and Fred L. Israel, eds., *History of American Presidential Elec-tions, 1789–1968*, 4 vols. (New York: Chelsea House, 1971); Skowronek, *The Politics Presidents Make*, 153–54; Wilentz, *The Rise of American Democracy*, 482–518.

CHAPTER THREE: CONSERVATIVE INTENTIONS

1 Abraham Lincoln, "Eulogy on Henry Clay," July 6, 1852, in Abraham Lincoln, *The Collected Works of Abraham Lincoln*, ed. Roy P. Basler (New Brunswick, N.J.: Rutgers University Press, 1953–55), 2:126.

2 William Lloyd Garrison, *The Letters of William Lloyd Garri-son*, ed. Louis Ruchames and Walter M. Merrill (Cambridge, Mass.: Belknap Press of Harvard University Press, 1971–81), 3:118.

3 Stephen Douglas to the Editor of the Concord (New Hamp-shire) *State Capitol Reporter*, February 16, 1854, in Stephen A.

Douglas, *The Letters of Stephen A. Douglas*, ed. Robert W. Johannsen (Urbana: University of Illinois Press, 1961), 284.

4 Lincoln, "Speech at Peoria, Illinois," October 16, 1854, in Lincoln, *Collected Works*, 2:250.

5 Ibid., 2:275 (first and second quotations), 276 (third and fourth quotations).

6 Sean Wilentz, *The Rise of American Democracy: Jefferson to Lincoln* (New York: Norton, 2005), 675–77.

7 Lincoln to George Robertson, August 15, 1855, in Lincoln, *Collected Works*, 2:318.

8 Harry V. Jaffa, *A New Birth of Freedom: Abraham Lincoln and the Coming of the Civil War* (Lanham, Md.: Rowman & Littlefield, 2000), 179.

9 Lincoln to Joshua F. Speed, August 24, 1855, in Lincoln, *Collected Works*, 2:323.

10 Arthur M. Schlesinger and Fred L. Israel, eds., *History of American Presidential Elections, 1789–1968* (New York: Chelsea House, 1971), 2:1040.

11 Ibid., 2:1037.

12 Nicole Etcheson, *Bleeding Kansas: Contested Liberty in the Civil War Era* (Lawrence: University Press of Kansas, 2004).

13 James D. Richardson, ed., *A Compilation of the Messages and Papers of the Presidents, 1789–1897* (Washington, D.C.: U.S. Government Printing Office, 1897), 5:431 (second quotation), 432 (first, third, and fourth quotations).

14 *Dred Scott v. Sandford*, 60 U.S. 393 (1857).

15 Ibid., at 407 (first and second quotations), 410 (third quotation).

16 Lincoln, "Speech at Springfield, Illinois," June 26, 1857, in Lincoln, *Collected Works*, 2:404.

17 Ibid., 2:405 (first quotation), 406 (second through fourth quotations).

18   See, for example, Lincoln, "Speech at Chicago, Illinois," July 10, 1858, in ibid., 2:484–502.

19   Lincoln, "'A House Divided': Speech at Springfield, Illinois," June 16, 1858, in ibid., 2:461 (first and second quotations), 461–62 (third quotation).

20   "First Debate with Stephen A. Douglas at Ottawa, Illinois," August 21, 1858, in ibid., 3:16.

21   Ibid., 3:18.

22   Ibid., 3:9.

23   Ibid., 3:8.

24   "Third Debate with Stephen A. Douglas at Jonesboro, Illinois," September 15, 1858, in ibid., 3:116 (Douglas quotation), 117 (Lincoln quotations).

25   "Fifth Debate with Stephen A. Douglas at Galesburg, Illinois," October 7, 1858, in ibid., 3:216.

26   Ibid., 3:220.

27   "Sixth Debate with Stephen A. Douglas at Quincy, Illinois," October 13, 1858, in ibid., 3:274.

28   Ibid., 3:276.

29   Wilentz, *The Rise of American Democracy*, 741–44.

30   Stephen A. Douglas, *Speeches of Senator S. A. Douglas, on the Occasion of His Public Receptions by the Citizens of New Orleans, Philadelphia, and Baltimore* (Washington, D.C.: L. Towers, 1859), 12.

31   Stephen A. Douglas, "The Dividing Line between Federal and Local Authority: Popular Sovereignty in the Territories," *Harper's Magazine*, September 1859, 521.

32   Lincoln, "Address at Cooper Institute, New York City," February 27, 1860, in ibid., 3:530.

33   Ibid., 3:535.

34   Ibid., 3:537.

35   Harold Holzer, *Lincoln at Cooper Union: The Speech That*

Made Abraham Lincoln President (New York: Simon & Schuster, 2004).

36   Lincoln to George D. Prentice, October 29, 1860, in Lincoln, *Collected Works*, 4:134.

37   Jefferson Davis, *Relations of States: Speech of the Hon. Jefferson Davis, of Mississippi: Delivered in the Senate of the United States, May 7th, 1860, on the Resolutions Submitted by Him on 1st of March, 1860* (Baltimore: J. Murphy, 1860), 8 (first three quotations); Davis, "Inaugural Address of the President of the Provisional Government," February 18, 1861, in Jefferson Davis, *The Messages and Papers of Jefferson Davis and the Confederacy*, ed. James D. Richardson and Allan Nevins, new ed. (New York: Chelsea House–Robert Hector, 1966), 1:33 (fourth and fifth quotations).

38   Davis, "Inaugural Address," in Davis, *Messages and Papers*, 1:36.

39   Alexander Stephens, "Cornerstone Speech," March 21, 1861, in Alexander H. Stephens, *Alexander H. Stephens in Public and Private*, ed. Henry Cleveland (Philadelphia: National, 1866), 721.

40   Lincoln, "First Inaugural Address," March 4, 1861, in Lincoln, *Collected Works*, 4:264 (first and second quotations), 265 (fourth quotation), 269 (third quotation).

41   Ibid., 4:271.

42   Lincoln, "Reply to the Baltimore Committee," April 22, 1861, in ibid., 4:341.

43   Lincoln, "Annual Message to Congress," December 3, 1861, in ibid., 5:49.

44   Lincoln, "Message to Congress," March 6, 1862, in ibid., 5:145 (quotation). See also Lincoln, "Appeal to Border State Representatives to Favor Compensated Emancipation," July 12, 1860, in ibid., 5:317–19.

45   Lincoln to Horace Greeley, August 22, 1862, in Lincoln, *Collected Works*, 5:388 (first quotation); Lincoln, "Reply to the Emancipation Memorial Presented by Chicago Christians of All Denominations," September 13, 1862, in ibid., 5:423 (second quotation).

46   Sean Wilentz points this out in Sean Wilentz, "Who Lincoln Was," *New Republic*, July 15, 2009, 36.

47   Lincoln, "Preliminary Emancipation Proclamation," September 22, 1862, in Lincoln, *Collected Works*, 5:433–36.

48   Richard Hofstadter, *The American Political Tradition and the Men Who Made It* (New York: Knopf, 1973), 131 (first quotation); Lincoln, "Emancipation Proclamation," January 1, 1863, in Lincoln, *Collected Works*, 6:29 (second and third quotations), 29–30 (fourth quotation).

49   Lincoln, "Annual Message to Congress," December 1, 1862, in Lincoln, *Collected Works*, 5:537.

50   Lincoln, "Address Delivered at the Dedication of the Cemetery at Gettysburg," November 19, 1863, in Lincoln, *Collected Works*, 7:23.

51   Cragin is quoted in Mark Wahlgren Summers, "With a Sublime Faith in God, and in Republican Liberty," in *Vale of Tears: New Essays on Religion and Reconstruction*, ed. Edward J. Blum and W. Scott Poole (Macon, Ga.: Mercer University Press, 2005), 124.

52   George Bailey Loring, *Safe and Honorable Reconstruction: An Oration, Delivered at Newburyport, July 4, 1866* (South Danvers, Mass.: Charles D. Howard, 1866), 13.

53   Lincoln, "Last Public Address," April 11, 1865, in Lincoln, *Collected Works*, 8:403.

54   On the fundamental transformation of the Founders' conception of Union, see Eric Foner, *Reconstruction: America's Unfinished Revolution, 1863–1877* (New York: Harper &

Row, 1988); Bruce A. Ackerman, *We the People: Foundations* (Cambridge, Mass.: Belknap Press of Harvard University Press, 1991).

55   Andrew Johnson, "Third Annual Message to Congress," American Presidency Project, http://www.presidency.ucsb .edu/ws/index.php?pid=29508.

56   Jefferson Davis, *The Rise and Fall of the Confederate Government* (New York: D. Appleton, 1881); Alexander H. Stephens, *A Constitutional View of the Late War between the States: Its Causes, Character, Conduct and Results*, 2 vols. (Philadelphia: National, 1868); Merrill D. Peterson, *The Jefferson Image in the American Mind* (Charlottesville, Va.: Thomas Jefferson Memorial Foundation, 1998), 214–16.

57   Ulysses S. Grant, *Personal Memoirs of U. S. Grant* (New York: C. L. Webster, 1885), 1:220 (first quotation), 221 (all subsequent quotations).

CHAPTER FOUR: THE INTERREGNUM

1   For a celebrated satire of the unfinished monument, from which I have drawn part of this description, see Mark Twain, *The Gilded Age and Later Novels* (New York: Library of America, 2002), 178–79.

2   For the few references to the Founders in the presidential rhetoric of the era, consult the American Presidency Project, http://www.presidency.ucsb.edu.

3   On the Populist rhetoric about the Founders, see Charles Postel, *The Populist Vision* (New York: Oxford University Press, 2007), 11, 163 (quotations). For an example of Bryan's rhetoric, see William Jennings Bryan, *The First Battle: A Story of the Campaign of 1896* (Chicago: W. B. Conkey,

1896), 518–22. On the way that this interdependency changed the conception of individual obligation to undermine Jeffersonian independence, see Thomas L. Haskell, *The Emergence of Professional Social Science: The American Social Science Association and the Nineteenth-Century Crisis of Authority* (Urbana: University of Illinois Press, 1977).

4 John Bach McMaster, *With the Fathers: Studies in the History of the United States* (New York: D. Appleton, 1896), 71; Paul Leicester Ford, *The True George Washington* (Philadelphia: J. B. Lippincott, 1896); Sydney George Fisher, *The True Benjamin Franklin* (Philadelphia: J. B. Lippincott, 1899).

5 See Stephen Skowronek, *The Politics Presidents Make: Leadership from John Adams to Bill Clinton* (Cambridge, Mass.: Belknap Press of Harvard University Press, 1997), 228–59.

6 Janet Podell and Steven Anzovin, eds., *Speeches of the American Presidents* (New York: H. W. Wilson, 1988), 325.

7 Woodrow Wilson, *Constitutional Government in the United States* (New York: Columbia University Press, 1908), 46 (first two quotations), 57 (third and fourth quotations).

8 Woodrow Wilson, "A News Report of an Address in Washington," February 23, 1906, in Woodrow Wilson, *The Papers of Woodrow Wilson*, ed. Arthur S. Link and Alfred D. Chandler (Princeton, N.J.: Princeton University Press, 1966–94), 16:315–16 (first quotation); Wilson, "A News Report of an Address on Americanism at Oberlin College," March 22, 1906, in ibid., 16:341 (second quotation); Wilson, "A News Release of a Speech on Thomas Jefferson," April 17, 1906, in ibid., 16:359 (third quotation), 360 (fourth quotation).

9 Charles A. Beard, *An Economic Interpretation of the Constitution of the United States* (New York: Macmillan, 1913).

10 Herbert David Croly, *The Promise of American Life* (New York: Macmillan, 1909), 5 (first two quotations); Walter E.

Weyl, *The New Democracy: An Essay on Certain Political and Economic Tendencies in the United States* (New York: Macmillan, 1912), 108 (third quotation); Walter Lippmann, *A Preface to Politics* (New York: M. Kennerley, 1913), 14 (fourth quotation), 31 (fifth quotation).

11 Podell and Anzovin, *Speeches of the American Presidents*, 339 (first and second quotations); Theodore Roosevelt to Hugo Münsterberg, February 8, 1916, in Theodore Roosevelt, *The Letters of Theodore Roosevelt*, ed. Elting E. Morison and Alfred D. Chandler (Cambridge, Mass.: Harvard University Press, 1951–54), 8:1018 (third quotation).

12 Herbert Croly, *Progressive Democracy* (New York: Macmillan, 1914), 378.

13 Richard Bernstein first pointed out that Harding coined the phrase "Founding Fathers." See Richard B. Bernstein, *The Founding Fathers Reconsidered* (New York: Oxford University Press, 2009), 3–5.

14 Podell and Anzovin, *Speeches of the American Presidents*, 416 (first two quotations), 418 (third quotation).

15 Warren G. Harding, *President Harding's Address at the Dedication of the Lincoln Memorial* (Washington, D.C.: U.S. Government Printing Office, 1922), 4 (first quotation), 6 (second quotation); Chester Arthur, "Dedication of the Washington National Monument," December 6, 1884, in Podell and Anzovin, *Speeches of the American Presidents*, 255.

16 William E. Woodward, *George Washington, the Image and the Man* (New York: Boni & Liveright, 1926), 9 (first two quotations), 453 (third, fourth, and fifth quotations); "Restoring the Family," *New Republic*, November 28, 1914, 9 (sixth quotation).

17 On the 1920s and the economy, see Mike O'Connor, *A Commercial Republic: America's Enduring Debate over*

Democratic Capitalism (Lawrence: University Press of Kansas, 2014), 120–31.

18 William E. Leuchtenburg, *Franklin D. Roosevelt and the New Deal, 1932–1940* (New York: Harper Perennial, 2009), 18–25.

19 Skowronek, *The Politics Presidents Make*, 260–85 (quotation on p. 264).

20 Franklin Delano Roosevelt, "Address at Oglethorpe University," May 22, 1932, in Franklin Delano Roosevelt, *The Public Papers and Addresses of Franklin D. Roosevelt*, ed. Samuel I. Rosenman (New York: Random House, 1938–50), 1:642.

21 Ibid., 1:642 (second quotation), 646 (first and third quotations).

22 Roosevelt, "The Governor Accepts the Nomination for the Presidency," July 2, 1932, in ibid., 1:648 (first quotation), 649 (second quotation), 659 (third and fourth quotations).

CHAPTER FIVE: A MORAL AND EMOTIONAL PURPOSE

1 William E. Leuchtenburg, *Franklin D. Roosevelt and the New Deal, 1932–1940* (New York: Harper Perennial, 2009), 38–40 (quotations on p. 39).

2 Roosevelt, "Inaugural Address," March 4, 1933, in Franklin Delano Roosevelt, *The Public Papers and Addresses of Franklin D. Roosevelt*, ed. Samuel I. Rosenman (New York: Random House, 1938–50), 2:11 (first and second quotations), 12 (third and fourth quotations).

3 Ibid., 2:15.

4 Roosevelt, "First Press Conference," March 8, 1933, in ibid., 2:30–31.

5 Theodore G. Joslyn, *Sunday Star*, Washington, D.C., March

4, 1934, excerpted in ibid., 2:41 (first quotation), 45 (second quotation).

6   Roosevelt, "First 'Fireside Chat,'" March 12, 1933, in ibid., 2:61–66 (second quotation on p. 61); Lawrence W. Levine and Cornelia R. Levine, eds., *The People and the President: America's Conversation with FDR* (Boston: Beacon Press, 2002), 29 (first quotation).

7   Leuchtenburg, *Franklin D. Roosevelt*, 61–62.

8   Ibid., 67–69; George Wolfskill, *The Revolt of the Conservatives: A History of the American Liberty League, 1934–1940* (Boston: Houghton Mifflin, 1962), 10–13.

9   Leuchtenburg, *Franklin D. Roosevelt*, 90–91.

10 Kim Phillips-Fein, *Invisible Hands: The Businessmen's Crusade against the New Deal* (New York: Norton, 2009), 3–13 (quotation on p. 5).

11 William H. Stayton, "Confidential Memorandum to Former Members of the Executive Committee of the Association against the Prohibition Amendment," August 24, 1934, Papers of Pierre S. du Pont, Longwood Manuscripts, Group 10/A, File 1023–48, Box 1557, Folder "William H. Stayton, 1934," Hagley Museum and Library, Wilmington, Delaware.

12 Wolfskill, *The Revolt of the Conservatives*, 112 (first four quotations), 113 (fifth and sixth quotations).

13 Ibid., 56–70 (quotations on p. 62).

14 Roosevelt, "The One Hundred and Thirty-Seventh Press Conference," August 24, 1934, in Franklin Delano Roosevelt, *The Roosevelt Reader: Selected Speeches, Messages, Press Conferences, and Letters*, ed. Basil Rauch (New York: Holt, Rinehart, Winston, 1957), 127. Also see "Roosevelt Twits Liberty League as Lover of Property," *New York Times*, August 25, 1934, pp. 1–2.

15 James C. Pitney, "American Liberty League, Inc." (bachelor's thesis, Princeton University, 1948), 66–67.

16 *Railroad Retirement Board et al. v. Alton Railroad Co. et al.*, 295 U.S. 330 (1935), at 346 (first quotation), 347 (second quotation), 375 (third quotation).

17 *A.L.A. Schechter Poultry Corp. et al. v. United States*, 295 U.S. 495 (1935).

18 Roosevelt quoted in Leuchtenburg, *Franklin D. Roosevelt*, 145.

19 Roosevelt, "The Two Hundred and Ninth Press Conference," May 31, 1935, in Roosevelt, *Public Papers and Addresses*, 4:200 (first quotation), 205 (second quotation), 209 (third and fourth quotations).

20 Ibid., 4:209 (first two quotations), 210 (third and fourth quotations).

21 Ibid., 4:221 (first two quotations), 222 (third through sixth quotations).

22 Walter Lippmann, *Public Opinion* (New York: Harcourt, Brace, 1922), 248.

23 Harold D. Lasswell, "The Theory of Political Propaganda," *American Political Science Review* 21 (August 1927): 627 (third quotation), 630 (first and second quotations).

24 Wolfskill, *The Revolt of the Conservatives*, 163.

25 Thurman W. Arnold, *The Symbols of Government* (New York: Harcourt, Brace & World, 1962), v (first quotation), 18 (second quotation), 269 (third and fourth quotations).

26 Edward S. Corwin, "The Constitution as Instrument and as Symbol," *American Political Science Review* 30 (December 1936): 1074 (first quotation), 1075 (second quotation).

27 Michael Kammen, *Mystic Chords of Memory: The Transformation of Tradition in American Culture* (New York: Knopf, 1991), 451.

28 Leuchtenburg, *Franklin D. Roosevelt*, 118–66.

29 Roosevelt, "A Message to Congress on Tax Revision," June

19, 1935, in Roosevelt, *Public Papers and Addresses*, 4:271–72 (first quotation), 272 (second and third quotations).

30   Turner Catledge, "Roosevelt Speech Politics, Say G.O.P.," *New York Times*, January 2, 1936, p. 1.

31   Roosevelt, "Annual Message to Congress," January 3, 1936, in Roosevelt, *Public Papers and Addresses*, 5:14.

32   Ibid., 5:12 (first, second, and fourth quotations), 12–13 (third quotation), 17 (fifth and sixth quotations).

33   Turner Catledge, "Calls for an Open Fight," *New York Times*, January 4, 1936, p. 1.

34   *United States v. Butler et al.*, 297 U.S. 1 (1936) at 68 (first two quotations); Roosevelt, "F.D.R. Miscellany," January 24, 1936, in Franklin Delano Roosevelt, *The Roosevelt Letters, Being the Personal Correspondence of Franklin Delano Roosevelt*, ed. Elliott Roosevelt (London: G. C. Harrap, 1952), 3:167 (third quotation).

35   Roosevelt, "Address at the Jackson Day Dinner," January 8, 1936, in Roosevelt, *Public Papers and Addresses*, 5:40 (first two quotations), 41 (third and fourth quotations).

36   Wolfskill, *The Revolt of the Conservatives*, 142–43, 149–50.

37   Alfred E. Smith, *The Facts in the Case: Speech of Alfred E. Smith, American Liberty League Dinner, Washington D.C., January 25, 1936* (Washington, D.C.: American Liberty League, 1936), 4 (first quotation), 14 (second quotation), 18 (third quotation).

38   Turner Catledge, "Smith Threatens a Revolt," *New York Times*, January 26, 1936, p. 36 (quotation); Pitney, "American Liberty League, Inc.," 78–79.

39   Roosevelt to Breckenridge Long, February 22, 1936, in Roosevelt, *Letters*, 3:171 (first two quotations); Roosevelt to James Farley, March 26, 1936, in ibid., 3:175 (third quotation). On the decision to focus on the Liberty League over

the Republican Party, see James A. Farley, *Behind the Ballots: The Personal History of a Politician* (New York: Harcourt, Brace, 1938), 292–95.

40 Roosevelt, "Address at the Thomas Jefferson Dinner," April 25, 1936, in Roosevelt, *Public Papers and Addresses*, 5:178 (first two quotations), 181 (third quotation).

41 Roosevelt, "A Greeting on the Centenary of the Death of James Madison," May 8, 1936, in ibid., 5:185–86.

42 Roosevelt, "Address at Little Rock Arkansas," June 10, 1936, in ibid., 5:199 (first quotation), 200 (second quotation).

43 For these titles and others, see the complete list of Liberty League publications in Wolfskill, *The Revolt of the Conservatives*, 283–89; Raoul E. Desvernine, *A Reply to Secretary Wallace's Question—Whose Constitution? The Dominant Issue of the Campaign* (Washington, D.C.: American Liberty League, 1936), 20 (final two quotations).

44 Roosevelt, "The Three Hundredth Press Conference," June 2, 1936, in Roosevelt, *Public Papers and Addresses*, 5:191–92.

45 Arthur Krock, "Campaign Issue Defined," *New York Times*, June 28, 1936, pp. 1, 25.

46 Roosevelt, "Acceptance of the Renomination for the Presidency," June 27, 1936, in Roosevelt, *Public Papers and Addresses*, 5:231 (first three quotations), 234 (fourth through seventh quotations).

47 Krock, "Campaign Issue Defined."

48 Catledge, "Smith Threatens a Revolt," p. 1 (first quotation); Wolfskill, *The Revolt of the Conservatives*, ix (second quotation).

49 Ibid., 214–15 (quotation on p. 215).

50 Leuchtenburg, *Franklin D. Roosevelt*, 195–96.

51 Irving Brant, *Storm over the Constitution* (1936; reprint, New York: Charter Books, 1963), xiii, 19–34; Michael G. Kammen,

Selvages and Biases: The Fabric of History in American Culture (Ithaca, N.Y.: Cornell University Press, 1987), 146.

52   Brant, *Storm over the Constitution*, 242; Walter E. Weyl, *The New Democracy: An Essay on Certain Political and Economic Tendencies in the United States* (New York: Macmillan, 1912), 109.

53   Roosevelt, "Second Inaugural Address," January 20, 1937, in Roosevelt, *Public Papers and Addresses*, 6:1–2 (first quotation), 2 (all subsequent quotations).

54   Roosevelt, "The Three Hundred and Forty-Second Press Conference," February 5, 1937, in ibid., 6:35–50; Roosevelt, "The President Presents a Plan for the Reorganization of the Judicial Branch of Government," February 5, 1937, in ibid., 6:51–66.

55   Jeff Shesol, *Supreme Power: Franklin Roosevelt vs. the Supreme Court* (New York: Norton, 2010), 246; Richard L. Neuberger, "America Talks Court," *Current History* 46 (June 1937): 35–37; Leuchtenburg, *Franklin D. Roosevelt*, 231–38.

56   Roosevelt, "The Three Hundred and Forty-Fourth Press Conference," February 12, 1937, in Roosevelt, *Public Papers and Addresses*, 6:75 (first and second quotations), 76 (third quotation).

57   Roosevelt, "A 'Fireside Chat' Discussing the Plan for Reorganization of the Judiciary," March 9, 1937, in ibid., 6:123 (first quotation), 124 (second and third quotations), 126 (fourth quotation).

58   *National Labor Relations Board v. Jones & Laughlin Steel Corp.*, 301 U.S. 1 (1937) at 43.

59   Roosevelt, "The Three Hundred and Sixtieth Press Conference," April 13, 1937, in Roosevelt, *Public Papers and Addresses*, 6:153.

60   Phillips-Fein, *Invisible Hands*; Alan Brinkley, *The End of*

Reform: New Deal Liberalism in Recession and War (New York: Knopf, 1995); Bruce A. Ackerman, *We the People: Foundations* (Cambridge, Mass.: Belknap Press of Harvard University Press, 1991).

CHAPTER SIX: THE MONTAGE EFFECT

1   On the day's events and the prior preparations, see "On the March," *Newsweek*, September 2, 1963, 17–21.

2   E. W. Kenworthy, "200,000 March for Civil Rights," *New York Times*, August 29, 1963, p. 16; "Civil Rights," *Time*, August 30, 1963, 9.

3   Glenn T. Eskew, *But for Birmingham: The Local and National Movements in the Civil Rights Struggle* (Chapel Hill: University of North Carolina Press, 1997).

4   James Reston, "'I Have a Dream . . .': Peroration by Dr. King Sums up a Day the Capital Will Remember," *New York Times*, April 29, 1963, p. 17.

5   Ibid., 1.

6   Martin Luther King Jr., "I Have a Dream," in Martin Luther King, *A Testament of Hope: The Essential Writings of Martin Luther King, Jr.*, ed. James M. Washington (San Francisco: HarperCollins, 1986), 217.

7   Ibid., 218 (second quotation), 219 (first quotation).

8   "On the March," *Newsweek*, September 2, 1963, 18.

9   William F. Buckley Jr., "Our Mission Statement," *National Review*, November 19, 1955, http://www.nationalreview.com/articles/223549/our-mission-statement/william-f-buckley-jr; Barry M. Goldwater, *The Conscience of a Conservative* (Shepherdsville, Ky.: Victor, 1960), 34.

10   Reston, "'I Have a Dream . . . ,'" p. 17.

11 Rick Perlstein, *Before the Storm: Barry Goldwater and the Unmaking of the American Consensus* (New York: Hill & Wang, 2001), 363–70.

12 Ronald Reagan, "A Time for Choosing," *Reagan Foundation*, accessed August 2, 2013, http://www.reaganfoundation.org /tgcdetail.aspx?p=TG0923RRS&h1=0&h2=0&lm=reagan &args_a=cms&args_b=1&argsb=N&tx=1736.

13 Lou Cannon, *Reagan* (New York: G. P. Putnam's Sons, 1982), 94–97.

14 Reagan, "A Time for Choosing."

15 On the continuation of League supporters in other activities, see Kim Phillips-Fein, *Invisible Hands: The Businessmen's Crusade against the New Deal* (New York: Norton, 2010).

16 On Reagan's relationship to his backers, see ibid., especially 142–49. On changes within liberalism to support civil rights, see Gary Gerstle, "The Protean Character of American Liberalism," *American Historical Review* 99 (October 1994): 1043–73.

17 Reagan, "A Time for Choosing."

18 Ibid.

19 Arthur M. Schlesinger Jr., *The Vital Center: The Politics of Freedom* (Boston: Houghton Mifflin, 1949).

20 "Politics," *Time*, October 30, 1964, 27.

21 "VPA: The Making of an Avalanche—1964," *Newsweek*, November 9, 1964, 28.

22 "After the Fall: To the Mainstream?" *Newsweek*, November 9, 1964, 31 (first two quotations), 32 (third quotation).

23 Cannon, *Reagan*, 98–118.

24 Seth Rosenfeld, *Subversives: The FBI's War on Student Radicals, and Reagan's Rise to Power* (New York: Farrar, Straus & Giroux, 2012), 4.

25 Clay Risen, *A Nation on Fire: America in the Wake of the King Assassination* (Hoboken, N.J.: John Wiley & Sons, 2009).

26 Cannon, *Reagan*, 157–65.

27 Richard Nixon, "Address to the Nation on the War in Vietnam," November 3, 1969, in Richard Nixon, *Public Papers of Richard Nixon* (Washington, D.C.: U.S. Government Printing Office, 1971–75), 1969:909 (first quotation); Nixon, "Inaugural Address," January 20, 1969, in ibid., 1969:2 (second and third quotations).

28 Mike O'Connor, *A Commercial Republic: America's Enduring Debate over Democratic Capitalism* (Lawrence: University Press of Kansas, 2014), 217–25.

29 "The Spirit of '70: Six Historians Reflect on What Ails the American Spirit," *Newsweek*, July 6, 1970, 19.

30 Ibid., 20.

31 "On the March," *Newsweek*, September 6, 1963, 18 (first quotation); Donald Bremner, "Picking Up the Bicentennial Pieces," *Los Angeles Times*, July 1, 1973, VII:4 (second and third quotations).

32 Bremner, "Picking Up the Bicentennial Pieces," VII:4.

33 Ibid.

34 Robert Sherril, "The Dispirit of '76: A Bicentennial Divided Against Itself," *New York Times*, March 23, 1975, sec. 10, pp. 1,16.

35 Ibid.

36 Jeremy Rifkin and John Rossen, *How to Commit Revolution American Style: An Anthology* (Secaucus, N.J.: Lyle Stuart, 1973), 9 (first quotation), 18 (second and third quotations).

37 Nixon, "Second Inaugural Address," January 20, 1973, in Nixon, *Public Papers*, 1973:13 (third and fourth quotations), 15 (first and second quotations).

38 American Revolution Bicentennial Administration, *The Bicentennial of the United States of America: A Final Report to the People* (Washington, D.C.: U.S. Government Printing Office, 1977), 1:preface.

39   *Newsweek*, July 4, 1976; "The Big 200th Bash," *Time*, July 5, 1976, 14.

40   "The Big 200th Bash," *Time*, July 5, 1976, 14.

41   Cannon, *Reagan*, 187–202.

42   Ronald Reagan, "Let the People Rule," September 26, 1975, in Ronald Reagan, *Actor, Ideologue, Politician: The Public Speeches of Ronald Reagan*, ed. Davis W. Houck and Amos Kiewe (Westport, Conn.: Greenwood Press, 1993), 143.

43   Ibid., 143 (second and third quotations), 144 (first quotation).

44   Ibid., 144–45 (quotation on p. 144).

45   Cannon, *Reagan*, 203–209 (quotation on p. 204).

46   "Can Reagan Stop Ford?" *Newsweek*, November 24, 1975, 31 (first, third, and fourth quotations); "The Star Shakes Up the Party," *Time*, November 24, 1975, 17 (second quotation), 24 (fifth through seventh quotations). Also see "Does He Really Want It?" *Time*, November 24, 1975, 20.

47   Cannon, *Reagan*, 210–26.

48   Ibid., 227–40.

49   Meg Greenfield, "Choices and Echoes on the Right," *Newsweek*, October 27, 1975, 108; Stephen Skowronek, *The Politics Presidents Make: Leadership from John Adams to Bill Clinton* (Cambridge, Mass.: Belknap Press of Harvard University Press, 1997), 361–406.

50   "The New Right: A Special Report," *Conservative Digest*, June 1979, 9–21 (quotations on p. 10).

51   O'Connor, *A Commercial Republic*, 225–36.

52   Joseph Crespino, *In Search of Another Country: Mississippi and the Conservative Counterrevolution* (Princeton, N.J.: Princeton University Press, 2007), 1.

53   Cannon, *Reagan*, 269–303.

54   Sean Wilentz, *The Age of Reagan: A History, 1974–2008* (New York: HarperCollins, 2008), 121 (quotation); Elizabeth

Drew, *Portrait of an Election: The 1980 Presidential Campaign* (New York: Simon & Schuster, 1981), 108–11.

55 Drew, *Portrait of an Election*, 112–13; Theodore H. White, *America in Search of Itself: The Making of the President, 1956–1980* (New York: Harper & Row, 1982), 187 (quotation). For an example of the carefully muted jeremiad, see Reagan, "Republican Nomination Acceptance Speech," July 17, 1980, in Reagan, *Actor, Ideologue, Politician*, 158–66.

56 Wilentz, *The Age of Reagan*, 124–25.

57 Reagan, "Inaugural Address," January 20, 1981, in Ronald Reagan, *Public Papers of the Presidents of the United States: Ronald Reagan* (Washington, D.C.: U.S. Government Printing Office, 1982–91), 1981:1 (first two quotations), 2 (third quotation), 3 (fourth through sixth quotations).

CHAPTER SEVEN: CRACKPOT THEORIES

1 Reagan, "Opening Remarks at a Meeting with the Cabinet," January 21, 1981, in Ronald Reagan, *Public Papers of the Presidents of the United States: Ronald Reagan* (Washington, D.C.: U.S. Government Printing Office, 1982–91), 1981:27.

2 Reagan, "Address to the Nation on the Economy," February 5, 1981, in ibid., 1981:81.

3 "Remarks and a Question-and-Answer Session on the Program for Economic Recovery at a Breakfast for Newspaper and Television News Editors," February 19, 1981, in ibid., 1981:132.

4 Reagan, "Address before a Joint Session of Congress on the Program for Economic Recovery," February 18, 1981, in ibid., 1981:114.

5 "Remarks and a Question-and-Answer Session," February 19, 1981, in ibid., 1981:137.

6   Reagan, "Address before a Joint Session of Congress on the Program for Economic Recovery," April 28, 1981, in ibid., 1981:393.

7   Wright quoted in Sean Wilentz, *The Age of Reagan: A History, 1974–2008* (New York: HarperCollins, 2008), 142.

8   Ibid., 141–43.

9   "He Got What He Wanted," *Time*, July 6, 1981, 6.

10 Ibid.

11 "This May Hurt a Little," *Time*, July 13, 1981, 10.

12 Reagan, "Address to the Nation on the Federal Tax Reduction Legislation," July 27, 1981, in Reagan, *Public Papers*, 1981:668.

13 Wilentz, *The Age of Reagan*, 143.

14 "Yeas 238–Nays 195," *Time*, August 10, 1981, 12 (first quotation); Ronald Reagan, *The Reagan Diaries* (New York: HarperCollins, 2007), 34 (second quotation).

15 "Yeas 238–Nays 195," *Time*, August 10, 1981, 13.

16 Reagan, *Reagan Diaries*, 37.

17 Reagan, "Address to the Nation on the Program for Economic Recovery," September 24, 1981, in Reagan, *Public Papers*, 1981:836.

18 "President's News Conference," October 1, 1981, in ibid., 1981:867–74 (quotation on p. 870).

19 Wilentz, *The Age of Reagan*, 146–47.

20 William Greider, "The Education of David Stockman," *Atlantic*, December 1981, 29.

21 Ibid., 32.

22 Ibid.

23 Ibid., 38.

24 Ibid., 47.

25 Ibid., 54.

26 Steven R. Weisman, "Stockman Offers Reagan 'Regrets' and Keeps His Job," *New York Times*, November 13, 1981, D16.

27   Ibid.

28   "A Visit to the Woodshed," *Time*, November 23, 1981, 12.

29   "Transcript of David Stockman's Statement and His News Conference," *New York Times*, November 13, 1981, D16.

30   "After the Lost Weekend," *Time*, December 7, 1981, 16–19.

31   "The President's Men," *Time*, December 14, 1981, 22.

32   Reagan, *Reagan Diaries*, 53.

33   For a nice review of the coverage, see Morton Kondracke, "Reagan's I.Q.," *New Republic*, March 24, 1982, 9–12 (quotations on p. 9).

34   Ibid., 10.

35   "Interview with Reporters from the *Los Angeles Times*," January 20, 1982, in Reagan, *Public Papers*, 1982:54 (first quotation), 55 (second quotation).

36   Reagan, "Address before a Joint Session of Congress Reporting on the State of the Union," January 26, 1982, in ibid., 1982:72.

37   Reagan, *Reagan Diaries*, 61 (first quotation); Reagan, "Address before a Joint Session of Congress Reporting on the State of the Union," January 26, 1982, in Reagan, *Public Papers*, 1982:76 (second quotation).

38   Reagan, "Remarks at a Conservative Political Action Conference Dinner," February 26, 1982, in Reagan, *Public Papers*, 1982:228 (first quotation), 230 (second quotation).

39   Reagan, "Remarks at a Rally Supporting the Proposed Constitutional Amendment for a Balanced Federal Budget," July 19, 1982, in ibid., 1982:939.

40   Ibid., 1982:941.

41   Reagan, *Reagan Diaries*, 94; David Treadwell, "Reagan Says 1983 Deficit Could Hit $110–$114 Billion," *Los Angeles Times*, July 26, 1982, pp. 1, 8.

42   Wilentz, *The Age of Reagan*, 148–49. See also an entire issue

devoted to the question, "Has Reagan Deserted the Conservatives?," *Conservative Digest*, August 1982.

43 "Remarks and a Question-and-Answer Session with Reporters Following the House of Representatives Vote on the Proposed Constitutional Amendment for a Balanced Federal Budget," October 1, 1982, in Reagan, *Public Papers*, 1982:1246 (first quotation), 1247 (subsequent quotations).

44 On the political pressures Reagan was facing, see Reagan, *Reagan Diaries*, 123, 142.

45 Ibid., 145, 153 (quotations).

46 Ibid., 192, 201 (first and second quotations), 206 (third quotation).

47 See, for example, Robert Dallek, *Ronald Reagan: The Politics of Symbolism* (Cambridge, Mass.: Harvard University Press, 1984).

48 David S. Broder, "Was Lincoln Wrong?," *Washington Post*, February 12, 1984, B7. On Broder's apolitical writing personae, see Bruce Weber, "David Broder, Political Journalist and Pundit, Dies at 81," *New York Times*, March 10, 2011, A29.

49 "Interview with Midwest Regional Reporters on Foreign and Domestic Issues," March 20, 1984, in Reagan, *Public Papers*, 1984:392 (first quotation), 393 (second quotation).

50 "President's News Conference," July 24, 1984, in ibid., 1984:1077.

51 Reagan, "Remarks at the Southern Republican Leadership Conference in Atlanta, Georgia," January 26, 1984, in ibid., 1984:104.

52 Reagan, "Toasts at a White House Dinner Honoring the Nation's Governors," February 26, 1984, in ibid., 1984:262.

53 Reagan, "Remarks at the Annual Convention of the National Association of Evangelicals in Columbus, Ohio," March 6, 1984, in ibid., 1984:305.

54 Reagan, "Remarks Accepting the Presidential Nomination at the Republican Convention in Dallas, Texas," August 23, 1984, in ibid., 1984:1180.

55 Michael Kramer, "A Modern Babbitt," *New York*, August 6, 1984, 16.

56 Reagan, "Remarks at a Reagan-Bush Rally in Portland, Oregon," October 23, 1984, in Reagan, *Public Papers*, 1984:1624.

57 Reagan, "Remarks at a Reagan-Bush Rally in Fairfield, Connecticut," October 26, 1984, in ibid., 1984:1656.

58 Wilentz, *The Age of Reagan*, 174–75.

59 Reagan, *Reagan Diaries*, 282.

60 Reagan, "The President's News Conference," January 9, 1985, in Reagan, *Public Papers*, 1985:25.

61 Reagan, "Interview with Ann Devroy and Johanna Neuman of *USA Today*," January 17, 1985, in ibid., 1985:46.

62 Reagan, "Inaugural Address," January 21, 1985, in ibid., 1985:55 (first through third quotations), 56 (fourth and fifth quotations).

63 For the debt ceiling raises, see table 7.3 at "Historical Tables | The White House Office of Management and Budget," http://www.whitehouse.gov/omb/budget/Historicals/, accessed August 14, 2013.

64 Reagan, *Public Papers*, 374.

65 See David Sehat, *The Myth of American Religious Freedom* (New York: Oxford University Press, 2011), 221–22, 267–68 (quotation on p. 268).

66 *Trimble v. Gordon*, 430 U.S. 762 (1977) at 777.

67 Antonin Scalia, *A Matter of Interpretation: Federal Courts and the Law: An Essay*, ed. Amy Gutmann (Princeton, N.J.: Princeton University Press, 1997), 24.

68 Reagan, "Remarks on the Resignation of Supreme Court Chief Justice Warren E. Burger and the Nominations of

William H. Rehnquist to Be Chief Justice and Antonin Scalia to Be Associate Justice," June 17, 1986, in Reagan, *Public Papers*, 1986:785.

69 Reagan, "Remarks at the Swearing-in Ceremony for William H. Rehnquist as Chief Justice and Antonin Scalia as Associate Justice of the Supreme Court of the United States," September 26, 1986, in ibid., 1986:1270.

70 Thurgood Marshall, *Thurgood Marshall: His Speeches, Writings, Arguments, Opinions, and Reminiscences*, ed. Mark V. Tushnet (Chicago: Lawrence Hill Books, 2001), 281 (first quotation), 282 (all subsequent quotations).

71 Reagan to William F. Buckley Jr., July 15, 1981, in Ronald Reagan, *Reagan: A Life in Letters*, ed. Kiron K. Skinner, Annelise Graebner Anderson, and Martin Anderson (New York: Free Press, 2003), 63–64.

72 Robert H. Bork, *Slouching Towards Gomorrah: Modern Liberalism and American Decline* (New York: Regan Books, 1996).

73 Neal E. Devins and Wendy L. Watson, eds., *Federal Abortion Politics: A Documentary History* (New York: Garland, 1995), 3:71.

74 Reagan, "Remarks Announcing America's Economic Bill of Rights," July 3, 1987, in Reagan, *Public Papers*, 1987:739–44 (quotation on p. 741); Reagan, "Radio Address to the Nation on the Supreme Court Nomination of Robert H. Bork and the Economic Bill of Rights," July 4, 1987, in ibid., 1987:793–94.

75 Wilentz, *The Age of Reagan*, 196–203; Michael Schaller, *Reckoning with Reagan: America and Its President in the 1980s* (New York: Oxford University Press, 1992), 99–118.

76 Wilentz, *The Age of Reagan*, 208.

77 Ibid., 206; Schaller, *Reckoning with Reagan*, 69–71.

78   Wilentz, *The Age of Reagan*, 275–76; Schaller, *Reckoning with Reagan*, 71–79.

79   "Interview with Andrew Neil and Jon Connell of the *Sunday Times* of London," September 6, 1984, in Reagan, *Public Papers*, 1984:1254 (first quotation), 1255 (all subsequent quotations).

80   William Safire, "Read My Lips," *New York Times Magazine*, September 4, 1988, http://www.nytimes.com/1988/09/04/magazine/on-language-read-my-lips.html.

81   Andrew Rosenthal, "Bush Now Concedes a Need for 'Tax Revenue Increases' to Reduce Deficit in Budget," *New York Times*, June 27, 1990, http://www.nytimes.com/1990/06/27/us/bush-now-concedes-a-need-for-tax-revenue-increases-to-reduce-deficit-in-budget.html.

82   Bob Woodward, *The Agenda: Inside the Clinton White House* (New York: Simon & Schuster, 1994), 161.

83   Wilentz, *The Age of Reagan*, 323–407; James T. Patterson, *Restless Giant: The United States from Watergate to Bush v. Gore* (New York: Oxford University Press, 2005), 318–86.

84   Julian E. Zelizer, ed., *The Presidency of George W. Bush: A First Historical Assessment* (Princeton, N.J.: Princeton University Press, 2010).

CHAPTER EIGHT: THIS IS AMERICA!

1   "Santelli's Tea Party," CNBC.com, February 19, 2009, http://video.cnbc.com/gallery/?video=1039849853.

2   Eric Etheridge, "Rick Santelli: Tea Party Time," *New York Times*, Opinionator blog, February 20, 2009, http://opinionator.blogs.nytimes.com/2009/02/20/rick-santelli-tea-party-time/.

3   First and second quotations: Kathryn Jean Lopez, "Watch for the Palin-Santelli 2012 Signs," *National Review Online*, February 19, 2009, http://www.nationalreview.com/corner /177629/watch-palin-santelli-2012-signs/kathryn-jean -lopez. Third quotation: Etheridge, "Rick Santelli: Tea Party Time."

4   First four quotations: Liz Robbins, "Tax Day Is Met With Tea Parties," *New York Times*, April 15, 2009, http://www.nytimes .com/2009/04/16/us/politics/16taxday.html. Last quotation: "Governor Says Texans May Want to Secede From Union But Probably Won't," Fox News, April 15, 2009, http://www.fox news.com/politics/2009/04/15/governor-says-texans-want -secede-union-probably-wont.

5   Eric Ostermeier, "Michele Bachmann on D.C.: 'I'm a Foreign Correspondent On Enemy Lines,'" *Smart Politics*, March 22, 2009, http://blog.lib.umn.edu/cspg/smartpolitics/2009/03 /michele_bachmann_on_dc_im_a_fo_1.php.

6   First quotation: David Frum, "The Reckless Right Courts Violence," *Week*, August 12, 2009, http://theweek.com /article/index/99474/the-reckless-right-courts-violence. Second quotation: Thomas Jefferson to William Stephens Smith, November 12, 1787, in Thomas Jefferson, *The Papers of Thomas Jefferson*, ed. Julian P. Boyd (Princeton, N.J.: Princeton University Press, 1950–), 12:356. Third quotation: Scott Wong, "Man with AR-15 Rifle at Obama Rally Sparks Concerns," *Arizona Central Republic*, PHX blog, August 17, 2009, http://www.azcentral.com/insiders/phxbeat/2009/08/17 /man-with-ar-15-rifle-at-obama-rally-sparks-concerns/. Also see Albert R. Hunt, "Tough Slog on Health Care Plan Gets a Little Easier," *New York Times*, August 16, 2009, http://www.nytimes.com/2009/08/17/us/17iht-letter.html; Scott Foster, "More Men with Guns at Obama Event," NBC

News, August 17, 2009, http://firstread.nbcnews.com/_news /2009/08/17/4427421-more-men-with-guns-at-obama-event.

7   First quotation: Adam Nagourney et al., "G.O.P. Used Energy and Stealth to Win Seat," *New York Times*, January 20, 2010, http://www.nytimes.com/2010/01/21/us/politics /21reconstruct.html. Second quotation: Mark Leibovich, "Massachusetts: Political Kingmaker, Political Heartbreaker," *New York Times*, January 23, 2010, http://www.nytimes.com /2010/01/24/weekinreview/24leibovich.html.

8   David Brooks, "The Tea Party Teens," *New York Times*, January 4, 2010, http://www.nytimes.com/2010/01/05/opinion /05brooks.html; "Palin's Tea Party Speech," *New York Times*, Caucus blog, February 7, 2010, http://thecaucus.blogs .nytimes.com/2010/02/07/palins-tea-party-speech/.

9   "Ron Paul: The Founding Fathers Were Libertarians," http:// www.ronpaul.com/2010-05-21/ron paul-the-founding -fathers-were-libertarians/, accessed August 1, 2013; "Sarah Palin on National Day of Prayer Controversy," Fox News, May 7, 2010, http://www.foxnews.com/story/0,2933,592422, 00.html.

10   Adam Liptak, "The Tea Party and the Constitution," *New York Times*, March 13, 2010, http://www.nytimes.com/2010 /03/14/weekinreview/14liptak.html.

11   Jill Lepore, *The Whites of Their Eyes: The Tea Party's Revolution and the Battle over American History* (Princeton, N.J.: Princeton University Press, 2010), 16.

12   Mark Lilla, "The Tea Party Jacobins," *New York Review of Books*, May 27, 2010, http://www.nybooks.com/articles /archives/2010/may/27/tea-party-jacobins/.

13   David Barstow, "Tea Party Lights Fuse for Rebellion on Right," *New York Times*, February 15, 2010, http://www .nytimes.com/2010/02/16/us/politics/16teaparty.html.

14   Greg Sargent, "Sharron Angle Floated Possibility of Armed Insurrection," *Washington Post*, Plum Line, June 15, 2010, http://voices.washingtonpost.com/plum-line/2010/06 /sharron_angle_floated_possibil.html.

15   Barstow, "Tea Party Lights Fuse for Rebellion on Right."

16   First quotation: Caitlin Taylor, "Conservatives Decry Home-land Security Report on 'Rightwing' Extremism," April 15, 2009, ABC News, http://abcnews.go.com/blogs/politics /2009/04/conservatives-d/. All subsequent quotations: Robert Pear, "Spitting and Slurs Directed at Lawmakers," *New York Times*, Prescriptions blog, March 20, 2010, http://prescriptions .blogs.nytimes.com/2010/03/20/spitting-and-slurs-directed -at-lawmakers/.

17   Kenneth R. Bazinet, "Democrats Who Voted for Health Care Reform Get Police Protection as Threats Turn Ugly," New York *Daily News*, March 24, 2010, http://www.nydaily news.com/news/politics/democrats-voted-health-care -reform-police-protection-threats-turn-ugly-article-1.171425.

18   First quotation: Igor Volsky, "McCain Refuses to Con-demn Palin's 'Reload' Rhetoric," Think Progress, March 25, 2010, http://thinkprogress.org/politics/2010/03/25/88643 /mccain-palin-crosshairs/. Second quotation: Katharine Q. Seelye, "Palin Invokes Tea Party Origins," *New York Times*, Caucus blog, April 14, 2010, http://thecaucus.blogs.nytimes .com/2010/04/14/palin-invokes-tea-party-origins/.

19   David M. Herszenhorn, "Congress Now Has a 'Tea Party Caucus,'" *New York Times*, Caucus blog, July 20, 2010, http:// thecaucus.blogs.nytimes.com/2010/07/20/congress-now -has-a-tea-party-caucus/.

20   "Polling the Tea Party," *New York Times*, April 14, 2010, http://www.nytimes.com/interactive/2010/04/14/us /politics/20100414-tea-party-poll-graphic.html. Quotation:

Kate Zernike, "Tea Party Supporters Doing Fine, but Angry Nonetheless," *New York Times*, April 17, 2010, http://www.nytimes.com/2010/04/18/weekinreview/18zernike.html.

21   "Election Results 2010—The New York Times," http://elections.nytimes.com/2010, accessed August 1, 2013.

22   Jennifer Steinhauer, "Constitution Has Its Day (More or Less) in the House," *New York Times*, January 6, 2011, http://www.nytimes.com/2011/01/07/us/politics/07constitution.html.

23   Chris Good, "Should Congress Have Read the WHOLE Constitution? Jesse Jackson, Jr. Makes the Case," *Atlantic*, January 6, 2011, http://www.theatlantic.com/politics/archive/2011/01/should-congress-have-read-the-whole-constitution-jesse-jackson-jr-makes-the-case/68983/.

24   Jack M. Balkin, "Read the Whole Constitution," Balkinization, January 6, 2011, http://balkin.blogspot.com/2011/01/read-whole-constitution.html; Adam Serwer, "Huck Finning the Constitution," *Washington Post*, Plum Line, January 6, 2011, http://voices.washingtonpost.com/plum-line/2011/01/huck_finning_the_constitution.html; Adam Kirsch, "The First Drafts of American History," *New York Times*, January 7, 2011, http://www.nytimes.com/2011/01/08/opinion/08kirsch.html.

25   Adam J. White, "Misreading the Constitution," *Weekly Standard* blog, January 6, 2011, http://www.weeklystandard.com/blogs/misreading-constitution_526807.html; Alana Goodman, "New Complaint: The GOP 'Sanitized' the Constitution," *Commentary*, January 6, 2011, http://www.commentarymagazine.com/2011/01/06/new-complaint-the-gop-'sanitized'-the-constitution/.

26   Frum, "The Reckless Right Courts Violence."

27   Jake Sherman, Jonathan Allen, and Molly Ball, "Rep. Gabrielle Giffords Shooting Sparks National Debate," *Politico*,

January 8, 2011, http://www.politico.com/news/stories/0111/47244.html.

28 Matthew Continetti, "The Two Faces of the Tea Party," *Weekly Standard*, June 28, 2010, http://www.weeklystandard.com/articles/two-faces-tea-party.

29 Jonah Goldberg, "On Continetti's Tea Party Problem," *National Review Online*, June 29, 2010, http://www.national review.com/corner/232561/continettis-tea-party-problem-jonah-goldberg.

30 Michael D. Shear, "Republicans Set to Wield New Power in Washington," *New York Times*, Caucus blog, January 25, 2011, http://thecaucus.blogs.nytimes.com/2011/01/05/republicans-prepare-to-wield-new-power-in-washington/.

31 Nate Silver, "How Boehner's Bill Has Hurt, and How It Could Help, Republicans," *New York Times*, FiveThirtyEight blog, July 29, 2011, http://fivethirtyeight.blogs.nytimes.com/2011/07/29/how-boehners-bill-has-hurt-and-how-it-could-help-republicans/.

32 Alan Silverleib and Tom Cohen, "House Passes GOP Debt Measure; Obama Praises Compromise Plan," CNN, July 19, 2011, http://www.cnn.com/2011/POLITICS/07/19/debt.talks/index.html; Jeanne Sahadi, "The Problem with 'Cut, Cap and Balance,'" *CNNMoney*, July 19, 2012, http://money.cnn.com/2011/07/18/news/economy/cut_cap_balance/index.htm.

33 Thomas Sowell, "Ideals vs. Realities," *Real Clear Politics*, July 28, 2011, http://www.realclearpolitics.com/articles/2011/07/28/ideals_versus_realities_110742.html; Roger Pilon, "We're in This for the Long Haul," Cato Institute, July 29, 2011, http://www.cato.org/blog/were-long-haul.

34 Michael Sokolove, "Dick Armey Is Back on the Attack," *New York Times Magazine*, November 4, 2009, http://www.nytimes.com/2009/11/08/magazine/08Armey-t.html.

35   "The GOP's Reality Test," *Wall Street Journal*, July 27, 2011, http://online.wsj.com/news/articles/SB100014240531119035 91104576470061986837494.

36   Carl Hulse and Helene Cooper, "Obama and Leaders Reach Debt Deal," *New York Times*, July 31, 2011, http://www.nytimes.com/2011/08/01/us/politics/01FISCAL.html.

37   Ibid.

38   Sam Tanenhaus, "Jefferson's Tea Party Moment," *New York Times*, July 31, 2011, http://www.nytimes.com/2011/07/31/sunday-review/us-has-lovehate-relationship-with-debt.html.

39   Bill Keller, "Is the Tea Party Over?," *New York Times*, October 9, 2011, http://www.nytimes.com/2011/10/10/opinion/is-the-tea-party-over.html.

40   Kate Zernike, "Tea Party Gets Early Start on G.O.P. Targets for 2012," *New York Times*, January 29, 2011, http://www.nytimes.com/2011/01/30/us/politics/30teaparty.html.

41   Jacob Weisberg, "Face It: Romney's the Nominee," *Slate*, January 4, 2012, http://www.slate.com/articles/news_and_politics/the_big_idea/2012/01/mitt_romney_s_the_nominee_the_republican_primary_race_is_over_.html.

42   Keller, "Is the Tea Party Over?"

43   Michael D. Shear, "G.O.P. Hopefuls Vying for Tea Party's Support," *New York Times*, September 5, 2011, http://www.nytimes.com/2011/09/06/us/politics/06repubs.html.

44   Glenn Kessler, "Fact Checker: Rep. Paul Ryan's Budget Blueprint," *Washington Post*, April 9, 2011, http://www.washingtonpost.com/politics/fact-checker-rep-paul-ryans-budget-blueprint/2011/04/09/AF7lmM9C_story.html. Quotations: Paul Ryan, "The Republican Response," *New York Times*, January 25, 2011, http://www.nytimes.com/2011/01/26/us/politics/26repubs-text.html.

45   Nate Silver, "The Simple Case for Why Obama Is the Favorite,"

New York Times, FiveThirtyEight blog, September 5, 2012, http://fivethirtyeight.blogs.nytimes.com/2012/09/05/sept-4-the-simple-case-for-why-obama-is-the-favorite/.

46 "Romney Prepared Victory Speech for Election, but Delivered Concession Speech Instead," *Washington Post*, November 7, 2012, http://www.washingtonpost.com/politics/decision2012/romney-prepared-victory-speech-for-election-but-delivered-concession-speech-instead/2012/11/07/74dd5b96-28a0-11e2-b4e0-346287b7e56c_story.html.

47 Ibid.; Tom Scocca, "Eighty-Eight Percent of Romney Voters Were White," *Slate*, November 7, 2012, http://www.slate.com/articles/news_and_politics/scocca/2012/11/mitt_romney_white_voters_the_gop_candidate_s_race_based_monochromatic_campaign.html.

48 Jana Kasperkevic, "The Petition to Let Texas Secede from the U.S. to Be Reviewed by the White House," *Houston Chronicle*, Texas on the Potomac blog, November 12, 2012, http://blog.chron.com/txpotomac/2012/11/the-petition-to-let-texas-secede-from-the-u-s-to-be-reviewed-by-the-white-house/; Trip Gabriel, "Tea Party, Its Clout Diminished, Turns to Narrower Issues," *New York Times*, December 25, 2012, http://www.nytimes.com/2012/12/26/us/politics/tea-party-its-clout-diminished-turns-to-fringe-issues.html. Quotation: Jana Kasperkevic, "Rick Perry Might Not Want Texas to Secede, but Ron Paul Believes 'Secession Is an American Principle,'" *Houston Chronicle*, Texas on the Potomac blog, November 14, 2012, http://blog.chron.com/txpotomac/2012/11/rick-perry-might-not-want-texas-to-secede-but-ron-paul-believes-secession-is-an-american-principle/.

49 Sam Tanenhaus, "Original Sin: Why the GOP Is and Will Continue to Be the Party of White People," *New Republic*, February 10, 2013, http://www.newrepublic.com/article/112365/.

50 Ibid.

51 Ibid.

52 Ibid.

53 "President Obama's Inaugural Address," *New York Times*, January 21, 2013, http://www.nytimes.com/interactive/2013 /01/22/us/politics/22obama-inaugural-speech-annotated .html.

54 Ibid.

55 Ibid.

56 Ibid.

57 "A Guide to Mass Shootings in America," *Mother Jones*, http:// www.motherjones.com/politics/2012/07/mass-shootings -map, accessed January 8, 2013; "Gunman at Minneapolis Sign Company Said 'Oh Really,' Then Started Shooting," Associated Press, October 5, 2012, http://www.foxnews .com/us/2012/10/05/gunman-at-minneapolis-sign-company -said-oh-really-then-started-shooting/; Steven Yaccino, Michael Schwirtz, and Marc Santora, "Gunman Kills 6 at Sikh Temple in Wisconsin," *New York Times*, August 5, 2012, http://www.nytimes.com/2012/08/06/us/shooting-reported -at-temple-in-wisconsin.html; "Seattle Cafe Shooter Kills 5 and Himself," ABC News, May 31, 2012, http://abcnews .go.com/US/ian-stawicki-seattle-cafe-racer-shooter -kills-shoots-citywide/story?id=16463885; Norimitsu Onishi and Malia Wollan, "Troubled History Emerges for Suspect in Fatal Oakland Attack," *New York Times*, April 3, 2012, http://www.nytimes.com/2012/04/04/us/oikos-university -gunman-lined-up-victims.html; Joel Anderson, "Business Dispute, La. Gun Battle Eyed in Norcross Shooting," *Atlanta Journal-Constitution*, February 24, 2012, http://www .ajc.com/news/news/local/business-dispute-la-gun-battle -eyed-in-norcross-sh/nQRcn/; James Barron, "Gunman Kills

20 Schoolchildren in Connecticut," *New York Times*, December 14, 2012, http://www.nytimes.com/2012/12/15/nyregion /shooting-reported-at-connecticut-elementary-school.html; "151 Victims of Mass Shootings in 2012: Here Are Their Stories," *Mother Jones*, http://www.motherjones.com/politics /2012/12/mass-shootings-victims-2012, accessed January 8, 2013.

58   "NRA Foundation," http://www.nrafoundation.org/endow ment.aspx, accessed January 8, 2013.

59   Jennifer Steinhauer, "Senate Hearing on Guns Suggests an Uphill Fight on New Limits," *New York Times*, January 30, 2013, http://www.nytimes.com/2013/01/31/us/politics/senate -hearing-to-focus-on-gun-violence.html.

60   "Fireworks: Ted Cruz vs. Dianne Feinstein on Gun Rights," *Real Clear Politics*, March 14, 2013, http://www.realclear politics.com/video/2013/03/14/fireworks_ted_cruz_vs _dianne_feinstein_on_gun_rights.html.

61   Ibid.

62   Ibid.

63   Ibid.

64   Ibid.

65   Ibid.

66   Ed O'Keefe and Philip Rucker, "Gun-Control Overhaul Is Defeated in Senate," *Washington Post*, April 17, 2013, http:// www.washingtonpost.com/politics/gun-control-overhaul -is-defeated-in-senate/2013/04/17/57eb028a-a77c-11e2-b029 -8fb7e977ef71_story.html.

67   First quotation: Kevin Liptak, "Cruz Hates on Republicans and Democrats Alike," CNN, Political Ticker blog, May 22, 2013, http://politicalticker.blogs.cnn.com/2013/05/22/cruz -hates-on-republicans-and-democrats-alike/. Second quotation: "Day 3: McCain vs. Tea Party Senators," *CNN*, Political

Ticker blog, May 23, 2013, http://politicalticker.blogs.cnn
.com/2013/05/23/day-3-mccain-vs-tea-party-senators/.

68 Rachel Weiner, "Ted Cruz Mocks Senate Republican," *Washington Post*, April 29, 2013, http://www.washingtonpost.com
/blogs/post-politics/wp/2013/04/29/ted-cruz-mocks
-squishes-in-republican-party/; Katy Steinmetz, "The Meaning of 'Squish' and Other Fun-to-Say Political Slights," *Time*,
May 1, 2013, http://newsfeed.time.com/2013/05/01/the
-meaning-of-squish-and-other-fun-to-say-political-slights/.

69 Gary Gutting, "You Say You Want a Revolution," *New York Times*, July 2, 2013, Opinionator blog, http://opinionator
.blogs.nytimes.com/2013/07/02/you-say-you-want-a
-revolution/.

70 Fredreka Schouten, "Boehner: Judge Congress on How Many Laws It Repeals," *USA Today*, July 21, 2013, http://
www.usatoday.com/story/news/politics/2013/07/21/bochner
-congress-repeal-health-care-unpopularity/2572839/.

71 Ross Douthat, "Good Populism, Bad Populism," *New York Times*, September 21, 2013, http://www.nytimes.com
/2013/09/22/opinion/sunday/douthat-good-populism-bad
-populism.html.

72 Ashley Parker, "Pelosi Derides 'Tea Party Shutdown,'" *New York Times*, October 1, 2013, http://www.nytimes.com
/news/fiscal-crisis/2013/10/01/pelosi-derides-tea-party
-shutdown/.

73 Ibid.

74 First quotation: Ross Douthat, "Is Republican Intransigence Reasonable?," *New York Times*, Ross Douthat blog, September 30, 2013, http://douthat.blogs.nytimes.com/2013/09/30
/is-republican-intransigence-reasonable/. Second quotation:
Ross Douthat, "The Costs of Fantasy Politics," *New York Times*, Ross Douthat blog, October 11, 2013, http://douthat

.blogs.nytimes.com/2013/10/11/the-costs-of-fantasy -politics/. Third and fourth quotations: Ross Douthat, "Why the Right Fights," *New York Times*, Ross Douthat blog, October 2, 2013, http://douthat.blogs.nytimes.com/2013/10/02 /why-the-right-fights/.

75 Mark Murray, "NBC/WSJ Poll: Shutdown Debate Damages GOP," NBC News, October 10, 2013, http://firstread.nbc news.com/_news/2013/10/10/20903624-nbcwsj-poll-shut down-debate-damages-gop.

76 Jared Bernstein, "The Shutdown Shuts Down," *New York Times*, Economix blog, October 17, 2013, http://economix .blogs.nytimes.com/2013/10/17/the-shutdown-shuts-down/.

77 Jonathan Weisman, "In Defeat for Tea Party, House Passes $1.1 Trillion Spending Bill," *New York Times*, January 15, 2014, http://www.nytimes.com/2014/01/16/us/politics/in-defeat -for-tea-party-house-passes-1-1-trillion-spending-bill.html.

78 Bernstein, "The Shutdown Shuts Down."

AFTERWORD

1 Tony Judt, "Interview with Donald A. Yerxa," *Historically Speaking: The Bulletin of the Historical Society* 7 (January/ February 2006), http://www.bu.edu/historic/hs/judt.html.

2 Richard Hofstadter, *Anti-Intellectualism in American Life* (New York: Knopf, 1963), 43.

3 Walter Lippmann, *Drift and Mastery: An Attempt to Diagnose the Current Unrest* (New York: Mitchell Kennerley, 1914), 266 (first quotation), 267 (second quotation).

INDEX

Index

ABOUT THE AUTHOR

David Sehat is Associate Professor of History at Georgia State University. His first book, *The Myth of American Religious Freedom*, won the Frederick Jackson Turner Award from the Organization of American Historians. Learn more about David at www .davidsehat.net.